FERRARI ENGINES

15 iconic Ferrari engines from 1947 to the present

Dedication

For Dad, to reciprocate a dedication from 26 years ago, also in a Ferrari book.

COVER IMAGE: A view of the assembled 2.8-litre V8 twin-turbo F114 B engine and transmission from the legendary 1984 Ferrari GTO (288).
(Francesco Reggiani)

© Francesco Reggiani 2018

All rights reserved. No part of this publication may be reproduced or stored in a retrieval system or transmitted, in any form or by any means, electronic, mechanical, photocopying, recording or otherwise, without prior permission in writing from Haynes Publishing.

First published in October 2018

A catalogue record for this book is available from the British Library.

ISBN 978 1 78521 208 6

Library of Congress control no. 2018938898

All photographs appearing in this book are copyright of Francesco Reggiani

Published by Haynes Publishing,
Sparkford, Yeovil,
Somerset BA22 7JJ, UK.
Tel: 01963 440635
Int. tel: +44 1963 440635
Website: www.haynes.com

Haynes North America Inc.,
859 Lawrence Drive, Newbury Park,
California 91320, USA.

Printed in Malaysia.

FERRARI ENGINES

15 iconic Ferrari engines from 1947 to the present

Enthusiasts' Manual

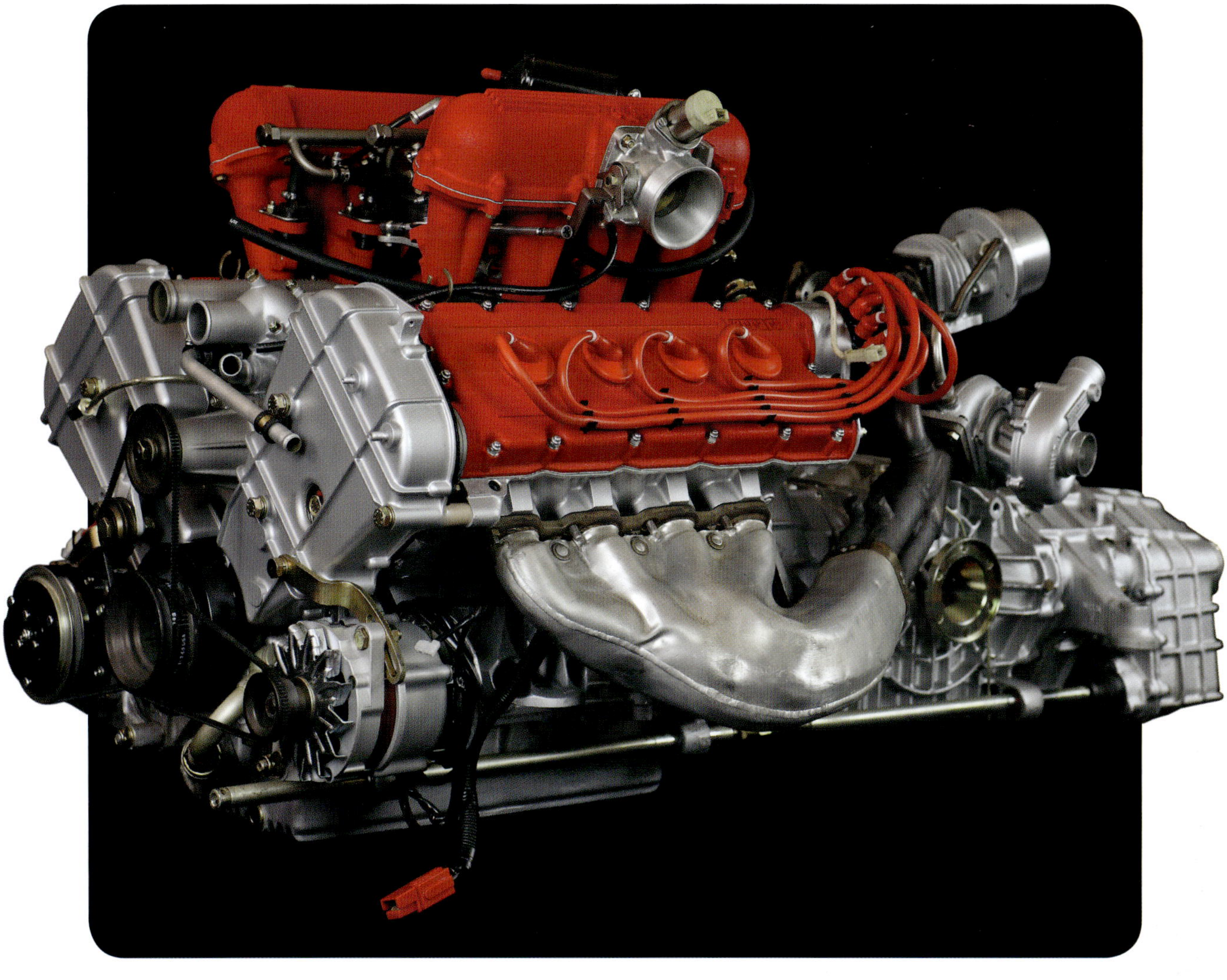

A photographic insight into the design, engineering and mechanical art of Ferrari road-car engines

Francesco Reggiani with Keith Bluemel

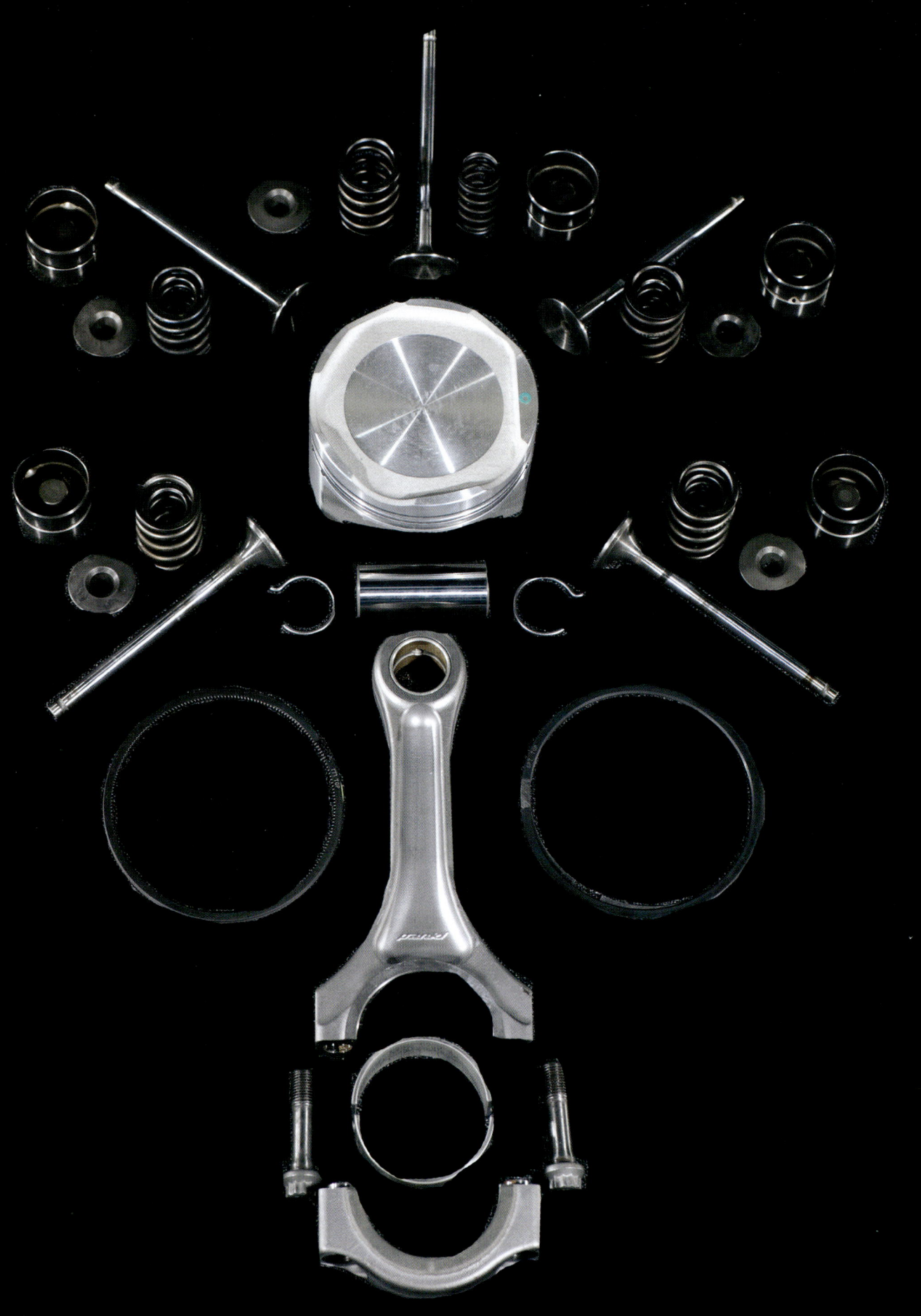

Contents

INTRODUCTION	**6**
ACKNOWLEDGEMENTS	**9**

195 INTER   **10**
The first-generation Ferrari V12 (1949)

340 AMERICA   **26**
The 'long block" V12 (1950)

250 CALIFORNIA   **42**
A classic V12 icon (1957)

250 LM   **58**
The first rear-engined' Ferrari 'road car' (1963)

275 GTB   **74**
The transaxle arrives (1964)

330 GTS   **90**
Increasing the capacity (1966)

DINO 246 GTS   **106**
The Fiat partnership (1972)

365 GT4 BB   **122**
The first flat-12-engined Ferrari road car (1973)

308 GTB   **138**
The arrival of the V8 (1975)

208 TURBO   **154**
The first Ferrari turbo road car (1982)

GTO (288)   **170**
Twin-turbo supercar (1984)

512 TR   **186**
The end of the flat-12 era (1992)

456 GT M   **202**
V12 return to the front (1998)

360 MODENA   **218**
The V8 reborn (1999)

FF   **234**
The first Ferrari engine in a 4WD car (2011)

MORE ROAD ENGINES   **250**

COMPETITION ENGINES   **252**

Introduction

Enzo Ferrari's dream and vision was the V12 engine configuration, mounted in beautiful and light sport cars, which could be used in competition, but also were equally at home for road use, providing performance and excitement for the driver. After driving for Alfa Romeo, and then managing its racing team under his own Scuderia Ferrari name, Ferrari parted ways with Alfa Romeo due to irreconcilable differences with the company's management.

During the period that Ferrari was managing the Alfa Romeo team, the *Cavallino Rampante* symbol began to appear on the team's cars. The emblem was presented to Ferrari as a gift by the mother of World War I fighter pilot Francesco Baracca. Baracca had been shot down and killed in 1918, and in memory of his death, Enzo decided to place the black *Cavallino Rampante* symbol on a yellow shield representing the colour of Modena – the city in which Ferrari was born.

The severance contract that Ferrari agreed with Alfa Romeo precluded him from using his own name on a car for at least four years. So, after parting company with Alfa Romeo, in

↓↘ **All the photographs appearing in this book were taken on location at various Ferrari engineering specialists in Italy, who worked with the author to set up temporary 'studio' conditions.**

1939 he founded his first car-building business, naming it Auto Avio Costruzioni. The two 815 AAC spiders that he built featured in-line eight-cylinder engines, constructed by mating two Fiat 508 motors on a single crankshaft.

It was only in 1947 that Enzo Ferrari, free from the contract with Alfa Romeo, was able to build cars and engines bearing his own name. Over the years, the company would become one of the world's most prestigious, admired and famous producers of speedy dreams for driving enthusiasts. The famous V12 engines (but also in-line 4, in-line 6, V6, V8 and V10 engines) – designed by ingenious engineering masters such as Gioachino Colombo, Giuseppe Busso, Aurelio Lampredi, Vittorio Jano, Giotto Bizzarrini, Mauro Forghieri, Nicola Materazzi, Giuliano de Angelis, Angelo Bellei and Franco Rocchi – became more than just aesthetic masterpieces of mechanical art, providing (and still provide today) exceptional performance, accompanied by the divine sound of a symphony orchestra, as was stated by the artistic manager of the Vienna Opera House, Herbert Von Karajan!

The idea for this book has been developed over an exciting past five years of work, during which I have followed the complete restoration of some of the most beautiful Ferraris built by the Maranello factory. Taking photographs to document the various fascinating steps of the restorations, I began to understand that it was not just the bodywork – the various shapes of which I knew well – that provided a unique aesthetic value, but also the mechanical components hidden inside the engine bay, which until I shot the dismantled engines I had never imagined would be so fascinating. I fell in love with the pulsating hearts of the creatures, and began to research these engineering masterpieces built by Ferrari, photographing the engine components both dismantled and assembled.

In this book, celebrating the foresight and talent of Enzo Ferrari, we have chosen 15 engines which represent significant landmarks in the story of Ferrari – engines of various configurations, capacities and fuel systems, and displaying various technical innovations. They could be considered the ideal overview to underline the genius and the artistic ability of the engineers that designed them, together with the aesthetic creativity of the coachbuilders and designers who produced the cars that clothed them.

Francesco Reggiani
July 2018

'When I began, against everyone's advice I wanted a 12-cylinder engine and that engine, which many people expected to put an end to my ambitions, is still recognisable in its numerous sons and grandsons. I have tried them all, eight-, six- and four-cylinder units, but I keep returning to the 12-cylinder, which remains my favourite.'

Enzo Ferrari
from *Caratteristiche Tecniche dei Motori Ferrari realizzati dal 1946 al 1985*, published by Ferrari in 1985

Acknowledgements

This book, which presents a selection of important engines to tell the story of Ferrari power over the years, would not have been feasible without the cooperation, willingness and patience of some of the most important engineering specialists working on the restoration and servicing of *Cavallino Rampante* engines.

I would like to offer a special thanks to the crew of Toni Auto workshop, namely Silvano Toni, Davide Toni and Andrea Toni, Vincenzo Conti, Marcello Silferi and Alessandro Ovile, who work just in front of the Ferrari factory at Via dell'Abetone Inferiore 41, in Maranello.

Special thanks are also due to all the specialised workshops that offered help to allow me to shoot some of the engines that are shown over the following pages: Corrado and Guido Patella at Autofficina Omega, Zanè (VI); Alessandro Peraro at Maranello Service, Calvatone (CR); Carlo and Renato Bonini at Autofficina Bonini, Cadelbosco di Sotto (RE); Aldo Carrabs at Forza Service, Torino (TO); Engineer Vincenzi at Motor Service, Modena (MO); Angelo Rizzoli of Autofficina Sauro, Bologna (BO); Maurizio Colpani at Colpani Motori, Poncarale (BS); Gesuita of Rosso Monza Officina Ferrari, Concorezzo (MB); and Tommaso Gelmini of GPS Classic, Soragna (PR).

Thanks are also due to Sergio Abate of Studio Ellisse, and Duerre Tubi Style Group S.p.A.

Thanks to Lorenzo Beltrami, Commissioner of the ASI (Automotoclub Storico Italiano) for sparing the time to share his knowledge and experience.

Many thanks to both Alberto Nobile and Pietro Gandolfi for the kind assistance of the Autodromo di Marzaglia.

Special thanks are also due to my friend Andrea Galletti, who hosted me several times during my visits to London.

Special thanks must also go to Ferrari expert Keith Bluemel for taking time out of his busy schedule to check the accuracy of my words and for adding insight and detail.

My heartfelt thanks go to Steve Rendle, for his belief in my idea from the first e-mail I sent him, and for his support during the complex realisation of this project.

And finally, to the owners of all the beautiful Ferraris displayed in this book, who accepted my often peculiar requests to photograph their cars.

Francesco Reggiani

↓ **An engineering work of art – the four triple-choke Weber 40 IF3C carburettors fitted to the Ferrari 365 GT4 BB.**

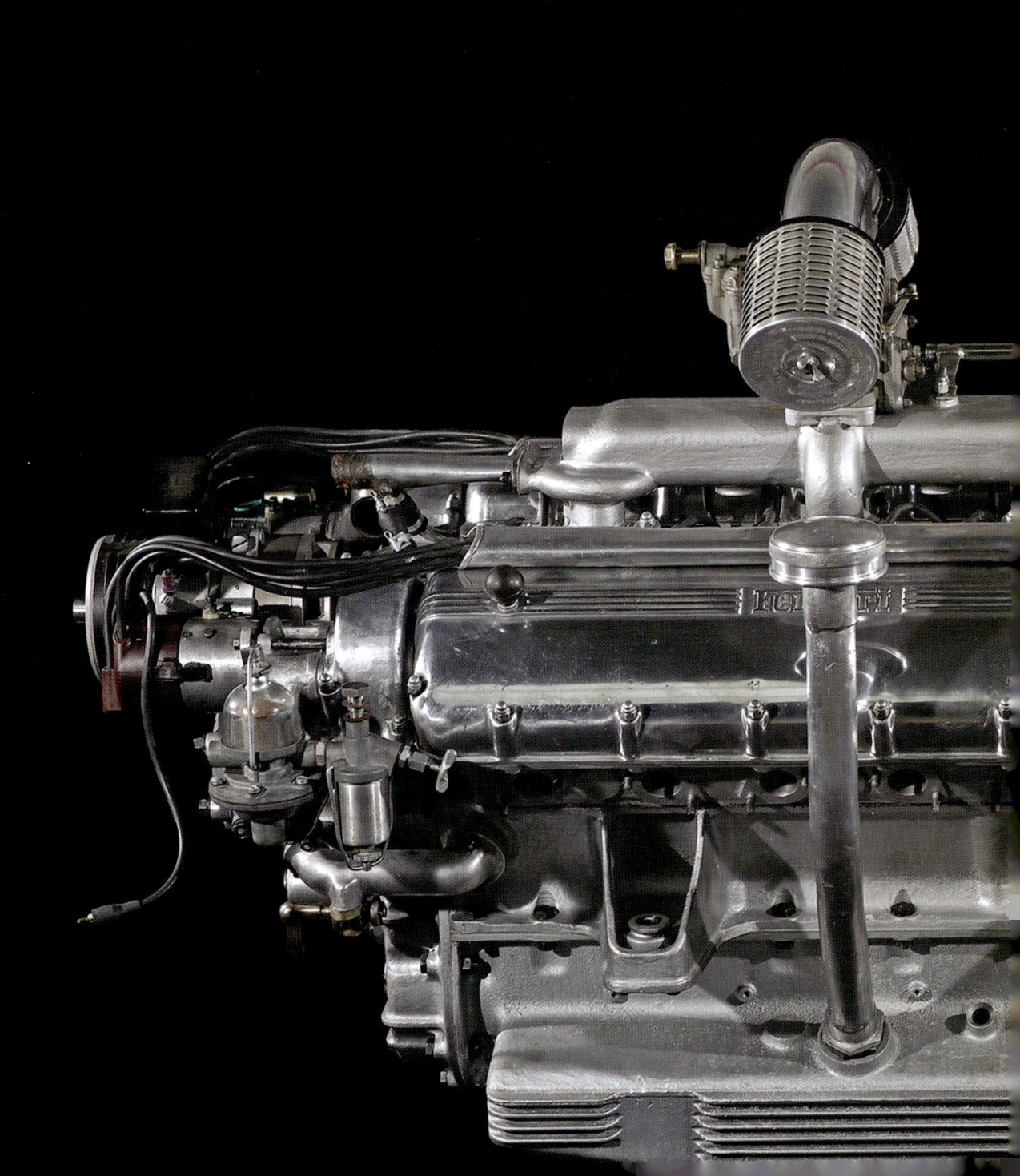

195 Inter
The first-generation Ferrari V12 (1949)

← The 195 engines still carried the code 166 (from the previous 2.0-litre engine) cast into the cylinder blocks.

↙ The big-ends of the steel connecting rods featured an oblique-angled split – typical for Ferrari engines of the fifties.

When Ferrari first started building engines, the car model designation numbers were derived from the swept volume of a single cylinder. So, to find the total cubic capacity of the engine it was necessary to multiply the designation by the number of cylinders. For example, for the 195 model, the overall capacity was 195 x 12 = 2,340cc. This system of nomenclature would characterise Ferraris for many years to come. Enzo Ferrari used several different coachbuilders to build the bodywork for his cars, and so the cars were referred to as *fuori serie* (specially built), because of the different shapes identifying each one. The very rare 195 engine, produced in 1950 and 1951, was fitted in just 32 cars, created by master Italian designers of the era including Ghia, Motto, Touring and Vignale. The 195 engine was very similar to the previous 166 (just 39 examples built), but with different pistons and an increased bore to reach a capacity of 2.3 litres instead of the 2.0 litres of the 166 unit. As with many other engines built by Ferrari, the 195 was directly derived from competition experience, and for this reason details of each of the road engines varied, as customers could specify modifications to increase power if they wished to race their Ferrari.

When Ferrari first started building cars V12 engines were rarer and arguably more fascinating than their present-day counterparts, not only because they were produced in much smaller numbers, but also because a V12 engine in the post-war years was like something from another planet! Motorsport competition was the *raison d'etre* for Enzo Ferrari's company, and Ferrari was founded on the V12 concept. The very first Ferrari V12 was the 1,497cc 125 engine, created by engineering genius Gioachino Colombo, whose design skills convinced Ferrari to trust in the V12 layout, and which was translated into reality by the head of the Ferrari technical department, Giuseppe Busso, during 1946. Only two examples of the type 125 V12 engine that powered the 'Alaspessa' Barchetta and the two-seater 'Sigaro' 125 S Competizione, were built.

↖ The famous Ferrari name is cast into the aluminium camshaft covers.

← The cast-aluminium lower rear engine casing (which fits behind the flywheel) to which the clutch bellhousing bolts.

The first limited-production Ferrari engine was the type 166 (1,995cc), which like the 125 unit was initially built for competition, and then mounted in coupés, berlinettas and spiders for road use. The spiders that were built by Carrozzeria Touring had body sides that curved under the car, which led to them being called barchettas (little boats) in the Italian motoring press of the day, a name that has been applied ever since. This engine provided excellent performance by the standards of the day and plenty of excitement for the drivers. Only forty 166 Sport and Inter models were produced, which were again clothed with bodies from various different coachbuilders. The 195 was an evolution of this 2.0-litre engine, first built in 1949, and unveiled at the Paris Motor Show in 1950, mounted in a 195 Inter Vignale Coupé. The total number of these engines produced was 32, of which four were competition units. These four upgraded engines provided improved performance, with a power output of 168bhp (125kW) at 7,000rpm. One of these engines equipped a special 166 MM Barchetta Touring (chassis No. 0020M) and the second was mounted in a 166 MM Touring Berlinetta, which won the 1950 Mille Miglia that year, driven by Giannino Marzotto and Marco Crosara (chassis No. 0026M). The third 166 MM, converted to use a 2.3-litre engine, was a Touring Barchetta

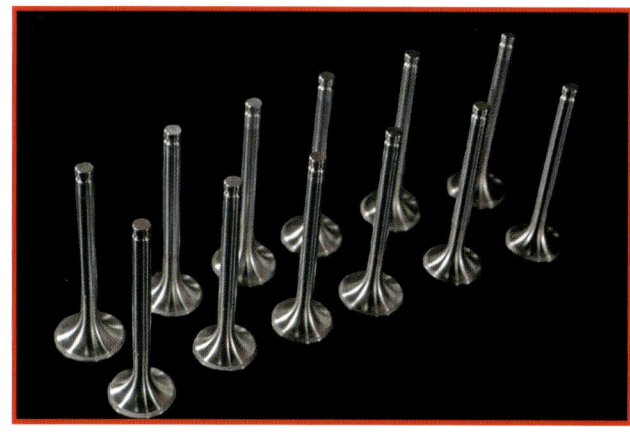

↑ **The valves from one of the cylinder heads – six inlet valves and six exhaust valves.**

(chassis No. 0038M), which took second place, driven by Serafini/Salani in the same Mille Miglia, finishing just ahead of the 2,500cc Alfa Romeo 6C driven by the legendary Juan

↓ **The 195 block is identical to the previous 166, with an increased bore size to provide a capacity of 2.3 litres.**

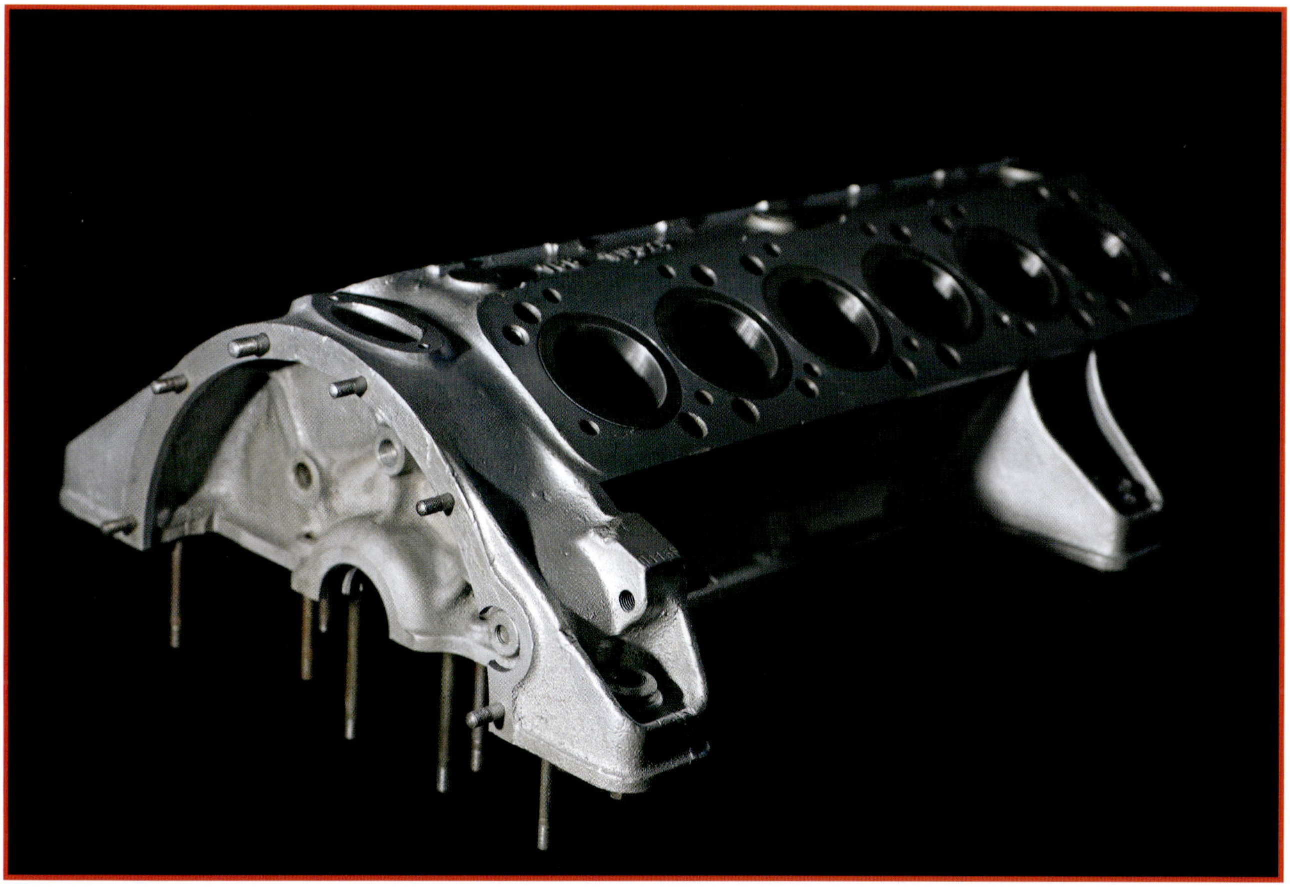

Manuel Fangio. The fourth and last car (chassis No. 0060M), was a Touring Berlinetta, which ran at Le Mans, driven by Dorino Serafini and Raymond Sommer, but did not finish the race. An interesting aside is that, in 1951, less than a year after it was delivered, a 166 Inter Coupé Touring (chassis No. 051 S) was sent back to Carrozzeria Vignale for conversion into a cabriolet, and at around the same time it was fitted with a brand-new 2,341cc V12 engine. A total of 25 cars actually started life as 195 Inters, and apart from those mentioned already, some other 166 Models had their engines upgraded to 195 specification. Both Ghia and Vignale produced coachwork for ten examples, whilst Touring bodied three cars, and Motto and Ghia Aigle produced one body apiece.

Incidentally, Ghia Aigle were a Swiss-based coachbuilder and were the first non-Italian coachbuilder to supply a body on a Ferrari, which was on a 195 EL (Export Lungo) chassis, which had a slightly longer, 2,550mm-wheelbase chassis, than the regular 2,500mm of the other cars in the series. This was 80mm longer than that of the 166, in order to create more room in the cockpit. The braking for these luxurious Ferraris was provided by a hydraulic drum-brake system with four huge 12-inch-diameter aluminium drums. Borrani wire wheels were standard and, depending on the coachwork, most Inters weighed around 1,000kg.

The first generation of 12-cylinder Ferrari engines was referred to as the 'short block' engine, because the distance

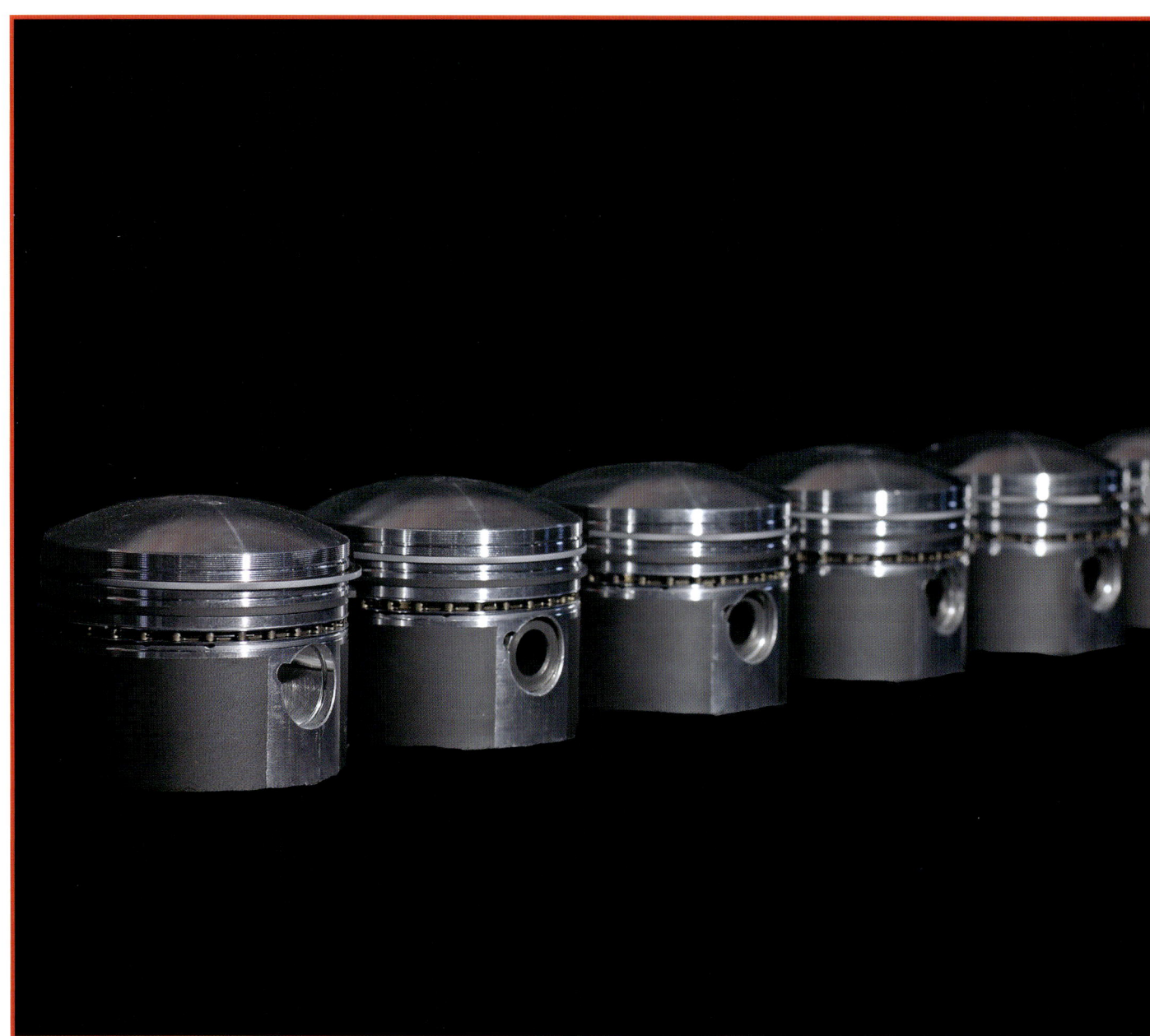

between the centres of adjacent cylinder bores was only 90mm. Apart from the Aurelio Lampredi engines, which featured a 'long block' layout, with 108mm between the cylinder-bore centres, the 'short block' 90mm configuration remained unchanged until the 1966 330 GTC, when an updated 'short block' engine was introduced with an increased bore-centre distance of 94mm. The engine code number 195 was still based on the original V12 project by Gioachino Colombo who, after the 125, also developed the 166 with Luigi Busso, before becoming an external consultant to Ferrari and engineering the 195 engine. To achieve the increase in capacity required for the 195, the Ferrari engineers increased the bore by 5mm (to 65mm, rather than the 60mm of the 166 engine), maintaining the same stroke (58.8mm). All the engines fitted to the Ferrari 195 Inter, and produced from 1950 to 1951, had an odd number sequence (as for all the road cars from Maranello), which in this case started with 081S and finished with 0195EL.

Strangely, possibly due to Ferrari's economic situation at the time, the 195 engine blocks still carried the code number (166) of the previous 2.0-litre engine, despite the larger bore. This, most likely, allowed Ferrari to use the engine blocks already cast but not yet built into completed engines, by simply increasing the bores for the cylinders liners. Also, to reduce the production cost for this rare V12, the crankshaft for the 195 was the same as that of the 166 – forged steel, with seven main bearings. Equally, the gearbox casing and most of the other mechanical components were the same as those for the 166 model.

The big-ends of the steel connecting rods featured the typical oblique-angled joint, which was an arrangement used by Ferrari through the fifties on the 'short block' V12 engines up to the 250 series D. Later, the big-ends were changed to the more common horizontal big-end joint on the connecting rods. Each pair of connecting rods (for pistons on opposing cylinder banks) shares a common big-end journal on the crankshaft, normal practice on a V12 engine. For the 195 engine, the firing order was 1–12–5–8–3–10–6–7–2–11–4–9.

The 60° V12, 195 engine had a capacity of 2,341cc, and produced 128bhp (95kW) at 6,000rpm, with a maximum torque of 154Nm (114lb/ft), and a compression ratio of 7.5:1. The lubrication was via a wet sump, with a mechanical oil pump. Pistons were cast aluminium, as were the cylinder block, timing chain covers, camshaft covers and transmission housing. The engine's steel valves (two per cylinder) were operated by finger followers, with a single chain-driven overhead camshaft per bank, gear-driven off the crankshaft. Ignition was provided by either twin distributors or twin magnetos, the latter normally being fitted to the competition versions. The 195 spark plugs, as for all V12 Ferraris previous to the 250 series with code number 128 D (in other words, before the arrival at Ferrari of engineer Giotto Bizzarrini), were mounted inside the V of the banks. On the road version of the 195, fuel delivery was normally provided by a single Weber 36 DCF twin choke carburettor (although a triple assembly could also be fitted), with a mechanical pump. The four 195 competition units (mentioned previously) featured triple Weber 36 DCF carburettors that increased the power output to 170bhp (127kW) at 7,000rpm. The 195's clutch was a dry

← The 'parade' of all 12 pistons, showing the details of their two compression rings and one oil-control ring.

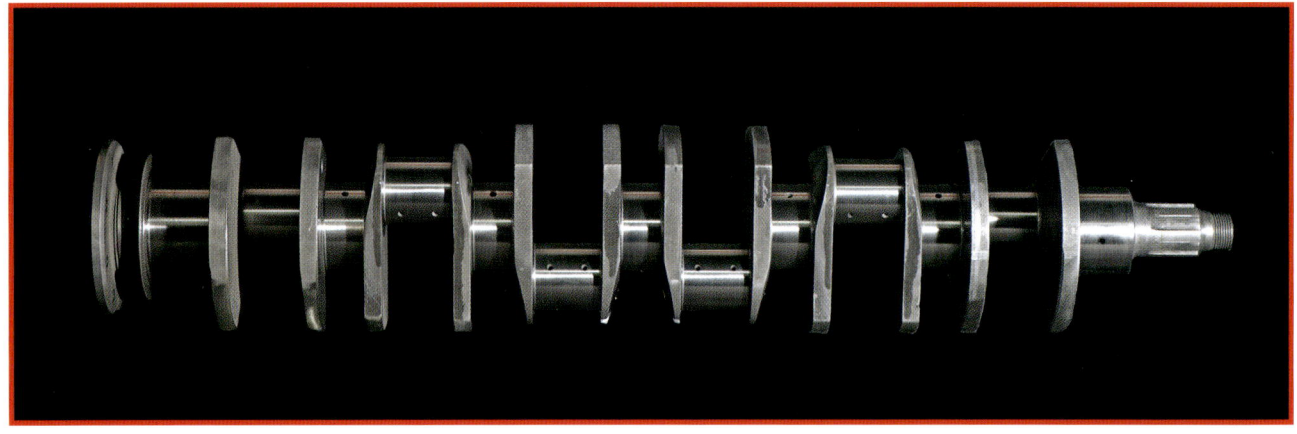

single-plate unit located on the flywheel, transmitting power through a five-speed gearbox via a propeller shaft to the rigid rear axle.

The engine shown in this book is mounted in a 195 Inter Vignale Coupé, designed by Giovanni Michelotti. Some specific details are unique to this particular coupé – such as duo-tone paintwork in dark green with a black roof. The quality of the interior finish is superb, putting this Ferrari firmly in the luxury category. The seats and door panels are covered with Connolly leather, with a Vignale emblem and chrome details. Wooden inserts in the door handles, a wood rim aluminium three-spoke steering wheel and gauges

↑ The cross-plane crankshaft for the 195 engine is similar to that of the 166 – forged steel, with seven main bearings.

→ With a little imagination, the cut-outs in the timing cover (viewed here inverted) make it look almost like a robotic face from another planet!

↓ The steel valves (two per cylinder) are operated via tappet fingers by a single overhead camshaft per bank. Here, the valves can be seen at the bottom, with the finger followers (and spacers) above, then the camshaft, with the pivots for the finger followers at the top.

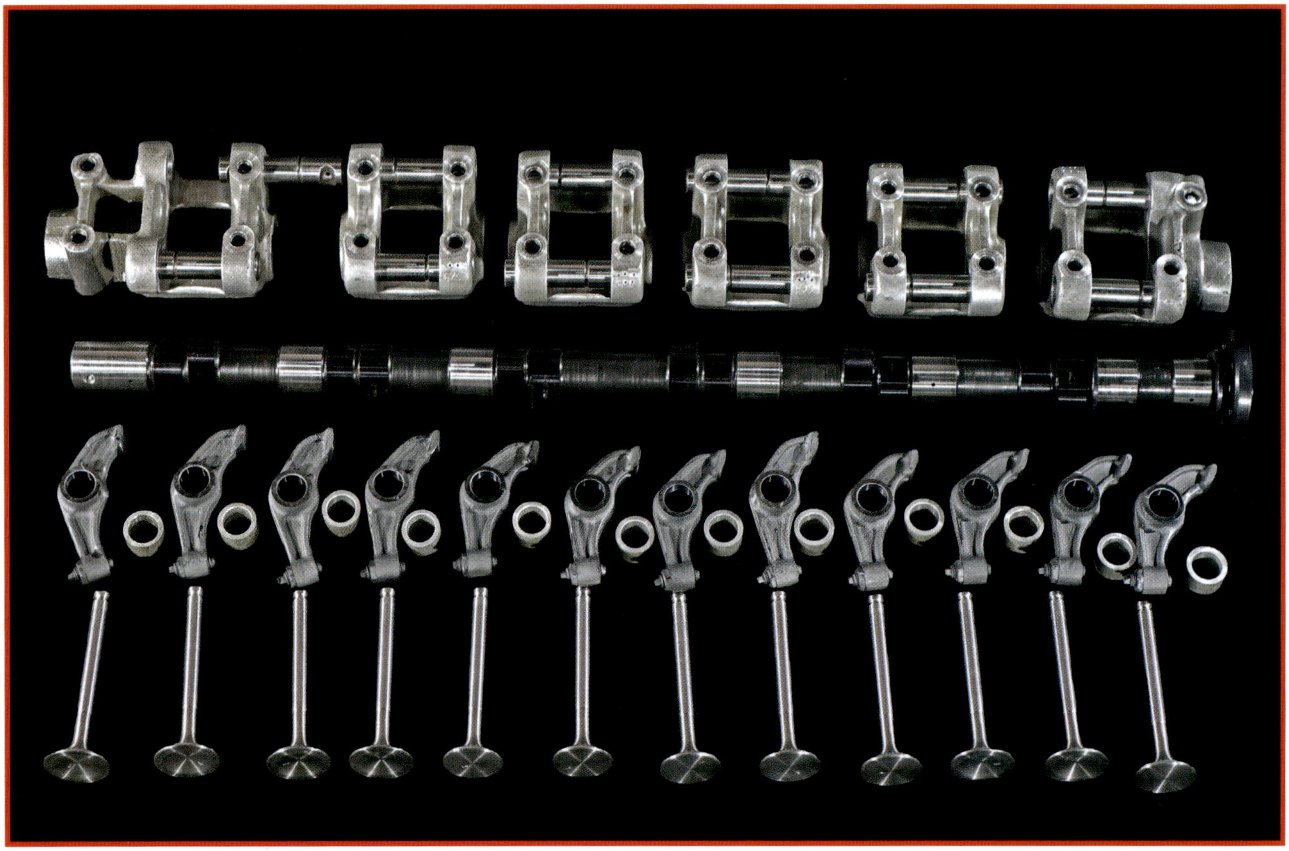

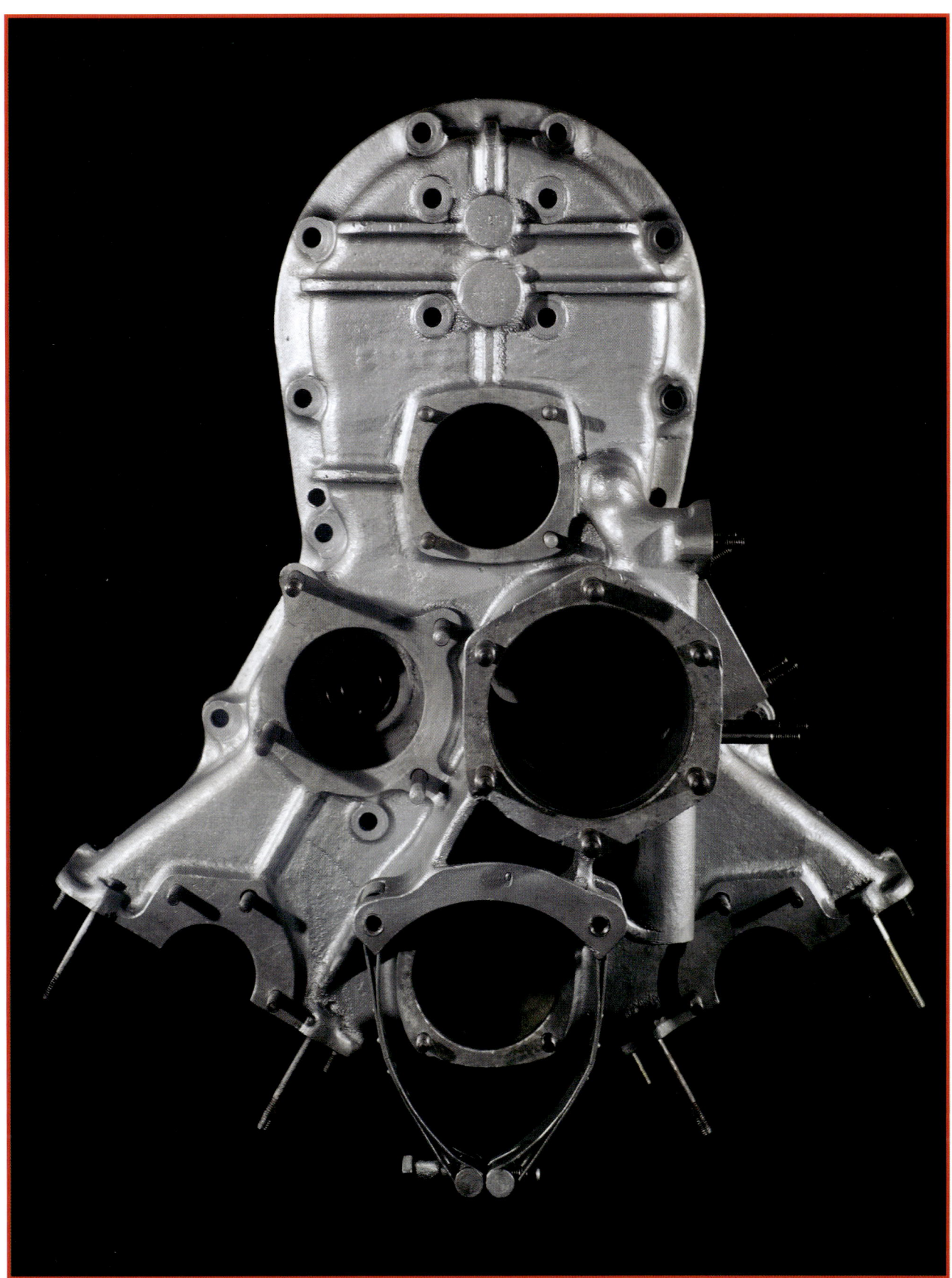

195 Inter: The first-generation Ferrari V12 (1949)

↑ The inverted cast-aluminium sump features integral cooling fins along its bottom and sides. The sump drain plug can be clearly seen in the bottom of the sump pan.

FERRARI 195 – TECHNICAL DATA

Engine code	195
Engine type	Front, longitudinal, V12, 60°
Bore and stroke	65 x 58.8mm (2.55 x 2.31in)
Total capacity	2,341.02cc (142.85cu in)
Unitary capacity	195.08cc (11.90cu in)
Compression ratio	7.5:1
Maximum power	128bhp (96kW) at 6,000rpm
Power per litre	55bhp/litre (41kW/litre)
Valve operation	Single overhead camshaft per bank, two valves per cylinder
Fuel feed	Single Weber 36 DCF carburettor
Ignition	Single spark plug per cylinder, twin distributors, single coil
Lubrication	Wet sump
Clutch	Dry, single plate
Maximum torque	154Nm (113.5lb ft) at 5,000rpm
Firing order	1–2–9–10–5–6–11–12–3–4–7–8

colour co-ordinated with the dashboard, provide an amazing elegance. In the engine bay, the cam covers featured the Ferrari script within longitudinal lines.

In the fifties, the operation and the reliability of the high-performances engines was often compromised by the cooling of the units, so Ferrari fitted large radiators behind large radiator grilles (the Ferrari factory's coachbuilders were renowned for producing masterpieces to grace the noses of its sport cars). The 195 Vignale Coupé follows this rule and was fitted with an artistically shaped radiator grille wearing a smile. This ensured adequate airflow for cooling the engine, and at the same time provided a sporty shape to the car. The 195's grille used all the space available, with the Marchal fog lights integrated below the rounded shape of the grille, and complementing the chrome-rimmed Marchal headlights. In spite of this large cooling opening, the 195, as with many other high performance engines of the period, was capable of running at high revs for long periods, which produced a lot of heat, so the water and oil temperature gauges needed to be watched with care by the driver. These engines were built to run fast, as were the cars in which they were mounted, and high speed was the only way to easily avoid overheating. So, although in the fifties the road traffic was far less busy than today, and the hold-ups due to traffic queues rare, going slowly was not a good idea for a 195 Ferrari!

↑ The domed 195 pistons, cast in aluminium, feature two compression rings and an oil-control ring.

↗ The flywheel features six dowels to locate the clutch assembly, and is secured to the crankshaft by eight bolts.

→ The single Weber 36 DCF carburettor, with air filters fitted. Some engines were fitted with three carburettors.

↓ The timing-chain gears, along with the alloy upper timing covers.

19

195 Inter: The first-generation Ferrari V12 (1949)

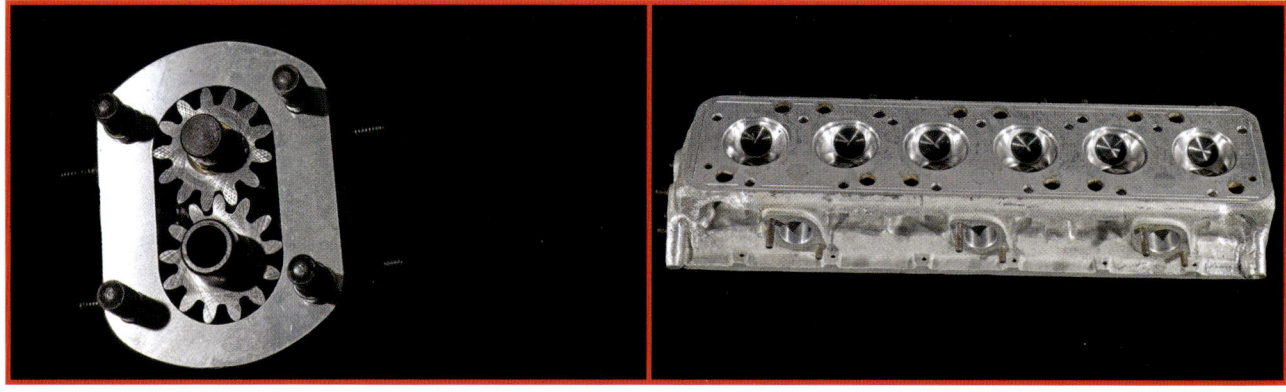

The 60° V12 'short block' Ferrari engines produced during the first five years of the Maranello factory's existence were very similar to one another, because of the materials used and the same basic design and layout. This first-generation 12-cylinder engine was special, due to both the period of post-war austerity in which it was conceived and constructed, and also due to it being a mechanical work of art. These details were frequently lost from the following 250 series engines, which often featured black-painted cam covers and carburettors hidden by bulky air filter housings. The charm of those first few and very rare V12 engines, including the 195, will remain incomparable forever.

↖ A view looking inside the twin-gear oil pump.

↑ A view of one of the cylinder heads, showing the 12 valves fitted to their valve seats in the combustion chambers, and the three shared inlet ports – one port for each pair of adjacent cylinders.

→ The cross-plane-configuration crankshaft has a pair of connecting rods (one for each cylinder bank) sharing each of the six big-end journals.

↓ The distance of only 90mm between the centres of adjacent cylinder bores inspired the 'short block' designation for the first generation of Ferrari V12 engines.

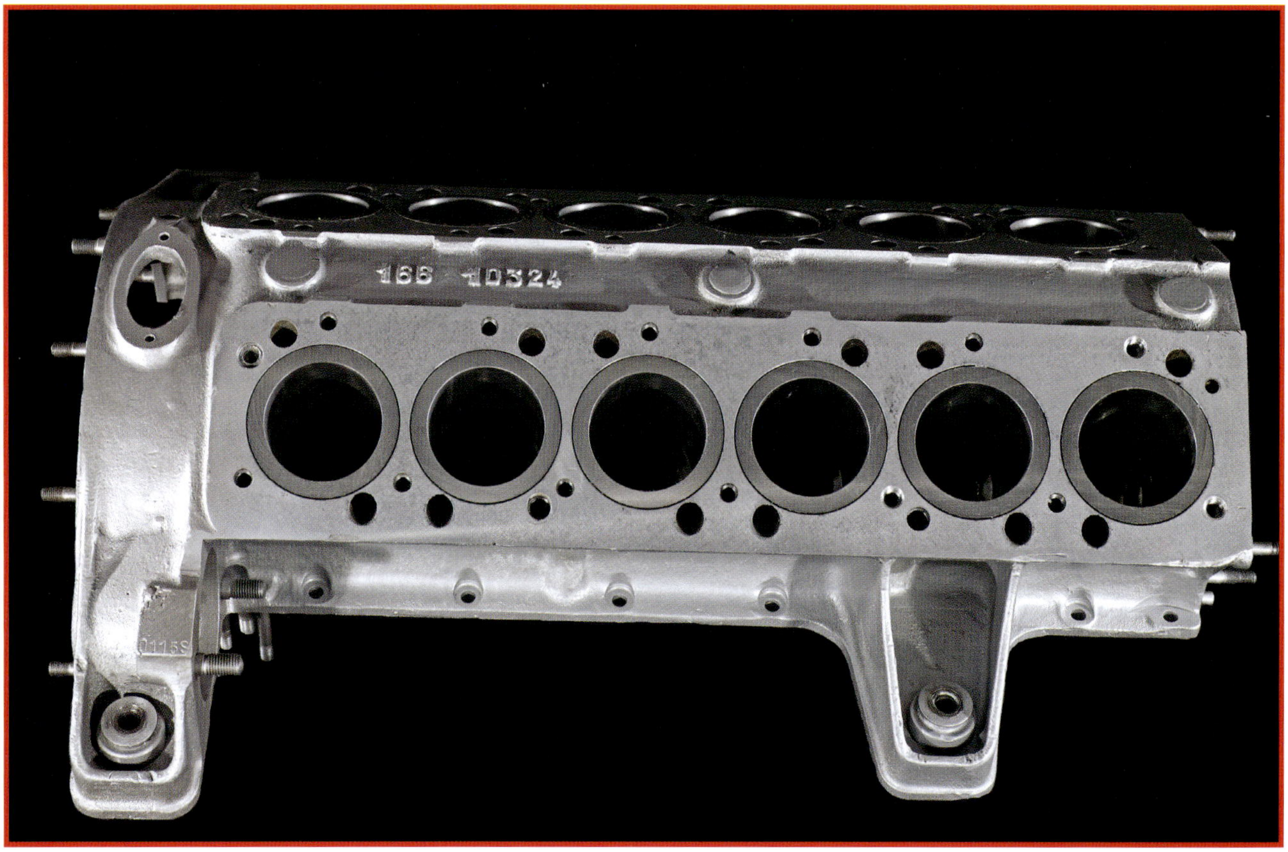

195 Inter: The first-generation Ferrari V12 (1949)

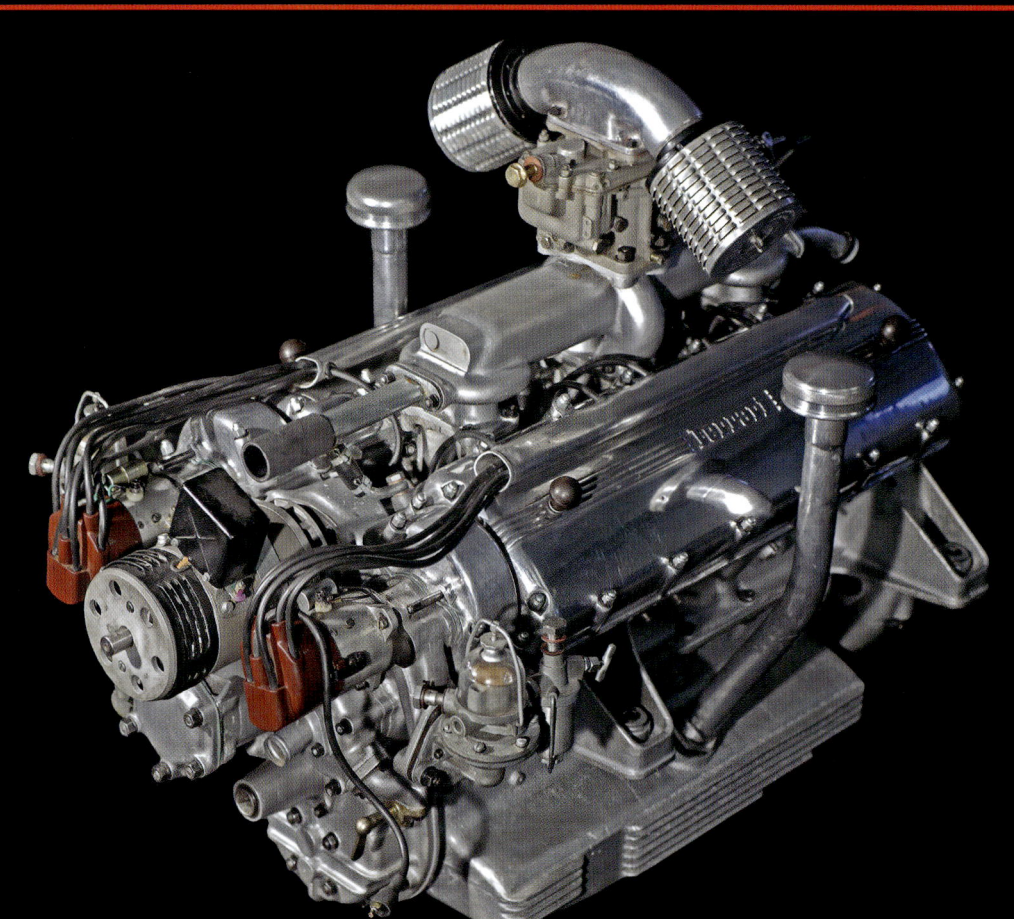

↑ A front view of this right-hand-drive 195, with its wide, smiling egg-crate grille curved to accommodate the fog lights.

↑ At the rear, the elegant styling features two chrome boot-release handles – one on either side.

➔ The elegant tail-light is located above the direction indicator, both lenses within a chrome surround.

↘ The Marchal fog lamps are integrated into the design of the front of the car, with recesses in the bumper and grille.

↘↘ The recessed aluminium door handles provide an elegant touch to this luxurious car.

↘↘↘ Borrani wire wheels were standard fitment, and a prominent feature of the design. The spare – located in the boot – was also a wire wheel.

↓ The 25 examples produced of the 195 featured bodywork by coachbuilders such as Ghia, Motto, Touring and Vignale.

25

195 Inter: The first-generation Ferrari V12 (1949)

340 America
The 'long block' V12 (1950)

← All in the detail – from the cast-in Ferrari branding to the domed nuts securing the camshaft covers.

↙ The cylinder liners screwed into position in the cylinder head, viewed from underneath.

The suffix that was used to name the first of Maranello's large-capacity engines came from Enzo Ferrari's overseas dream, and so the suffix 'A' (for 'America') appears on the long block of the 340 engine. With the idea of emulating the American 'big block' engines, engine designer Aurelio Lampredi planned a powerful and reliable power unit for the 340 America coupés and spiders. This unit was also installed (with minor changes from a competition viewpoint) in some race cars, such as the 340 Mexico (just four examples built) and the 340 Mille Miglia (ten examples built). Lampredi returned to Maranello after experience at Isotta Fraschini, where he had become an expert with large-capacity engines. He contributed to great innovations at Ferrari, including the use of cylinder liners screwed into the cylinder head (and sealed with O-rings at the bottom) for these engines, instead of the traditional arrangement of liners pressed into the cylinder block (with sealing provided by the cylinder-head gasket). This arrangement eliminated the possibility of a blown cylinder-head gasket. These engines became known as 'long block' units, as the screwed-in cylinder-liner arrangement necessitated more space between the bores than for a traditional layout. Thus, in 1950, the production of Ferrari cars with the 340 'long block' engine commenced, and they were installed in the 340 America series of road cars, aimed mainly at the US market, where big was best! This first series of large-capacity-engine 340 America Ferraris was succeeded by even larger-capacity versions of the same engine in the 375 America and 410 Superamerica series through the fifties. Then, with a return to a conventional cylinder head/liner arrangement, the large-capacity theme continued through the 400 Superamerica series, culminating with the 500 Superfast model that was produced between 1964 and 1966.

The origin of all the projects was, as ever, Enzo Ferrari's unbridled passion for motor racing. However, this engine also had the task of extending the overseas market for the

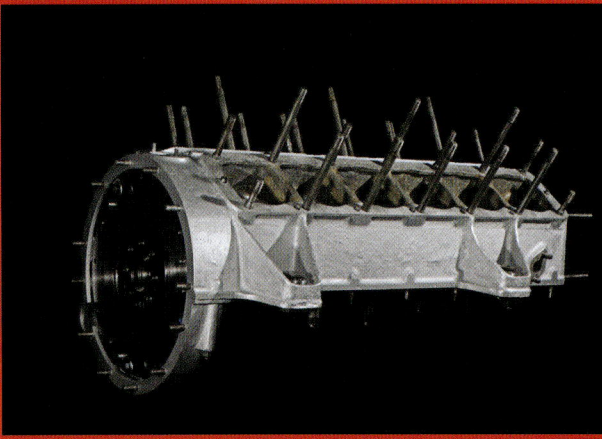

↘ On Lampredi's 'long block' V12, the distance between the centres of adjacent cylinder bores was 108mm, rather than the 90mm of the previous Colombo V12 units.

← The crankshaft sprockets, normally hidden by the timing cover.

Maranello factory, particularly in the USA. To turn the idea into reality, Enzo Ferrari brought the talented design engineer Aurelio Lampredi back to the company. He had worked for Ferrari briefly between late 1946 and early 1947, before leaving to work for Isotta Fraschini after a disagreement with Ferrari's Ing. Busso. Ferrari brought him back at the end of 1947, and gave him free rein on design, initially to refine, develop and improve the reliability of the Colombo-designed V12 engine, to ensure race wins. He did this in a number of ways, one of which was to increase the capacity of the engine, such that by the end of 1949 it had a capacity of 2.34 litres. He then embarked on his own V12 engine design which would evolve into the 340 'long block' engine. As an aside, he also designed the four-cylinder engines with which Alberto Ascari won the 1952 and 1953 World Drivers' Championships for Ferrari.

Lampredi's intuition, also influenced by knowledge of the American 'big-block' engines, led to the project for the first Ferrari long-block unit, with a distance between the centres of adjacent cylinder bores of 108mm, instead of 90mm for the previous V12 units. His new engine design was initially produced in 3.3-litre form, with a single-cylinder capacity of 275cc. The engine made its debut in the 1950 Mille Miglia, mounted in a pair of 275 S models with Touring bodies, and

↑ The engine number, with an 'A' suffix on the long block, as a reminder of Enzo Ferrari's overseas dream.

driven by Alberto Ascari/Senesio Nicolini and Gigi Villoresi/Pasquale Cassani. It was an unspectacular debut, as both cars retired with transmission failure. Following this, the

↓ This view of the cylinder block shows the length of the 'long block' conceived by Aurelio Lampredi.

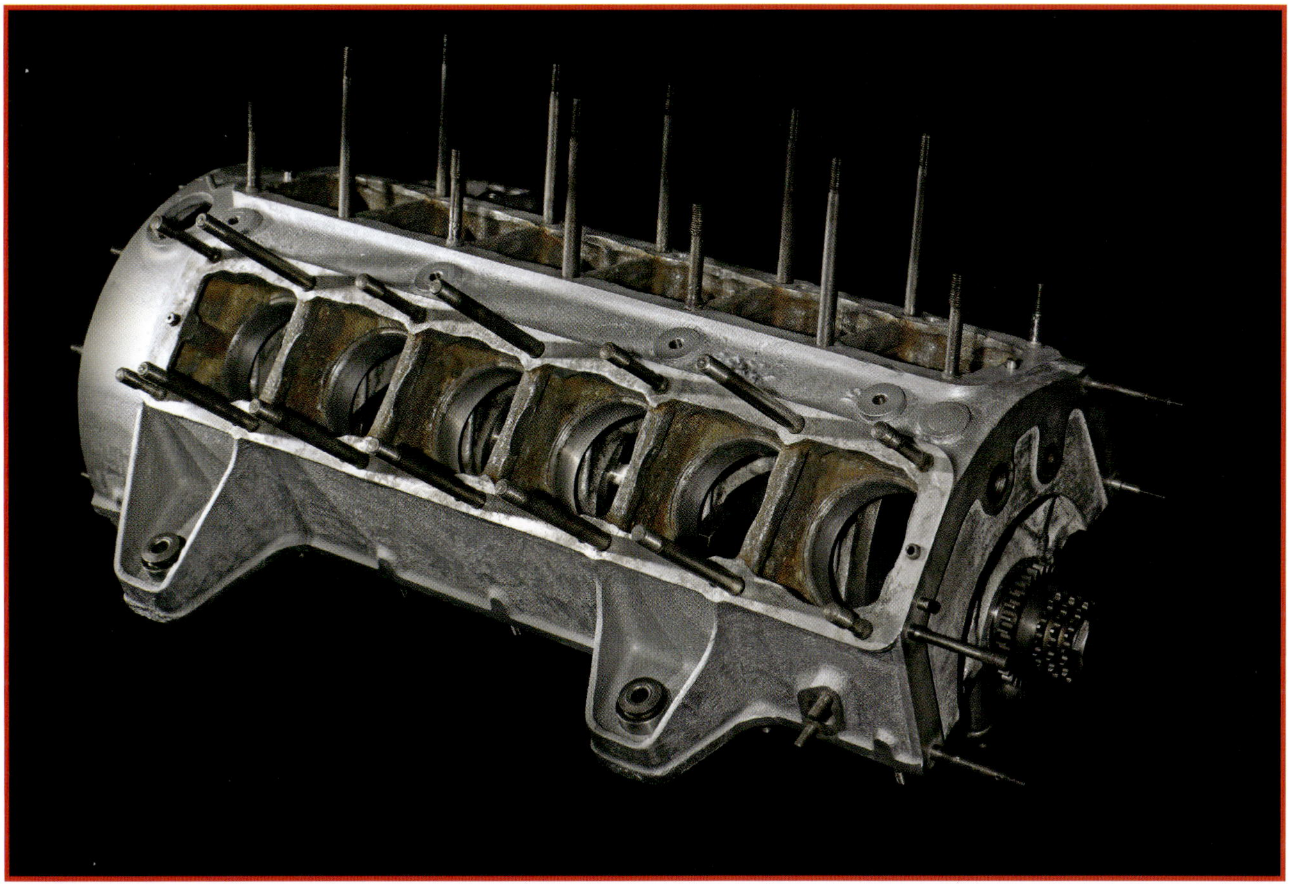

capacity was increased to provide a single-cylinder capacity of 341.8cc, and thus the first 340 engine was born. It was installed in an F1 Ferrari, driven by Alberto Ascari at the Gran Premio delle Nazioni, a non-championship F1 race in Geneva, Switzerland, in July 1950. Due to the increase in the length of the block, in comparison to the earlier Colombo V12 (which has become known as the 'short block'), the 340 looks like a giant! For this engine project, as previously mentioned, Lampredi used cylinder liners screwed into the cylinder heads, thus eliminating the head gasket and the possibility of leakage between combustion chambers, oil and water ways. The 340 engine had Ghisa cylinder liners, which had sealing rings at their base where they met the engine block.

After its first competitive outing, Ferrari decided that the 340 would be a great tool to strengthen marketing activities of his cars overseas. It would be particularly suitable for the USA, where 'big block' cars were the standard (and fuel costs were relatively low). A 4.1-litre Ferrari road car, for sure would draw the wealthy sports-car customers, giving rise to an expanded market for the *Cavallino Rampante* brand.

The first 340 engine (340/01) was unveiled in October 1950 at the Paris Motor Show, in chassis 0030MT, originally

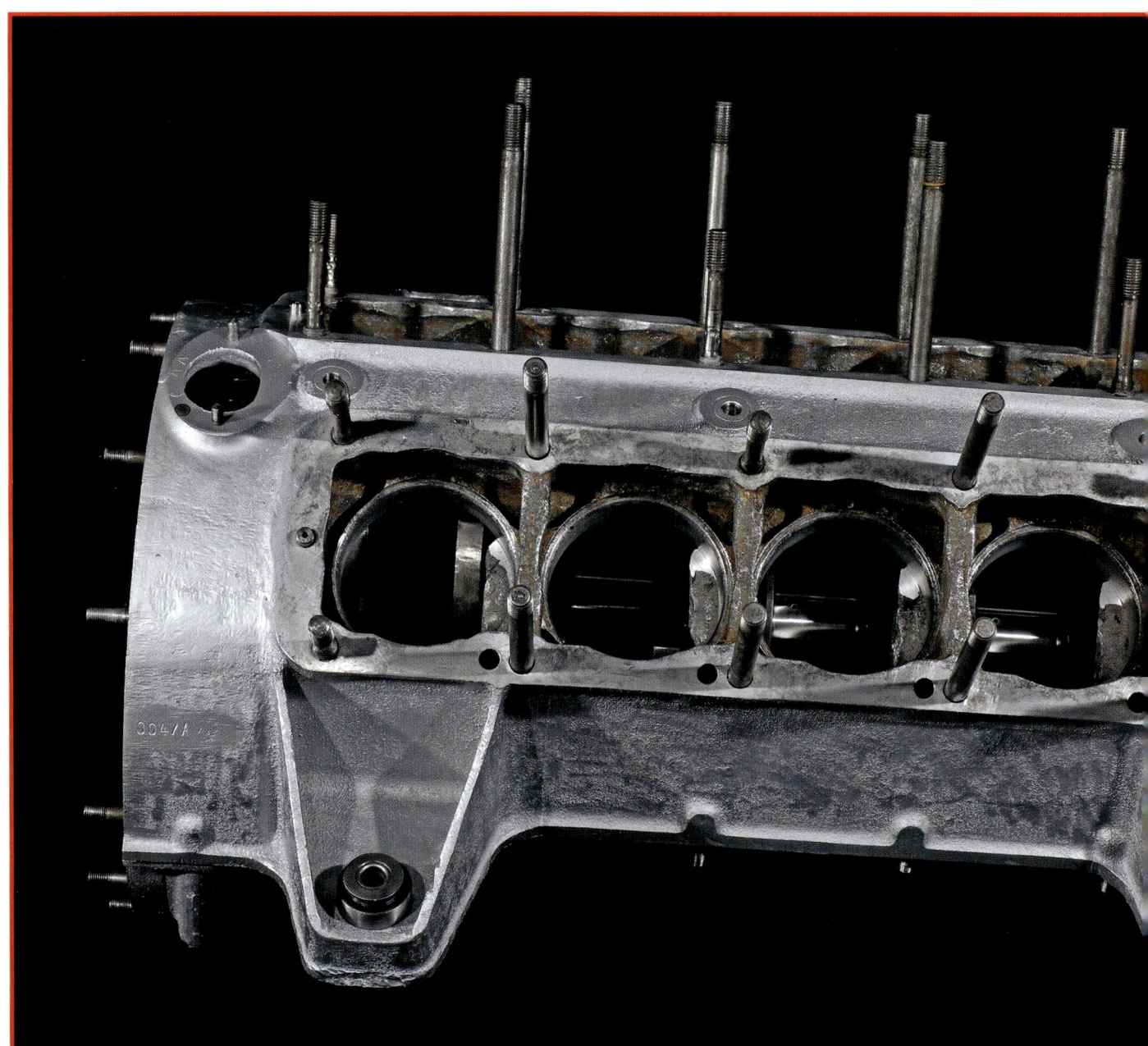

that of a 275 S, with new bodywork by Carrozzeria Touring. With the engine upgraded to 340 specification, the car was redesignated the 340 America. The test bed for the new engines series was the Mille Miglia, which ran from 28–29 April 1951, in which the works car – 340 Vignale Berlinetta chassi No. 0082A – emerged triumphant, driven by Gigi Villoresi and Pasquale Cassani. They covered the 1,000-mile route in 12 hours, 50 min and 18 sec. The mighty 60° V12 340 engine (code 250), had a total displacement of 4,101.66cc (25.3cu in), a bore of 80mm (3.1in) and a stroke of 68mm (2.68in), and it produced 220bhp (164kW) at 6,000rpm, with a torque of 260Nm (192lb ft) at 4,800rpm, which allowed this car to easily reach 150mph (240kmh), a significant speed in the fifties.

The series of 340 models that this engine was originally used in comprised of both competition variants, normally with a Touring Barchetta body, and also what, from their features and appearance, were clearly road cars. However, in one of those common quirks with Ferrari, all models carried chassis numbers in the 'even' competition car sequence.

The impressive block had square housings surrounding each cylinder liner, providing water jackets to facilitate adequate cooling. The block was cast in light alloy, as were the cylinder heads, with spark plugs located inboard within the vee. The large pistons were light alloy, manufactured by Borgo, with steel connecting rods. A single steel overhead camshaft was fitted per bank, driven by a triple chain from the front of the crankshaft, with a tensioner, all contained in a light-alloy housing. Fuel was supplied via three twin-choke Weber DCF3 downdraught carburettors mounted in the centre of the vee, and fed by twin mechanical fuel pumps. A separate distributor was used for each cylinder bank, with a single coil. Electrical power was provided by a 12-volt battery charged by a dynamo driven by a V-belt from the crankshaft. The firing order was 1–12–5–8–3–10–6–7–2–11–4–9. Specific features of Lampredi's 340 design included the external metal tubes, used for oil and water distribution (rather than internal galleries), and roller cam followers that replaced the previous finger type. The lubrication system was wet sump, with a crankshaft-driven mechanical oil pump which drew the oil from the sump and distributed it to the various parts of the engine, via the previously mentioned external metal tubes. As with all the Ferrari 12-cylinder engines built after 1957 (as with the short block of the 250 series 128 D and DF engines), the connecting-rod big-ends had a horizontal split, instead of the typical oblique split, and white-metal big-end bearings were used. The transmission used with this front-mounted longitudinal 340 engine was a five-speed manual non-synchromesh unit, with a light alloy casing, located to the rear of the clutch bellhousing. A dry single-plate clutch was used. To minimise production costs, the gearbox was the same as the unit used on the 166, 195 and 212 models. However, the version used with the 340 engine featured different gear ratios and a larger-diameter main shaft (80mm). The top of the casing, which supported the gear-lever housing, used the same casting as the 212 model. Power was transmitted to the rigid rear axle via a propeller shaft with universal joints at each end.

In 1952, Ferrari produced another four 340 models,

← **The large block featured square housings for the water jacket surrounding each cylinder liner, to ensure adequate cooling.**

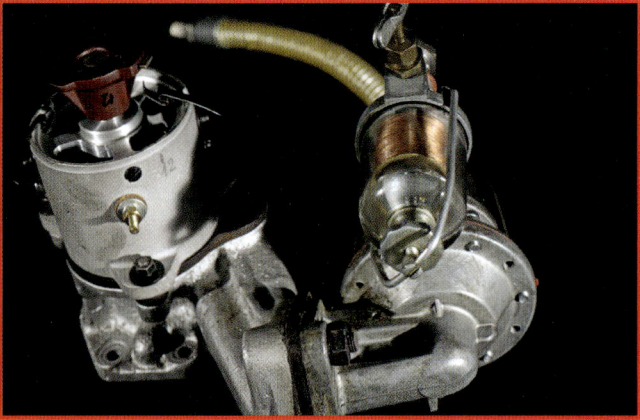

which were given the designation 'Mexico', with 340 as the number code. The engines for these cars produced a claimed 280bhp (209kW), the power increase being due to the fitment of Weber 40 DCF/3 twin-choke carburettors, different camshaft profiles and a higher compression ratio. The Mexico cars also featured a change to a multi-plate dry clutch, while the gear ratios were altered to suit the sustained high-speed sections in the race for which they were destined. These four cars were built on the instructions of Enzo Ferrari, to create a powerful and strong machine that would be capable of repeating the great result in the 1951 Carrera Panamericana road race, when a pair of

↖ The 340 America was fitted as standard with three Weber 36 DCF carburettors – available as an option for the 195.

↑ A separate mechanical fuel pump and distributor are fitted for each cylinder bank, mounted at the front of each cylinder head and driven from the end of the camshaft.

→ The big and heavy cast-iron flywheel, on which the dry, single-plate clutch is mounted.

↓ A side view of a cylinder head (inverted) showing the Ghisa cylinder liners, with grooves in their bases for the sealing rings.

33
340 America: The 'long block' V12 (1950)

↑ The large-capacity cast-aluminium sump features cooling fins and a cut-out to accommodate the starter motor.

FERRARI 340 AMERICA – TECHNICAL DATA

Engine code	250
Engine type	Front, longitudinal, V12, 60°
Bore and stroke	80 x 68mm (3.14 x 2.67cu in)
Total capacity	4,101.66cc (250.29cu in)
Unitary capacity	341.80cc (20.85 cu in)
Compression ratio	8:1
Maximum power	220bhp (162kW) at 6,000rpm
Power per litre	54bhp/litre (38kW/litre)
Valve operation	Single overhead camshaft per bank, two valves per cylinder
Fuel feed	Three twin-choke Weber 36 DCF carburettors
Ignition	Single spark plug per cylinder, twin distributors, single coil
Lubrication	Wet sump
Clutch	Dry, single plate
Maximum torque	260Nm (191.7lb ft) at 4,800rpm
Firing order	1–12–5–8–3–10–6–7–2–11–4–9

Ferrari 212 models finished first and second. The model name Mexico came from the name of the country that hosted the race. The four Mexico models were bodied by Vignale, one being a spider and the other three berlinettas. Luigi Chinetti and Jean Lucas drove one of the three Mexico Berlinettas to third place overall in the 1952 race, behind a pair of works-entered Mercedes-Benz 300SLs.

In 1953, Ferrari produced another ten examples of this latest update of the 340 engine, destined for a model with the suffix MM, of which four were Vignale-bodied Spiders, two featured coachwork by Carrozzeria Touring, and four had Pininfarina Berlinetta bodies. One of the 340 MM Vignale Spider's won the 1953 Mille Miglia (posting a new average speed record of more than 142kmh/88mph) completing the 939 miles (1,512km) in 10 hours, 37 min and 19 sec, driven by Giannino Marzotto and Marco Crosara. The 340 MM was the last evolution of the 340 series, built after the 340 America models had ceased production. The 340 MM was built for racing, as was proved by its results in competition, another 340 MM winning the Giro di Sicilia driven by Gigi Villoresi.

To satisfy customers who preferred a more gentle power unit for road use, rather than a race-tuned engine, Ferrari built a small series of six road cars designated the 342 America. There were three coupés and three cabriolets,

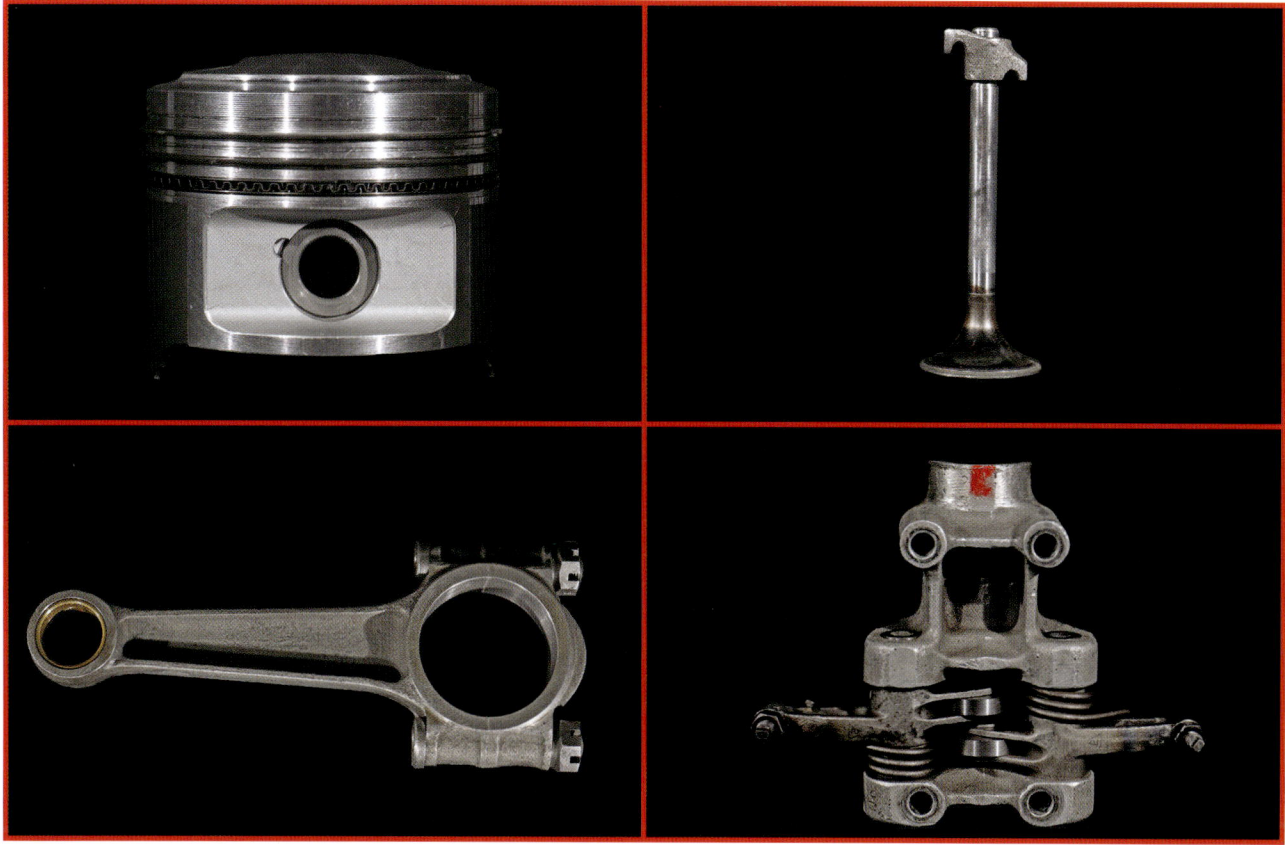

↑↑ The aluminium domed pistons (with two compression rings and an oil-control ring) were manufactured by Borgo.

↑ The connecting-rod big-ends had a horizontal split, rather than the then-typical oblique-angled split.

↑↑ The cam followers act on a cast lug fitted to the tops of the valve stems.

↑ For the 340 America engine, roller cam followers replaced the previous finger-follower system.

and despite clearly being road cars from their physical appearance, like the earlier cars, they carried chassis numbers in the even series competition-car range. The change of numbers in the model name should have signified an increase in cubic capacity, but in one of those quirks familiar in Ferrari history, the engine size was exactly the same as the 340 series. The 342 engine (code number 100), was identical to that of the 340 America, producing 230bhp (172kW) at 6,000rpm, the biggest mechanical change being to the gearbox, which was provided with syncromesh on all four ratios. The very last example of these six cars – chassis 0248 AL (America Lungo) – was actually fitted with a 4.5-litre engine, but still retained the 342 model reference, and was exhibited at the 1953 New York Auto Show. It is interesting to note, that from this evolutionary unit came the engine for the 375 America model that went into production in late 1953 – just after the end of 340 production – as a replacement model with newly styled bodywork.

The 340 models constituted the first ever supercar that Ferrari marketed specifically for the United States, even though it ended production before Enzo Ferrari had established an official concessionaire in the US. It is curious that one of the first official Ferrari overseas concessionaires was Australian, and the story of its emergence is as strange as it is interesting. Bill Lowe, a car enthusiast who had read about the Italian marque's exploits in national and international competition, asked Ferrari about buying a 212 Export model to run in Australian races. Ferrari could not fulfil Lowe's purchase request because of the lack of an Australian dealer. It took only a short time for Bill Lowe to come up with the idea of becoming the official dealer in Australia, and thus with Ferrari's blessing W.H. Lowe & Company in Melbourne became the official Ferrari dealer for Australia in 1952. With regard to the American market, although he had been selling Ferraris on a private basis since 1949, it was not until 1953 that Luigi Chinetti founded

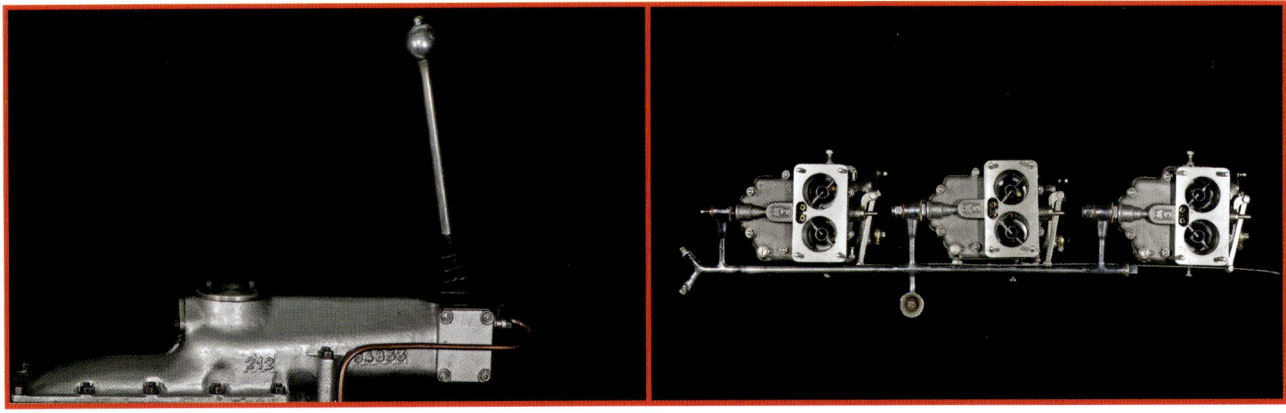

Luigi Chinetti Motors to become the official US dealer. He was one of the instigators of putting the Ferrari name on the international map, initially through his victory in the 1949 Le Mans 24 Hours, and later through his sales efforts on Ferrari cars in the US. Although further dealers were subsequently appointed in the western part of the US, the Chinetti name has remained synonymous with Ferrari ever since. Chinetti Motors ceased trading in 1977, and today import is through a fully Ferrari-owned subsidiary company, Ferrari North America, that runs the US operation, but it was the large-bore Lampredi-designed 340 series engine, and Luigi Chinetti, that realised Enzo Ferrari's American dream.

↖ The gear lever protrudes from the top of the alloy gearbox casing, which is located longitudinally at the rear of the engine.

↑ A view from above of the three Weber carburettors, showing the choke tubes and jets.

→ The alloy timing cover shows the 60° vee angle of this 4.1-litre engine designed by Aurelio Lampredi.

↓ The forged-steel crankshaft – seen here in position in Lampredi's 'long block' – is supported by seven main bearings.

37

340 America: The 'long block' V12 (1950)

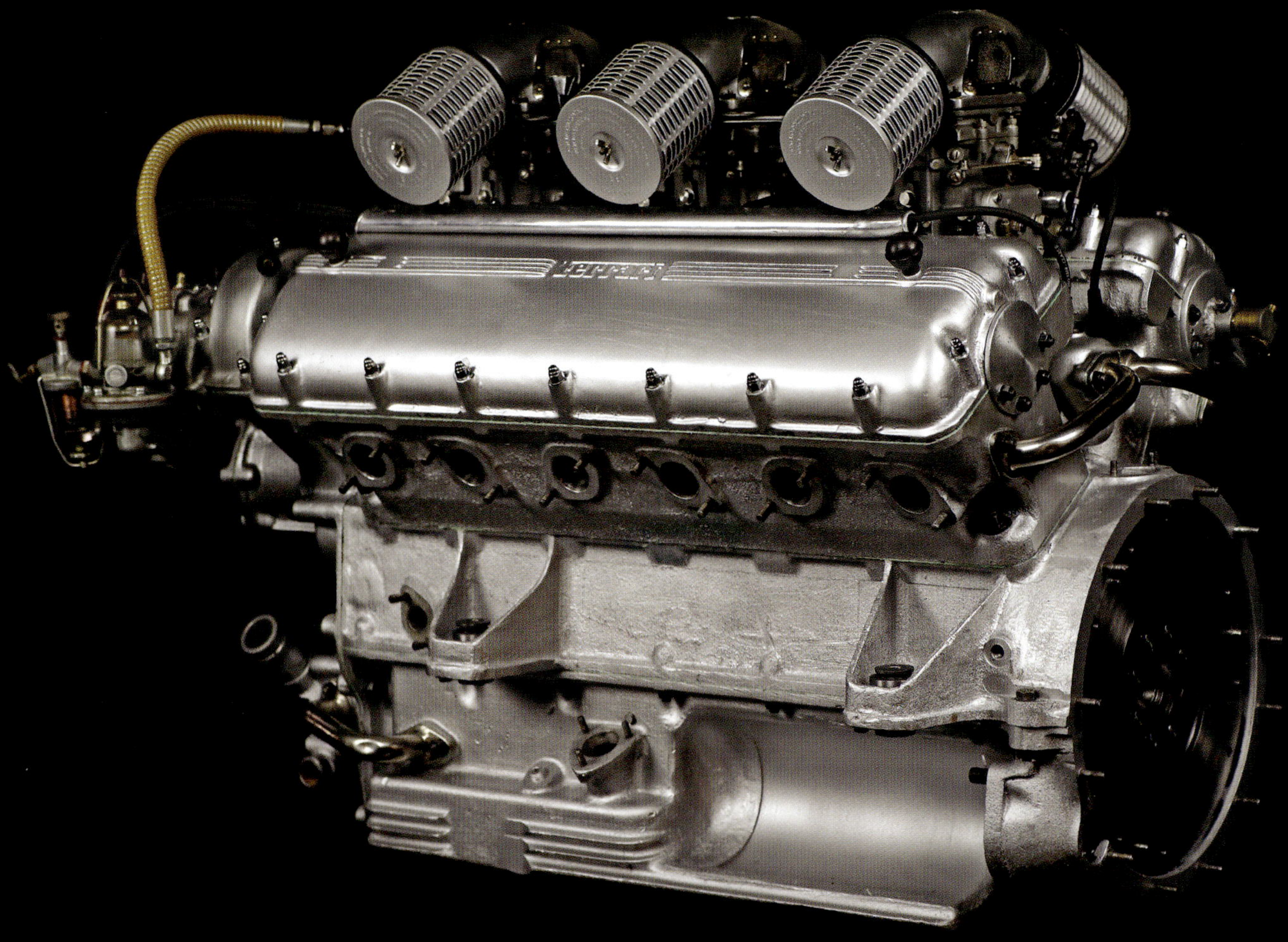

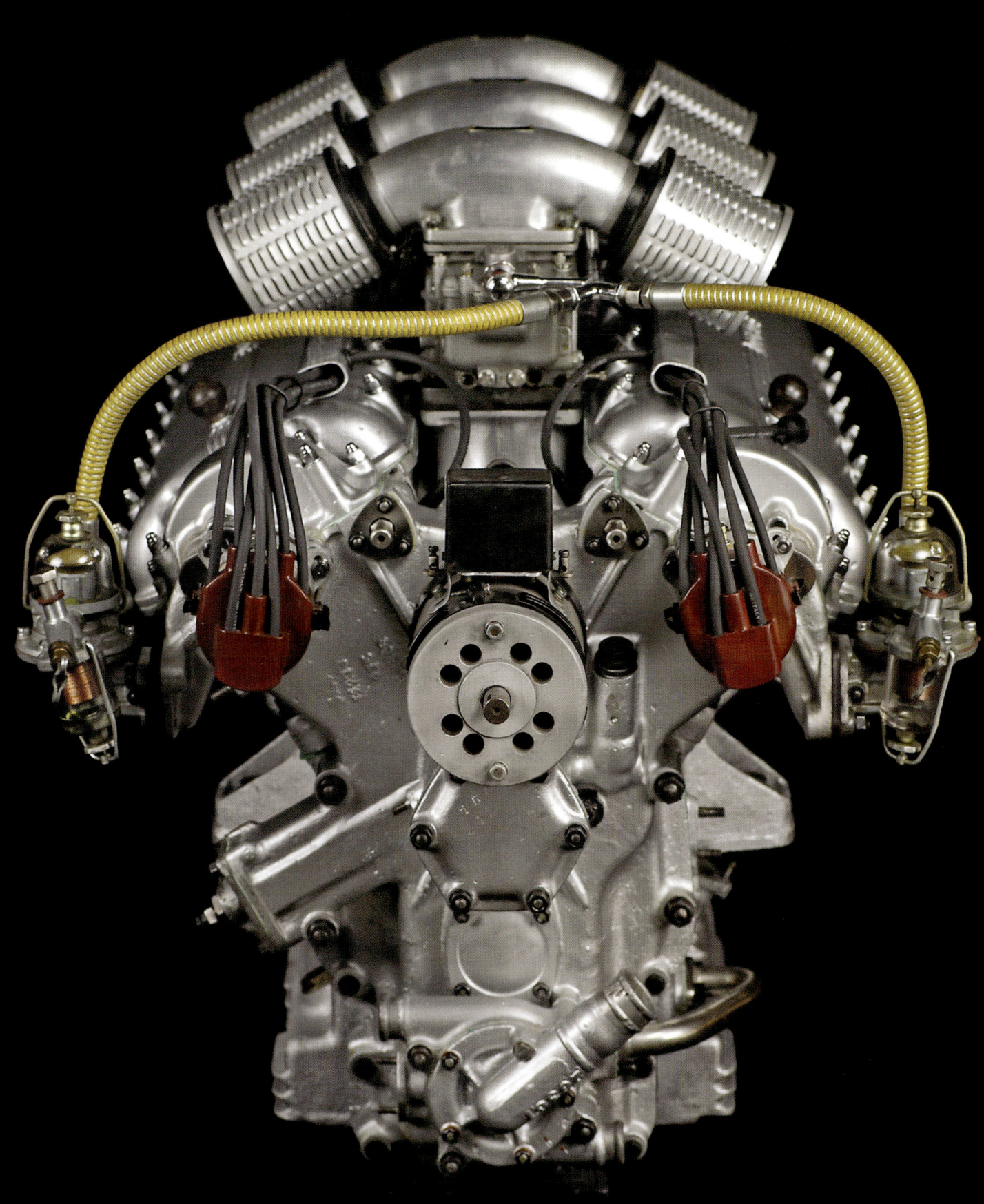

↑ The front view of the 340 America Ghia is characterised by a large egg-crate grille above a substantial chromed bumper.

↑ The perfect harmony of the rounded lines gives this luxurious berlinetta a refined elegance.

➔ The discreet Ferrari branding on the blue-painted bodywork of this 340 America sits well with the Ghia badge on the chrome of the number-plate surround.

↘ The detailing of the tail-light, with chrome surround, is an essential part of the elegant styling.

↘↘ The flush-fitting door handle underlines the class of this early Ferrari design.

↘↘↘ The chromed headlight, with the small sidelight below, complements the classic chromed grille.

↓ The elegance of the Ferraris for the American market was underlined by superb details throughout the styling.

41

340 America: The 'long block' V12 (1950)

250 California
A classic V12 icon (1957)

← The top of the domed piston with two cut-outs to accommodate the valves.

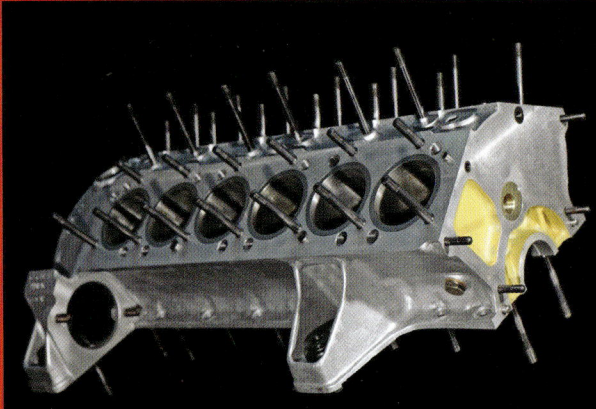

↙ The V12 60° ngine block shown with the cast-iron cylinder liners in place.

The 250 GT Spider California is, without any doubt, one of the most beautiful convertible cars ever built. Styled by Scaglietti (not Pininfarina, as sometimes mistakenly quoted) and aimed at the American market, hence the model name, it has become a classic icon of beauty. The 250 V12 'short block', Colombo-designed engine fitted under the California bonnet had the same technical specifications as the engines used in the 250 Berlinetta Tour de France (TdF). The idea to build a special Ferrari for the American market came from John Von Neumann, the Hollywood Ferrari dealer, who made contact with the head of North American Racing Team (NART), Luigi Chinetti, suggesting production of a spider using the chassis of the legendary 250 TdF Berlinetta. Enzo Ferrari, who was thinking about how to conquer the US market, surrendered gladly to pressure from Chinetti, hence beginning the fairy tale of this car. From late 1957, when the first California prototype appeared, 107 examples were built up until February 1963. The engine types that equipped these cars were the 128 C, 128 D, 128 DF, 128 F, 168 and 168/61.

The original Colombo-designed 128 C engine, revisited by Aurelio Lampredi, had a capacity of 2,953cc, with a single overhead camshaft per bank, and spark plugs located within the vee of the banks. The front, longitudinally mounted 3.0-litre V12 was located by four engine mountings on the cylinder block. The 128 C engine was the type fitted to the first eight 250 GT Californias built (until chassis No. 0939GT), and this engine was also used for various 250 series cars of that period, such as the 250 GT TdF Berlinetta, 250 GT Pininfarina Coupé/Cabriolet and 250 Boano and Ellena Coupés.

Among all the cars in which this engine was fitted, the most sought-after classic model is the spider California, whether it be a long-wheelbase (LWB) or a short-wheelbase (SWB) example. The chassis for all 107 examples (both LWB and SWB) were built on the same assembly line as the contemporary Tdf Berlinettas, with identical brakes,

↖ The camshafts (single camshaft per bank) are driven by a triplex chain from these sprockets at the front of the crankshaft.

← Each of the hollow cast-iron camshafts operates both the inlet and exhaust valves on one cylinder bank.

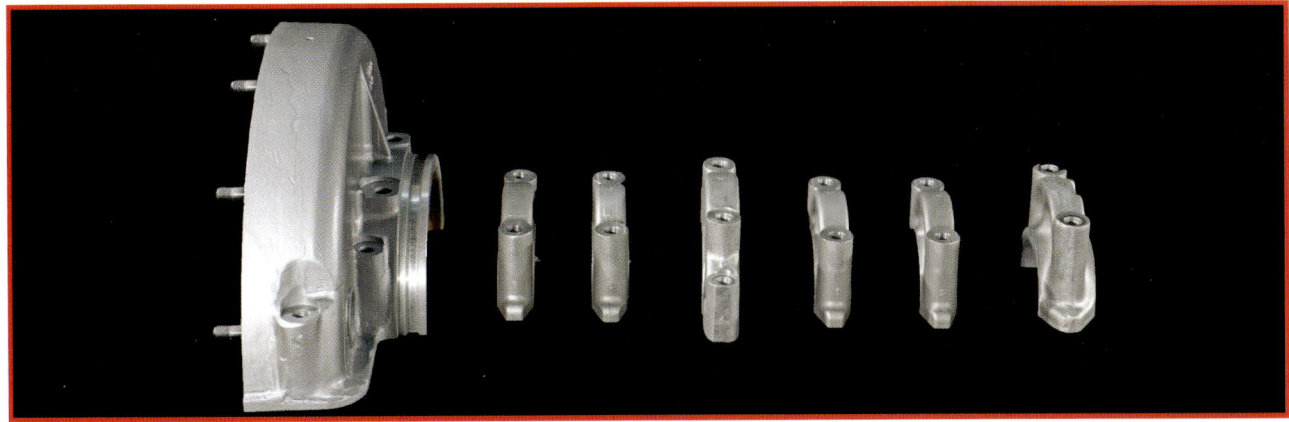

▲ The seven crankshaft main-bearing caps are located by dowels and studs and secured to the cylinder block by nuts.

suspension and other running gear. Apart from a single right-hand-drive SWB example, the Californias were only produced in left-hand-drive form. The 3.0-litre 60° V12 fitted to all these spiders was available in varying specifications. During over six years of production, only nine cars were produced featuring full alloy bodywork; all the other examples featured steel bodies with the doors, bonnet and boot lid in light alloy, whilst a hard top was available as an option. The desirability of the model is reflected in today's market price, with cars changing hands for up to US$20 million, depending on the model and history. On the late LWB cars, the engines (type 128 DF and 128 F) featured spark plugs located outside the vee of the bank, rather than inside as on previous engines. These units also featured twin coils, and

▼ The inverted 128 C cylinder block showing the main-bearing locations and the bearing-cap locating dowels and studs.

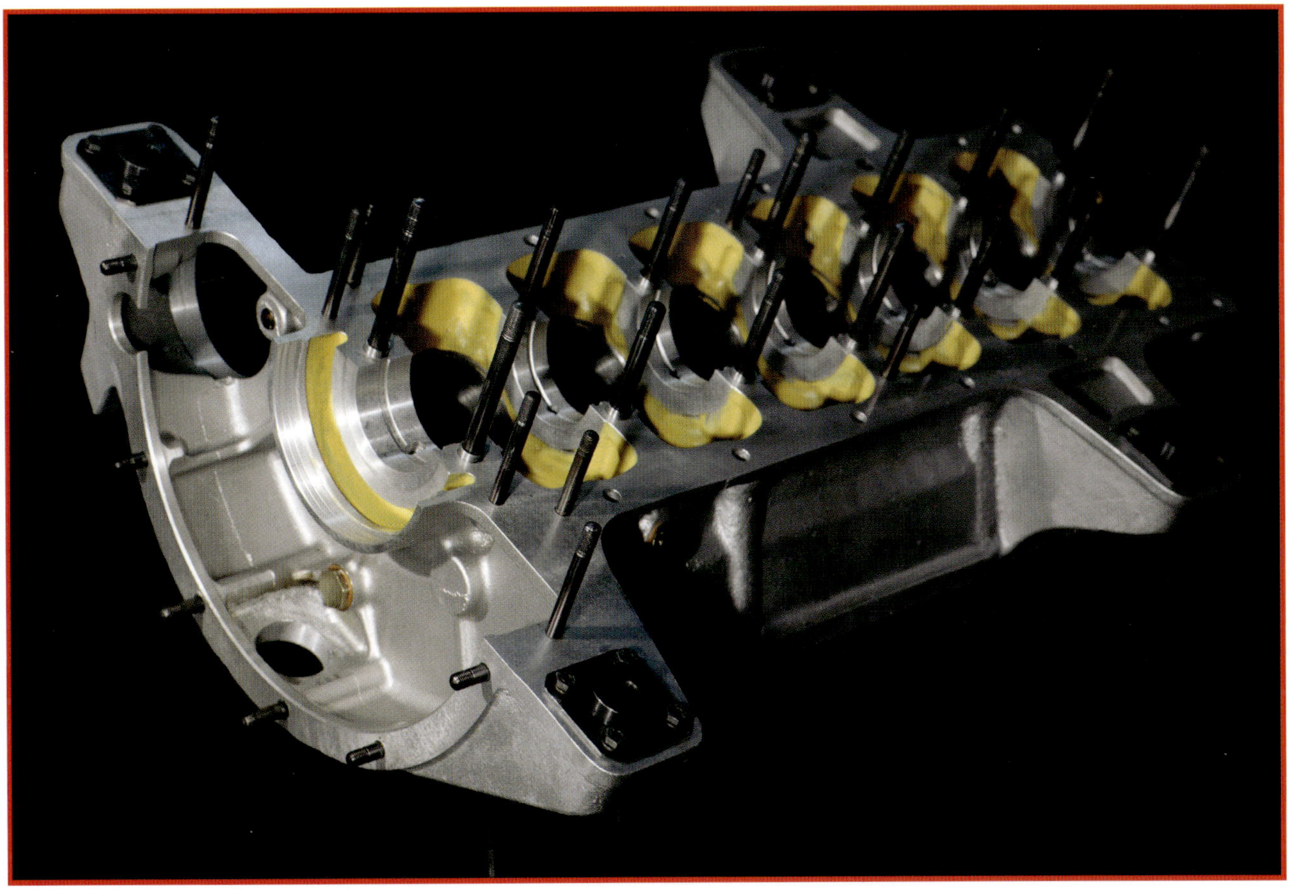

twin distributors, plus larger carburettors. Certain examples featured additional extra upgrades, with different camshafts, valve sizes, and carburettor set-ups, to boost the power output for fast road or competition use.

The cylinder block was manufactured from light alloy, as were the cylinder heads, pistons, timing covers, sump and clutch bellhousing. Valve operation was via a single overhead camshaft per bank, driven by a triplex chain via sprockets and a tensioner from the front of the crankshaft, with roller cam followers to the rocker arms. The nitrided crankshaft ran in seven main bearings, with white-metal shells to the connecting-rod big-end bearings. The connecting rods were steel, with a white-metal bearing to the piston gudgeon pin. The cast-iron cylinder liners featured the typical distance of all Colombo-derived 'short blocks' of 90mm between bore centres. Lubrication was via a wet sump. The clutch was a dry single-plate unit from Sachs, from which the drive went to a four-speed gearbox, then via a propeller shaft to a rigid rear axle. The ignition system for the type 128 C engine featured in this chapter comprised a single coil and single distributor, though later engines featured twin coils and twin distributors, as mentioned previously. Fuel was supplied via an electric pump and adjacent filter to a mechanical pump in the

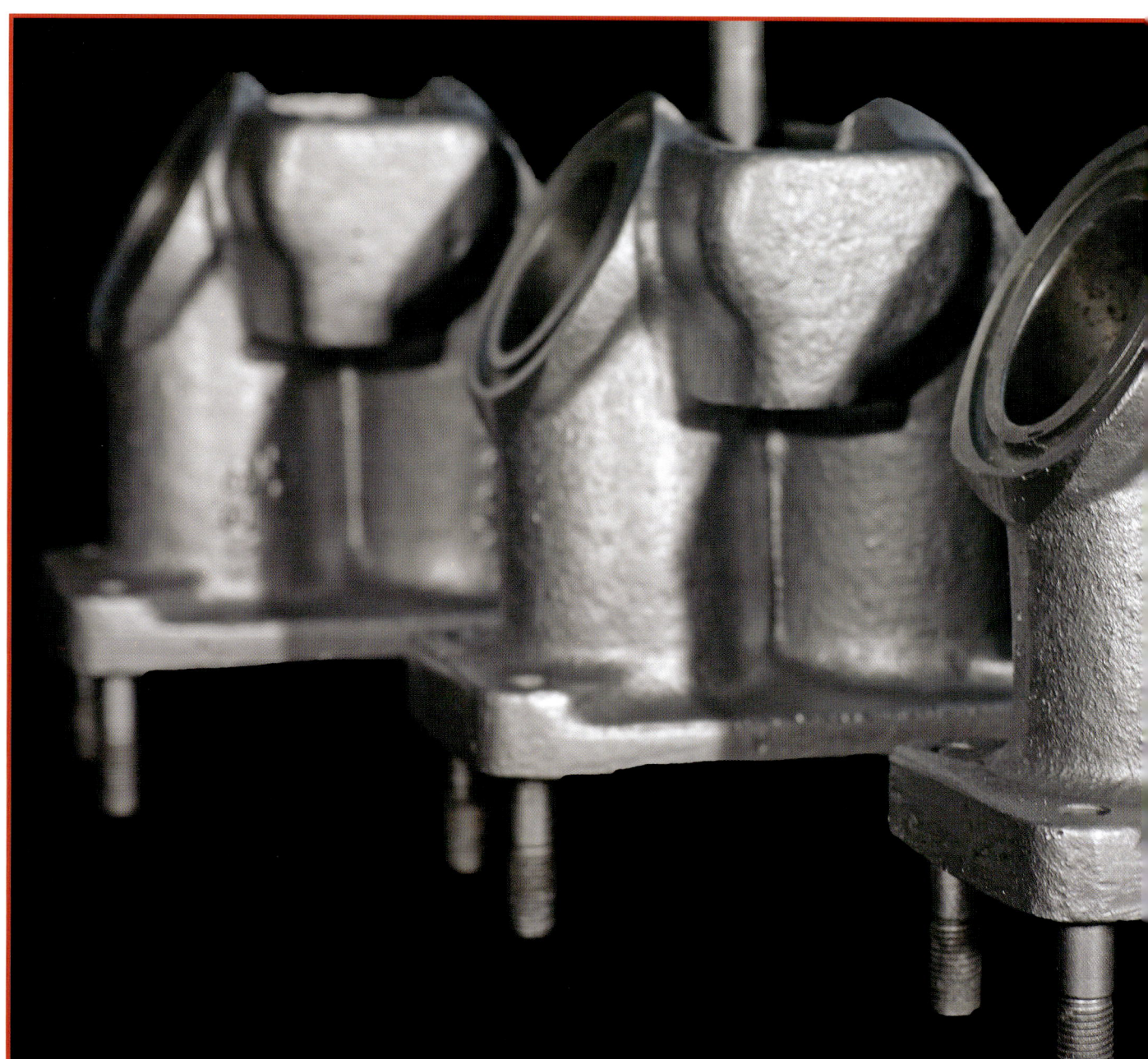

engine bay with a further filter assembly, then to three twin-choke Weber 36 DCL carburettors. This engine was capable of producing 237bhp (177kW) at 7,000rpm, with a torque of 245Nm (181lb ft) at 5,000rpm, and a compression ratio of 8.5:1. The firing order was 1–7–5–11–3–9–6–12–2–8–4–10.

Long-wheelbase 250 Californias (with 2,600mm wheelbase) were built from 1958 to 1960, although the prototype was produced in late 1957, and a total of 51 LWB cars were built. All 51 LWB examples were powered by type 128 engines, with different suffixes denoting progressive evolutions of the engine series. Factory engine code 128 C was the first engine, fitted to just eight LWB models, followed by type 128 D, fitted to 36 California Spiders. The final seven LWB cars built were fitted with engines coded 128 F or 168. Within these engine codes, various detailed changes were made. Instead of the 9mm valve lift and the 36 DCL3 Weber carburettors used on the early 128 engines, for the engine type 168, the camshaft lift became 10mm and the carburettors were 40 DCL6, taking the power over 270bhp (201kW). All the LWB models were built on chassis with factory reference numbers 508 C and 508 D (as on the concurrently produced TdF Berlinettas). The final cars produced in the series were fitted with four-wheel disc brakes, instead of the drum brake set-up of the early examples.

During the production period of the model the styling remained essentially the same, with early cars in the series being essentially a 250 GT TdF Berlinetta minus the roof. They featured the same small vertical rear light units and the same-style shaped aluminium exhaust air slots on the front wings, although the door handles were different, those on the California being flush units instead of the 'open' type on the berlinetta. Subsequently, the model was provided with a reshaped tail featuring a step below the boot lid, and a modified rear-wing line with larger rear light units, as fitted to the 250 GT PF Coupé, 'open'-type door handles, and the exhaust air slots on the front wings became more stylised, featuring three vertical blades covering a diamond mesh. The bodies of the 'SWB' series of cars were very similar to those of the outgoing 'LWB' version, but were mounted on a new 2,400mm-wheelbase chassis, that initially had factory reference number 539, and then 539/61, as on the concurrently produced 'SWB' berlinettas. The new chassis reduced the overall height of the car by 30mm, and although barely discernible, it gave the car a squatter appearance than the earlier examples, but they are still difficult to tell apart. The easiest methods of identifying a late 'LWB' example from an 'SWB' car is the design of the bonnet air intake, which on 'LWB' examples is proud of the bonnet line, whilst that on the 'SWB' rises from a depression in the bonnet line. The exhaust air outlet design on the front wings is also different, in that the 'SWB' version only has two vertical blades. As with the earlier 'LWB' variant, all 'SWB' examples were available with either open or Plexiglas-covered headlights, apart from 1959 Italian-market examples, which had to have open headlights due to new lighting legislation introduced in that country in that year.

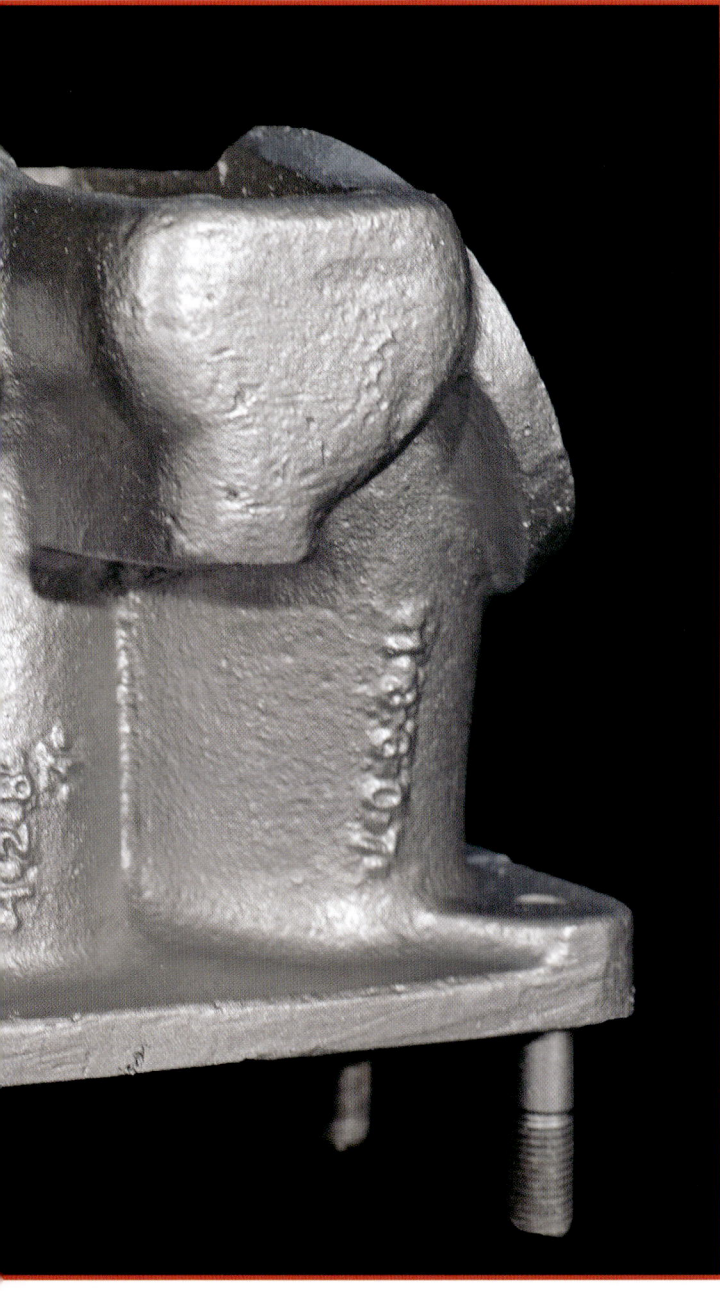

← Each of the inlet manifolds for the long-wheelbase California featured in this chapter is marked with the engine code 128.

The new 'SWB' California was unveiled in 1960 at the Geneva Motor Show, and the prototype that was displayed fitted with a 128 F engine, with 9mm camshaft lift and 40 DCL6 Weber carburettors. It was the last of the six 128 F engines built, of which five were used in 'LWB' cars. From the second 'SWB' car produced – chassis No. 1883GT – cars were fitted with type 168 engines (the same engine code as some 'LWB' models, but with different specifications). For the 168-type engine, power increased by around 20bhp (15kW), and the unit featured revised cylinder heads with larger intake valves. The competition version of the engine produced 280bhp (209kW), adopting

↑ The 12 light-alloy pistons were manufactured by Italian company Borgo. Note the oblique-angled split of the connecting-rod big-ends.

→ The cast-alloy timing cover (shown inverted here) carries the engine code 128 C. When the engine is assembled, the dynamo and cooling fan are mounted on the front of the cover.

↓ A wet-sump lubrication system was used, with a wide, cast-alloy sump.

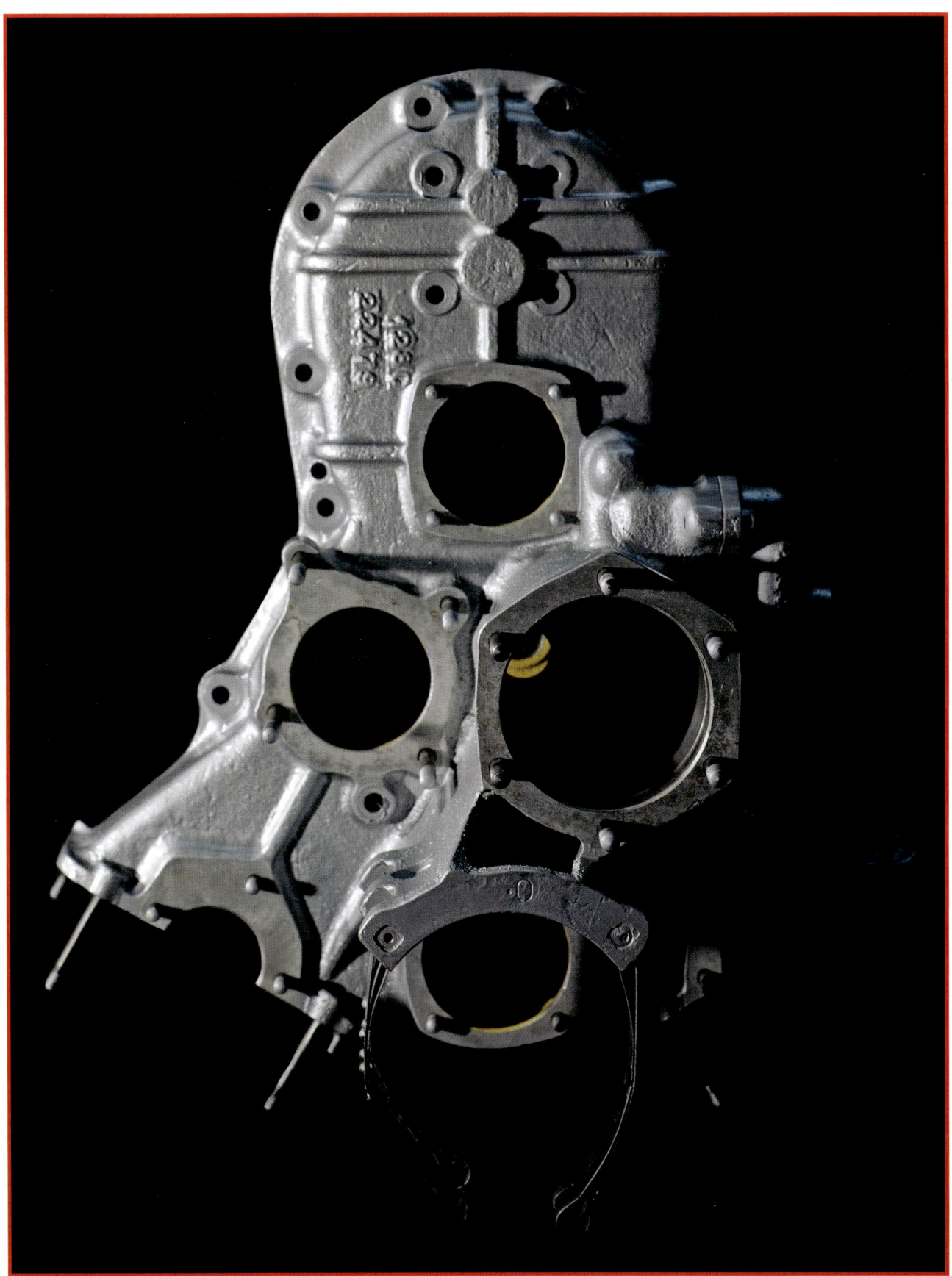

250 California: A classic V12 icon (1957)

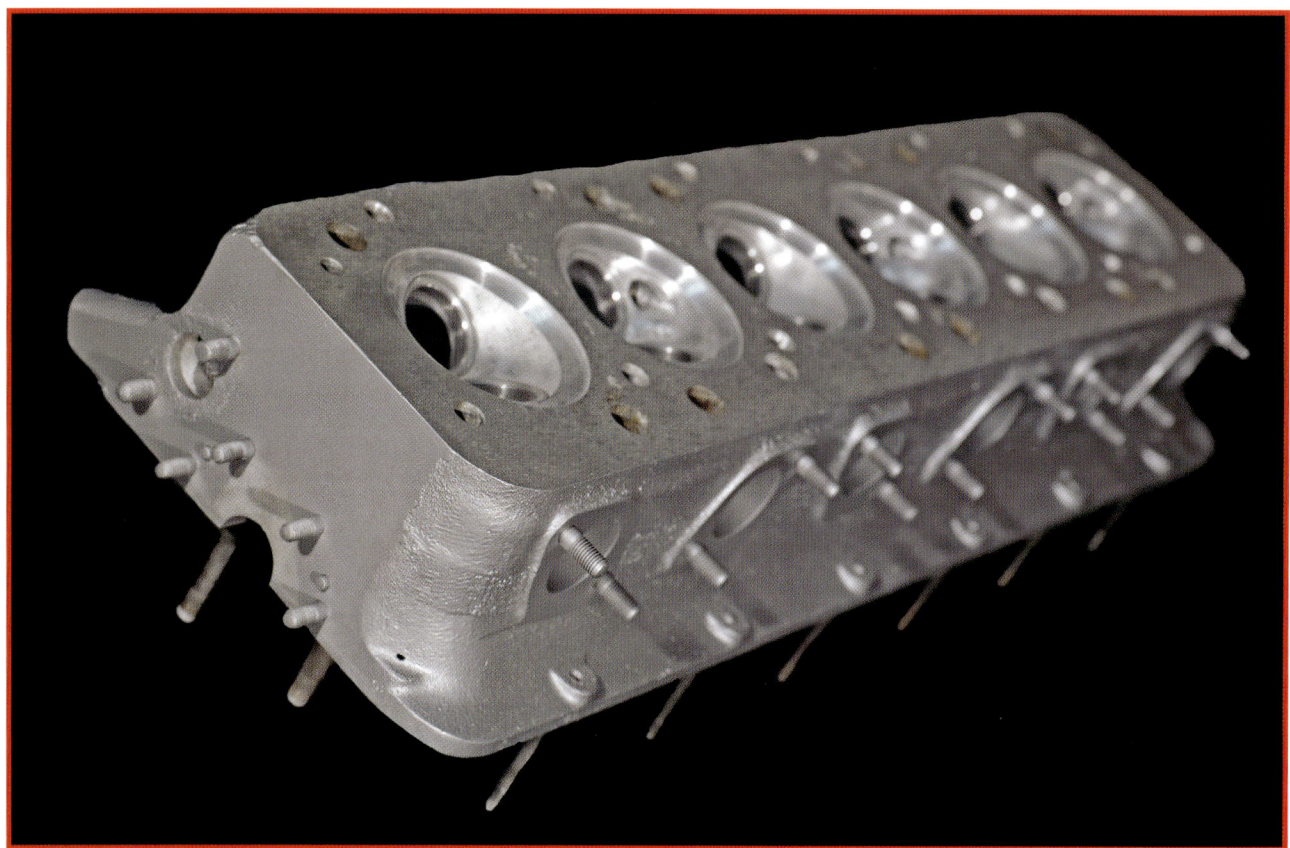

↑ A view of one of the cylinder heads, showing the combustion chambers, valve-seat locations and the six exhaust ports (on the right-hand side of the photograph).

FERRARI 250 CALIFORNIA – TECHNICAL DATA

Engine code	128 C
Engine type	Front, longitudinal, V12, 60°
Bore and stroke	73 x 58.8mm (2.87 x 2.31in)
Total capacity	2,953.21cc (180.21cu in)
Unitary capacity	246.10cc (15.01cu in)
Compression ratio	8.5:1
Maximum power	237bhp (176kW) at 7,000rpm
Power per litre	80bhp/litre (60kW/litre)
Valve operation	Single overhead camshaft per bank, two valves per cylinder
Fuel feed	Three twin-choke Weber 36 DCL carburettors
Ignition	Single spark plug per cylinder, single distributor, single coil
Lubrication	Wet sump
Clutch	Dry, single plate
Maximum torque	240Nm (177lb ft) at 4,800rpm
Firing order	1–7–5–11–3–9–6–12–2–8–4–10

features derived from the 250 Testarossa engine, with lighter camshafts, pistons and connecting rods. The last 250 GT California 'SWB's left the Maranello factory in February 1963. All the 107 Californias built featured odd chassis numbers, which in Ferrari tradition distinguished the road cars.

Even though the model was essentially a high-speed grand touring car, perfect for impressing the rich and beautiful on the Boulevard des Anglais in Nice, or in Hollywood, it also saw some owners putting it to competition use, and to good effect. One of those, chassis No. 2015GT, featured a special engine – type 168B – with high-compression cylinder heads and larger valves, increased power to 285bhp (213kW), and this finished second in class in the 12 Hours of Sebring in 1961, driven by Newmann/Publicker/Andrey. Other major competition achievements for this model were a class win at the 12 Hours of Sebring in 1959, with Ginther/Hively in chassis No. 1459 GT, which was followed by another class win in the Le Mans 24 Hours the same year, when Grossman/Tavano drove chassis No. 1451GT to fifth place overall. The following year there was a fifth overall, and third in class, at the 12 Hours of Sebring for chassis No. 1603GT, driven by Reed/Connell. Bob Grossman also had numerous good results in national

↑ Here, various components have been gathered together and laid out to create a 'face'.

↗ A close-up view of one of the domed light-alloy pistons, showing the piston rings and the bush for the gudgeon pin.

→ The interior of the cylinder head is painted with a special yellow sealing paint to seal the light-alloy castings ...

↓ ... as is the interior of the cast-alloy timing cover. The two upper timing covers fit over the studs at the top of this cover.

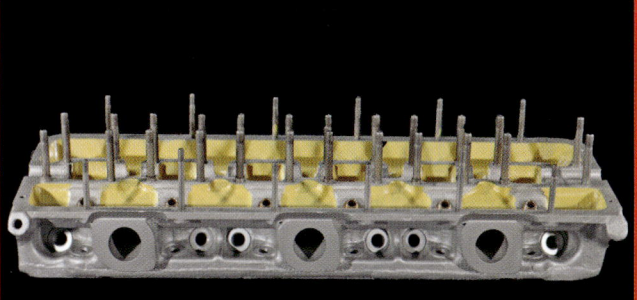

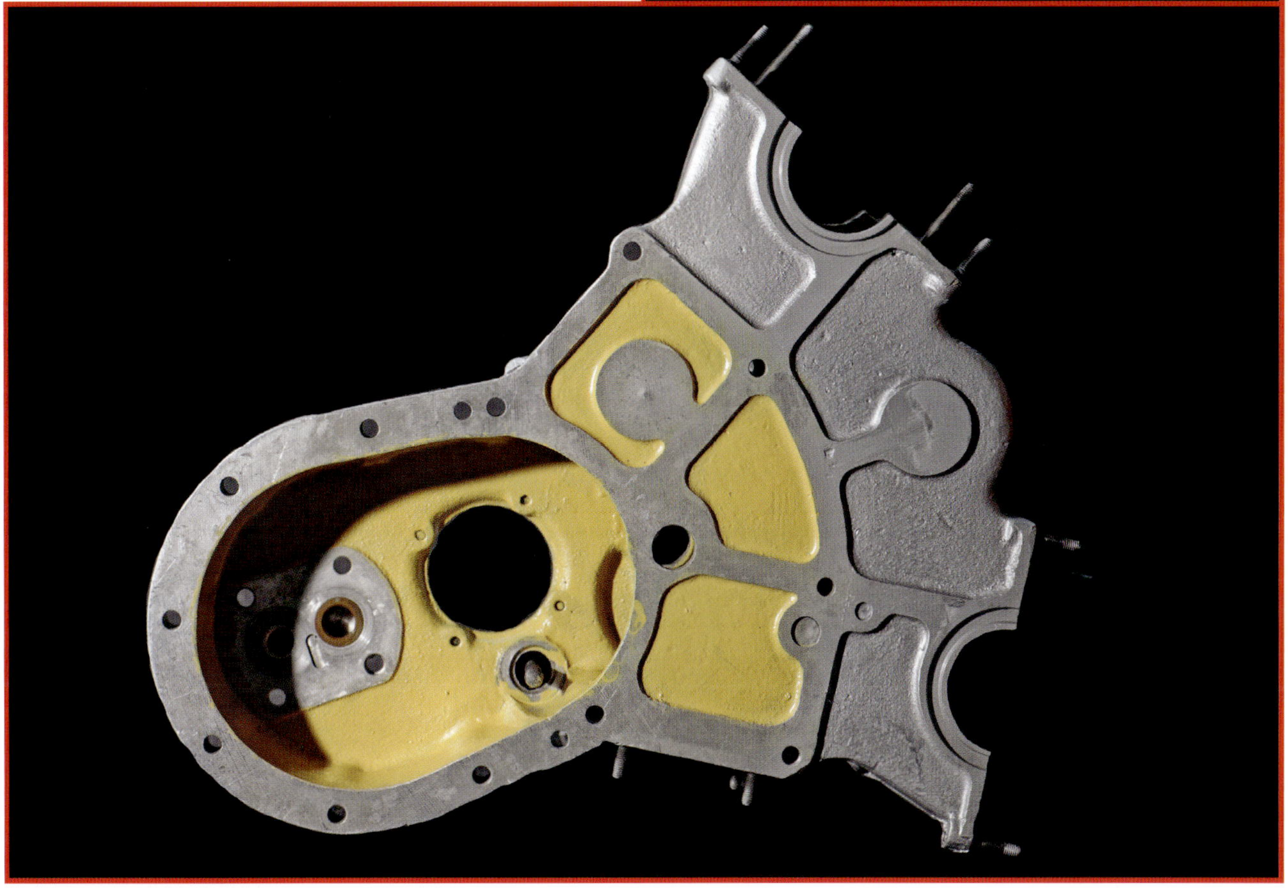

250 California: A classic V12 icon (1957)

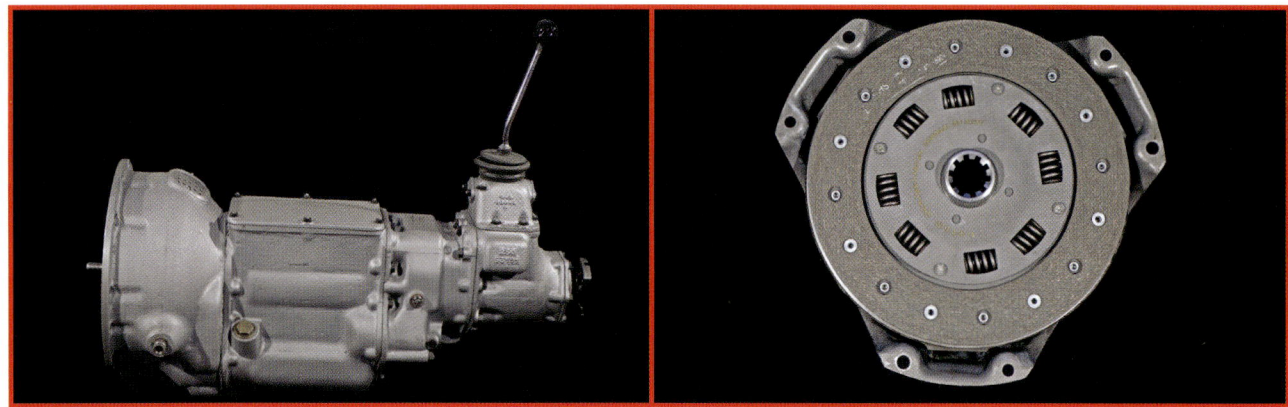

races in the USA during 1959 and 1960 in chassis No. 1451GT. However, as previously mentioned, the race track was not the California Spider's prime *raison d'etre*, it was more a wind-in-your-hair, high-speed grand touring car, and its elegant styling – whether in 'LWB' or 'SWB' form – captured the hearts of stars of stage and screen. These included American actor James Coburn, French heart-throb actor Alain Delon, playwright/novelist Francoise Sagan, actor/comedian Bob Hope, film director Roger Vadim, and French pop/rock star Johnny Hallyday. Over half a century later, the car continues to captivate modern-day collectors.

↖ The four-speed synchromesh gearbox. On some competition cars, the gearbox casing was finned for cooling.

↑ The dry, single-plate Fichtel & Sachs clutch assembly ready for fitting, complete with a new friction disc.

→ The connecting rods have the typical oblique-angled split of the Colombo engines, with the big-end bearing caps located on dowels and secured by two bolts.

↓ The nitrided steel crankshaft runs in seven main bearings, with two connecting rods located on each big-end journal.

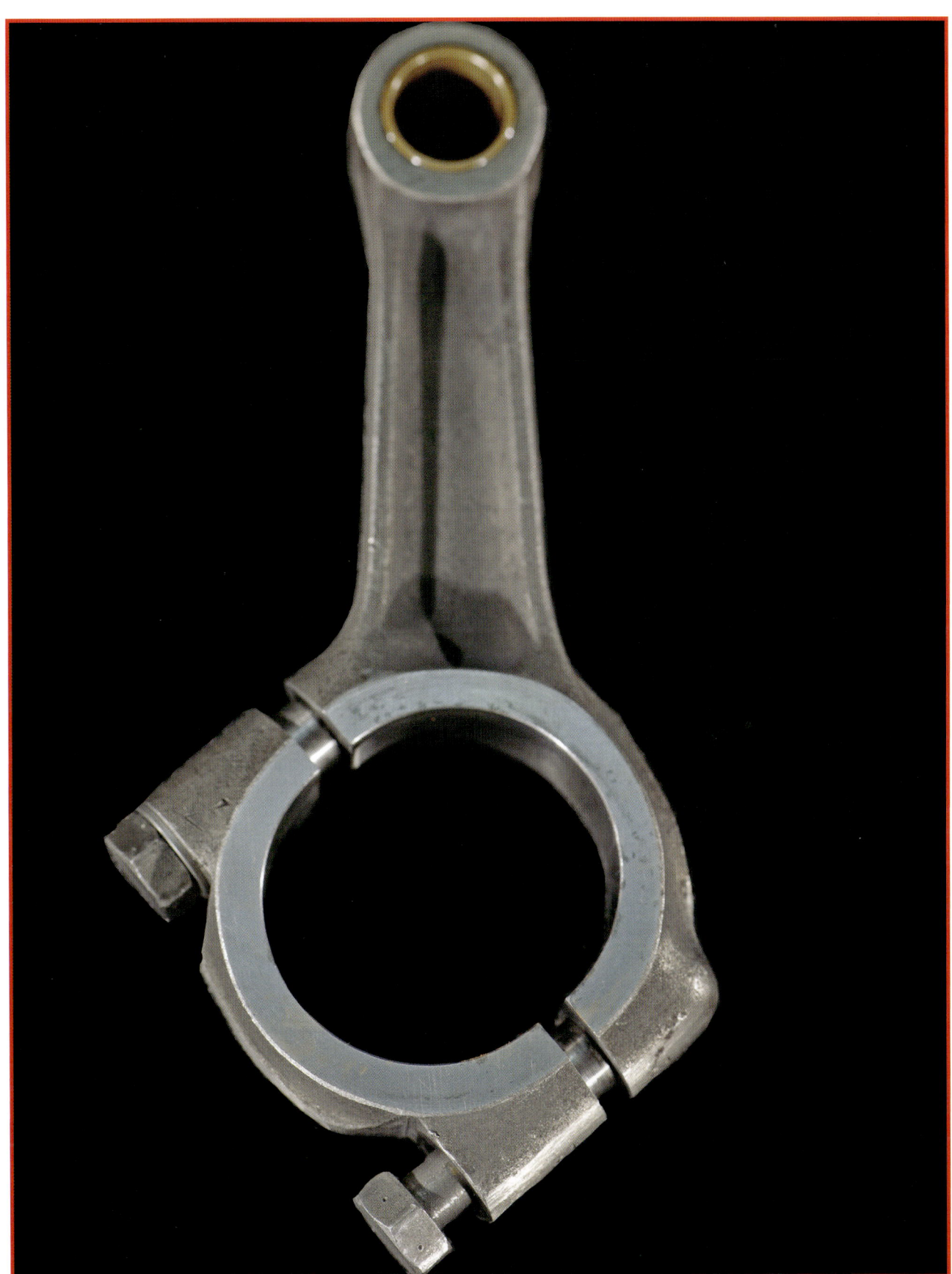

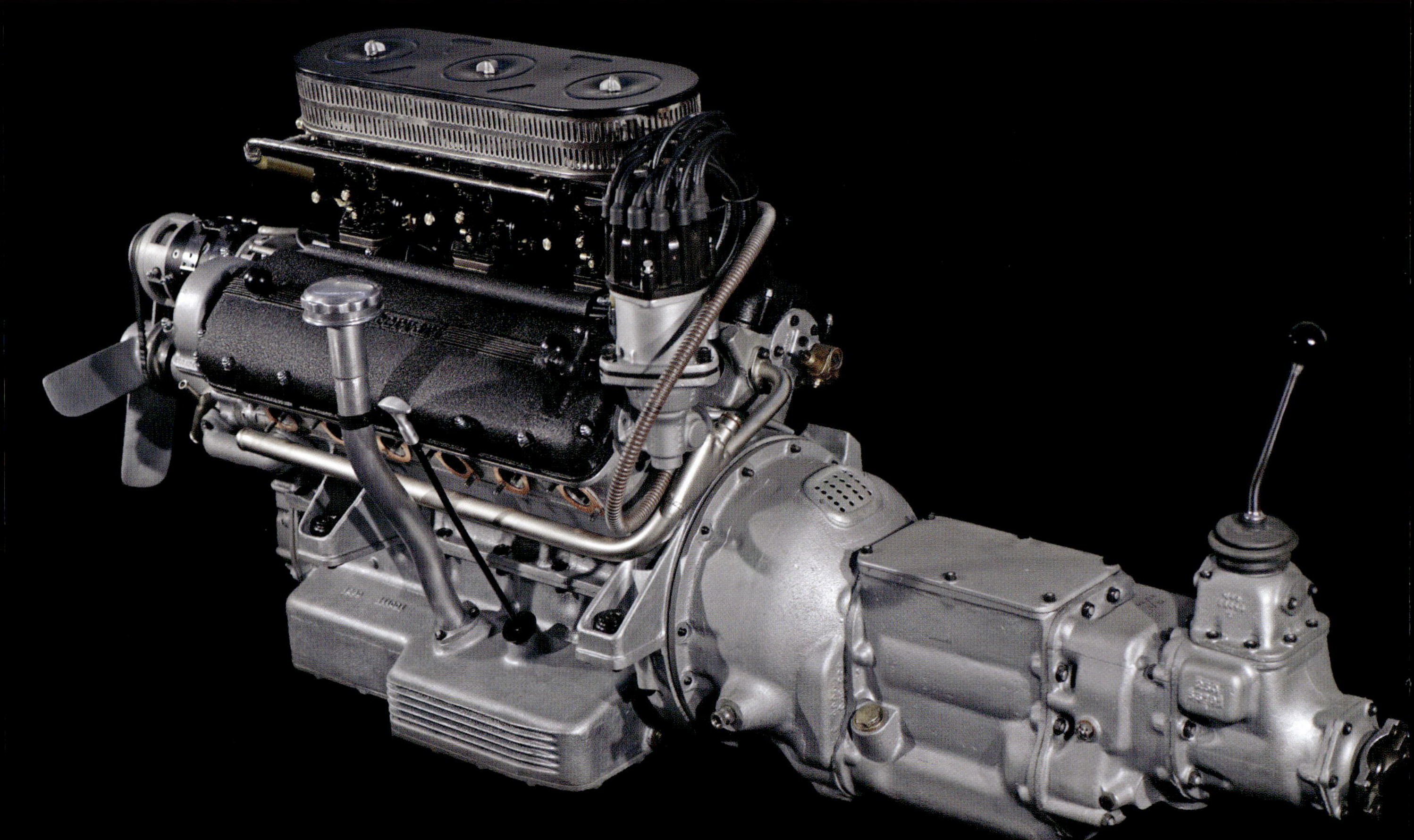

↑ The 250 California is one of the most sought-after classic models in most Ferrari collectors' wish lists.

↑ 'Details are not details – they make the design', as typified by the chromed trim surrounding the vertical tail-lights.

➜ A close-up view of the beautiful tapered tail of the 'LWB' California, showing the TdF (Tour de France) vertical light.

↘ The typical Marchal fog light and the Plexiglas headlight cover fitted to enhance the aerodynamics, as well as the styling.

↘↘ The aluminium air-outlet louvres on the front wings are a characteristic of this model, together with the TdF Berlinetta.

↘↘↘ A beautful Nardi wood-rim steering wheel, a comprehensive set of gauges, and Connolly leather trim adorn the interior.

↓ The 250 GT California is, without any doubt, one of the most beautiful spiders ever built, styled by Scaglietti and aimed at the American market.

250 LM
The first rear-engined Ferrari 'road car' (1963)

← The Ferrari logo cast prominently into the black-crackle finish of the camshaft covers.

↙ A close-up view of the vanadium inserts fitted into the crankshaft balance webs.

At the 1963 Paris Auto Show, the Maranello factory unveiled to the world its first longitudinal rear-engined 'road car', with a sentence that, then, would have been written in the classic *Ferrari Year Book*: 'The car for customers who want to go fast and know how to do it.' The revolution introduced with this 'berlinetta stradale' was the unconventional (until that year) location for the V12 engine, which for the first time in a Ferrari 'road car' was behind the driver's shoulders. At the beginning of the LM project, Enzo Ferrari's intention was to build a 'road car', based on the 250 P Sports Prototype, a Gran Turismo for customers who wanted to race.

Ferrari wanted to get the model homologated as a development of the 250 GTO, and one just has to compare the body style of the 1964 250 GTO to that of the 250 LM, to see the obvious similarity, despite the GTO being front-engined, and the LM having a mid-mounted engine. The FIA thought that this was pushing the boundaries of supposed development too far, and refused to homologate it as a GT car, so it had to run in the prototype class. This upset Ferrari somewhat, and he threatened to withdraw from motor racing, a threat that he eventually rescinded, despite having gone as far as handing back his entrant's competition licence. For this reason, the Ferrari F1 cars were painted white with a blue stripe for the last two races of the 1964 season and entered under Luigi Chinetti's NART (North American Racing Team) banner. To try and placate Ferrari, the ACI (the national motoring organisation in Italy) homologated the 250 LM as a national GT car in 1964, so that at least clients could compete in their 'road car'. In 1965, the FIA homologated the car under Appendix J as a Group 4 sports car, which essentially meant that it was considered a prototype GT car. Ever since the car's introduction, it has been known as the 250 Le Mans, despite only the first example (shown at the 1963 Paris Show) originally having a 3.0-litre engine, with all further examples being fitted with 3.3-litre engines from new. So, theoretically, as the model designation was that of the

↖ A close-up view of one of the hemispherical combustion chambers, with valve seats and inlet-valve guide visible.

← The cylinder-block casting with cylinder liners in place. The protruding studs secure the cylinder heads.

swept volume of a single cylinder, the car should have been designated the 275 Le Mans.

Technology and innovation at the Prancing Horse's factory resulted in the technical improvements that led to the serial production of the first 60° V12 mounted in a mid-rear longitudinal position in a Ferrari road car. This new and revolutionary Ferrari was also the first Ferrari whose shape was refined in a wind tunnel. Ferrari used the MIRA (Motor Industry Research Association) facility in England, where the aerodynamics were examined and refined on a clay scale model, to improve the drag coefficient. The 250 LM was a 'group project' realised by Ferrari's best engineers, including Forghieri, Rocchi, Maioli, Salvarani, Maffei and Marchetti, who were coordinated by Ing. Angelo Bellei, the engineer in overall charge of the 250 LM project. All these wonderful minds gave birth to one of the most powerful and delectable berlinettas ever made. As previously mentioned, it was presented at the 1963 Paris Auto Show, the show car being chassis No. 5149 – at the time a one-off model with Pininfarina bodywork and a 3.0-litre engine, and a unitary cylinder displacement of 250cc, corresponding to its name. In 1964 the engine capacity of the prototype was increased to 3.3 litres (the same displacement as the following 31 examples produced). The car also had some detail body differences to the cars

↑ **The twin alloy distributors (driven from the ends of the camshafts), shown without the caps and HT leads fitted.**

produced subsequently, notably the location of the inlets in the rear wings. After being presented at further auto shows, the prototype was fitted with the 3.3-litre engine and sold to

↓ **A view of the underside of the cylinder block shows the 12 cylinder bores and the crankshaft main-bearing housings.**

Luigi Chinetti's North American Racing Team (NART). The car was badly damaged by fire in the 12 Hours of Sebring in March 1964, and was then rebuilt with the later definitive 250 LM body style. Therefore, only the first 250 LM was born with a 3.0-litre engine, and was in that form for only a very short period of time.

The 250 LM mid-rear engine layout was derived from that of the 250 P sports-prototype model (and visually it was very similar to a 250 P, albeit with a roof). The car was named LM (Le Mans) as a tribute to the success of the 250 Prototipo in competition, which in June 1963, shortly before the unveiling of the 250 LM, had won the famous French race, driven by Lorenzo Bandini and Ludovico Scarfiotti. After chassis No. 5149, which was built by Pininfarina (as was the road car Speciale chassis No. 6025, which we will mention shortly), all the remaining 250 LM bodies were constructed by the famous coachbuilder Sergio Scaglietti in Modena. The artisan metalworkers at Scaglietti skilfully crafted aluminium sheets into the Pininfarina-designed marvel which is the much-admired 250 LM. Highlights included the one-piece rear body section, hinged at the roof, featuring oval air-intake scoops in the upper forward part of the rear wings, which fed cool air to the inboard rear brakes, and a shallow vertical rear screen located between short sail panel buttresses rising

from the flat rear deck, which flicked into a spoiler section where it met the Kamm tail. It is believed that Ferrari retained the '250' part of the model name, instead of changing it to the more logical '275', because the homologation request had already been submitted with these details, and changes would have complicated the situation. However, Dott. Franco Gozzi, Enzo Ferrari's personal assistant, is reported as having said that it was actually because Ferrari already had the sales material and catalogues printed with the 250 designation. This was probably an excuse, as although the brochures (there were three printings) state '250 Le Mans' as the model name on the cover, they all specify a 3.3-litre engine. When the model was finally homologated by the FIA in 1965, the paperwork stated the engine size was 3.3 litres, as did the previous ACI paperwork from 1964.

As mentioned previously, during the production run of this 'berlinetta', Pininfarina produced a Speciale road car – chassis No. 6025 – which was exhibited at the 1965 Geneva Motor Show. It featured electric windows, a leather-upholstered interior, a large curved Plexiglas rear screen that sloped down from the roof almost to the tail, with hinged roof sections above each door for easier access to the cabin, and a pair of vertical rubber-faced 'bumperettes' front and rear. This car was subsequently exhibited at the 1965 New York Motor Show and then sold in the USA through Luigi Chinetti. Another 250 LM, chassis No. 5995, was sold in 1964 to Conte Volpi di Misurata, the owner of Scuderia Serenissima, with whom it was raced for two years, before being converted to a Speciale road car in 1967. This LM was modified for road use, with a Plexiglas rear window, electric windows, air conditioning, and chrome front-quarter bumpers, with a matching full-width wraparound bumper at the rear. During the latter stages of the production run, some examples were fitted with glassfibre bodies, and Piero Drogo's Carrozzeria Sports Cars in Modena developed a long nose for the car, which both improved aerodynamics and increased front downforce.

The capacity of each cylinder for the 3.3-litre engine was 275cc, which was achieved by increasing the diameter of the bore to 77mm from the 73mm of the 250 engine, maintaining the same stroke of 58.8mm. The larger engine produced 320bhp (239kW) at 7,500rpm, whereas the 3.0-litre unit produced 300bhp (224kW) at the same engine speed. The torque increased commensurately, providing 314Nm (232lb ft) at 5,500rpm, up from 294Nm (217lb ft) at the same engine speed with the 3.0-litre unit. The only data that was inferior was the specific power per litre, which dropped from the 101bhp/litre (75.3kW/litre) to 97.3bhp/litre (72.6kW/litre). This power unit was a mechanical and technological leap for Ferrari with a road car, as Enzo Ferrari had famously been quoted as saying that, 'The horse pulls the cart, it doesn't push it', referring to the location of the engine.

The engine's performance was boosted by innovative solutions adopted from racing. One of the benefits was the use of a lighter nitrided steel crankshaft, with balance weights for smoother high-speed running. It weighed 18.8kg (41.4lb), and was supported in the block by seven main bearings. A light steel flywheel was used, weighing only 5.6kg (12.3lb). The LM engine block, cylinder heads, cam covers,

← **The rear-mounted longitudinal gearbox provides the mounting points for the inboard Dunlop rear disc brakes.**

↑ A line-up of the 12 pistons, featuring shallow convex crowns, with their steel connecting rods. Note the horizontally split big-end bearings.

inlet manifolds, sump, timing chain casing and ancillary castings were all cast in lightweight Silumin alloy, providing a total engine weight of 195kg (430lb). The cylinder heads featured a single overhead camshaft per bank, driven by a triplex chain via gears from the crankshaft at the front of the block. There were two valves per cylinder in a hemispherical combustion chamber, with the 38mm-diameter inlet valves in the centre of the V, and the 32.4mm-diameter exhaust valves on the outside. The engine had a bore of 77mm and a stroke of 58.8mm, and featured shallow convex-crown pistons, weighing 272 grams (9.6 ounces) each. The pistons were manufactured by Borgo and had two compression rings

→ The nitrided steel crankshaft weighs 18.8kg and runs in seven main bearings. Note the twin oil holes on the big-end journals for the twin connecting rods fitted to each journal.

↓ The cylinder heads feature two valves per cylinder in hemispherical combustion chambers. Nearest the camera are the six exhaust ports.

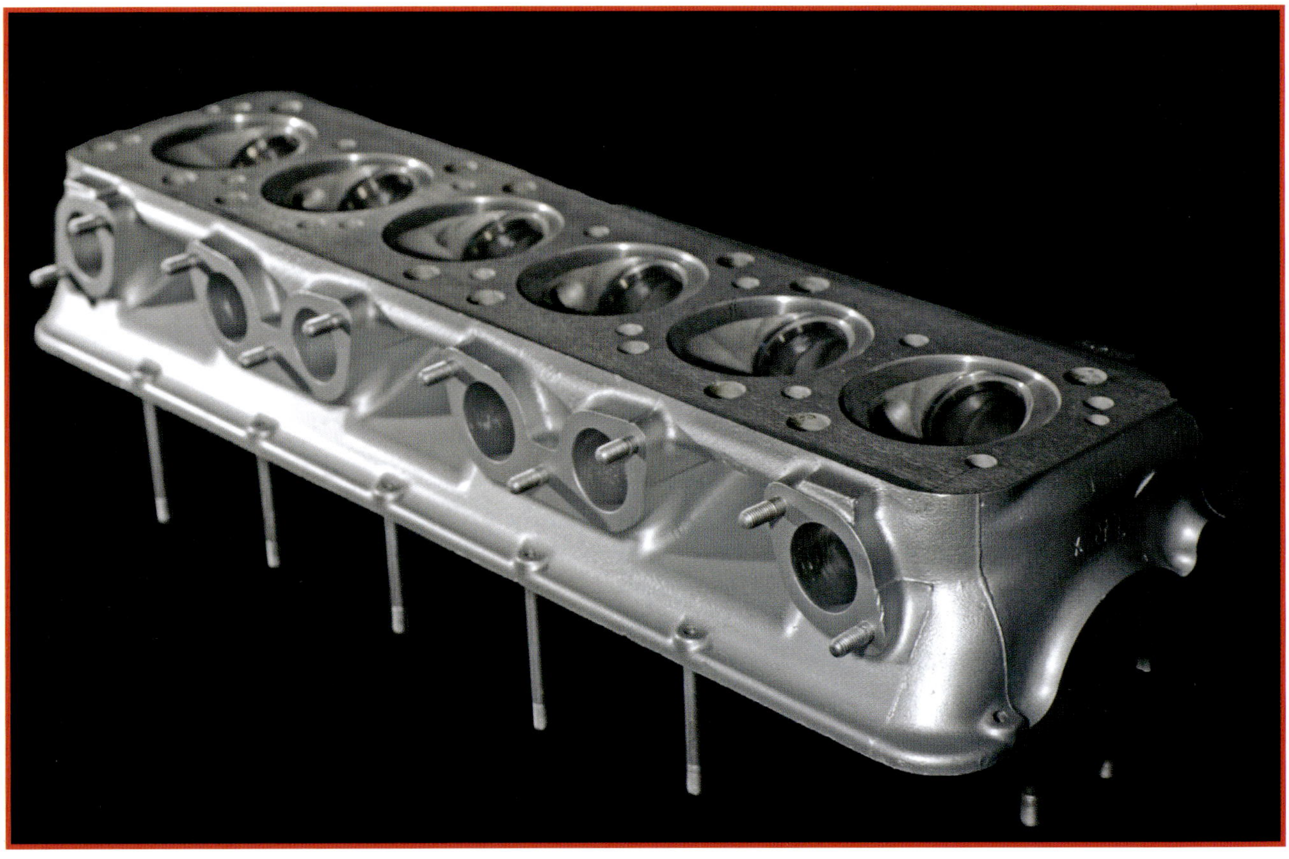

250 LM: The first rear-engined Ferrari 'road car' (1963)

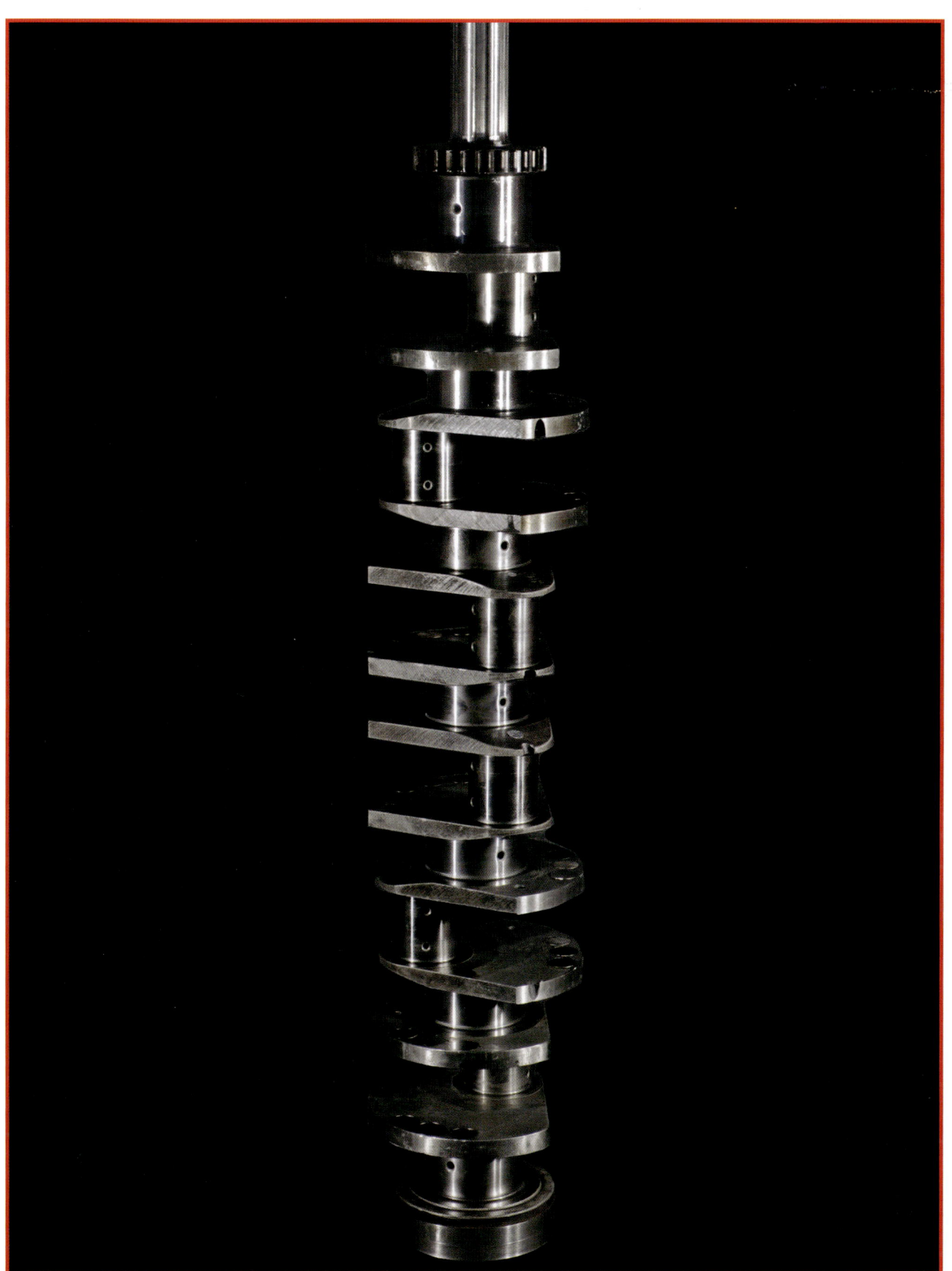

65

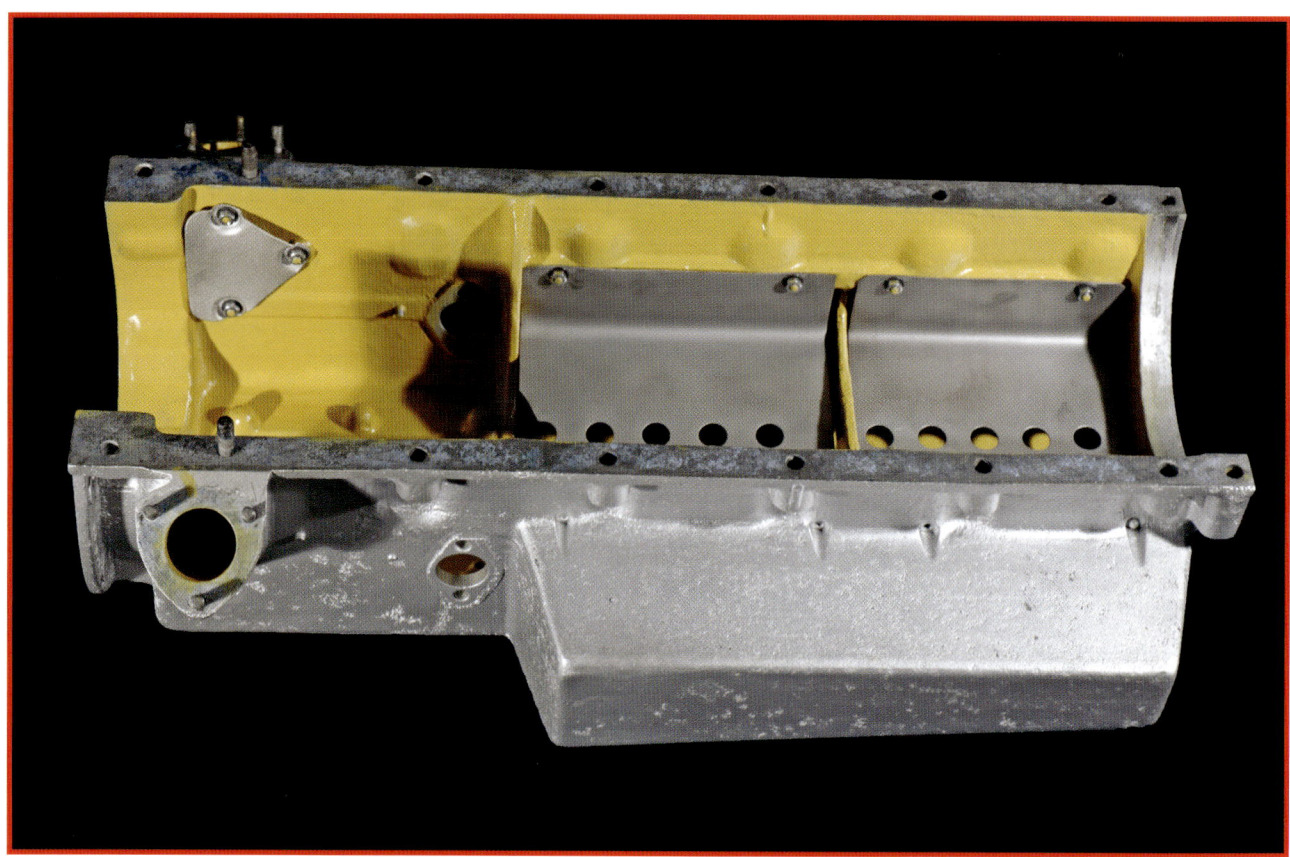

↑ To prevent oil surge when braking, accelerating and cornering, baffles are fitted inside the sump casting.

FERRARI 250 LM – TECHNICAL DATA

Engine code	210/211
Engine type	Rear, longitudinal, V12, 60°
Bore and stroke	77 x 58.8mm (3.03 x 2.31in)
Total capacity	3,285.72cc (200.50cu in)
Unitary capacity	273.81cc (16.70cu in)
Compression ratio	9.7:1
Maximum power	315bhp (235 kW) at 7,500rpm
Power per litre	96bhp/litre (71kW/litre)
Valve operation	Single overhead camshaft per bank, two valves per cylinder
Fuel feed	Six double-choke Weber 38/40 DCN carburettors
Ignition	Single spark plug per cylinder, two distributors, two coils
Lubrication	Dry sump
Clutch	Dry, single plate
Maximum torque	317Nm (233.8lb ft at 5,000rpm)
Firing order	1–7–5–11–3–9–6–12–2–8–4–10

and a single oil-control ring. The firing order was 1–7–5–11–3–9–6–12–2–8–4–10, with cylinder No.1 being the first on the right side, and No.7 the last on the left side of the block. The connecting rods had horizontally split big-ends (rods from opposing cylinders paired on the crank journals), and were manufactured from GMN steel, featuring a 'double-T' cross section, each one weighing 480g (1.1lb).

The induction system consisted of a bank of six Weber 38 DCN downdraught carburettors, mounted on duplex inlet manifolds in the centre of the engine vee, fed by a pair of Bendix electric fuel pumps from the twin 70-litre aluminium fuel tanks (with interconnecting balance pipe), one either side of the engine next to the cabin firewall. The 12-volt ignition system was by Magneti Marelli with a separate coil and distributor for each bank of cylinders. The camshaft-driven distributors were mounted vertically at the rear of the engine. The sparking plugs were fitted on the outside of the V, and the original equipment plugs were Marchal type HF33R. As on the competition cars, dry-sump lubrication was provided, as it provided more stable lubrication under all conditions. The oil tank, oil radiator and water radiator were fitted in the front compartment. An unusual feature of the LM was that the chassis tubes were used to carry the engine fluids (oil and water) from the engine to the front-mounted radiators and oil tank. A downside of this layout was the heat transfer

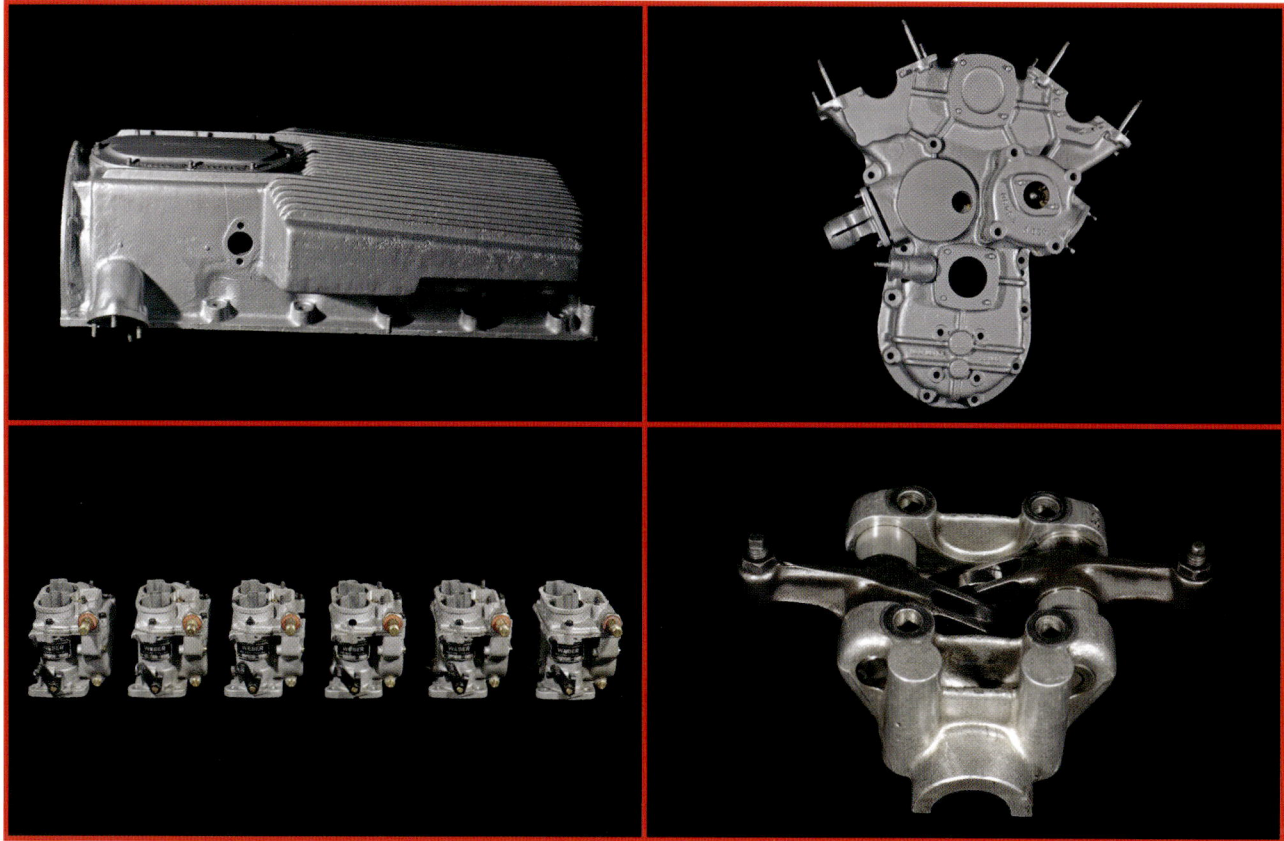

↑↑ A view of the upturned sump casting. The 'wings' at the sides increase the oil capacity without increasing the sump depth.

↑ Six twin-choke Weber 38/40 DNC carburettors are located in the centre of the 60° vee of the V12.

↑↑ The cast, light-alloy timing cover protects the triplex timing chains. The studs at the top secure the camshaft covers.

↑ Roller cam followers – shown here with their supports – are fitted to operate both the intake and exhaust valves.

from the tubes into the uninsulated cabin, which could make it uncomfortably warm.

The cooperation between Ferrari's Reparto Corse and Reparto Produzione (the competition and production departments) in Maranello made it possible – by using the layout of the 250 P – to produce a 'road car' with a rear-mounted transaxle layout, with the gearbox projecting rearward from the axle line. To centralise the mass, and also to reduce unsprung weight on the rear wheels, the Dunlop disc brakes were mounted inboard, close to the transmission casing, with cooling ducts from the rear-wing intakes. The five-speed non-synchromesh gearbox was mounted to the rear of the limited-slip differential, with which it shared an alloy casing. Four different rear axle ratios were available: 4.842:1, 4.426:1, 4.038:1 and 3.548:1. The gearbox featured a gear-driven lubrication pump, and the clutch was a single dry-plate unit mounted on the engine flywheel. The impressive performance of the rear-mounted 3.3-litre Ferrari V12 engine, coupled to the light weight of the 250 LM (820kg, dry) made it possible to achieve 0–62mph (0–100 kmh) in less than 5 seconds, an awesome performance for that time.

One of the racing drivers who knows more than most about these cars is David Piper, who drove a number of 250 LMs in period, and who has owned the last example built, chassis No. 8165, almost since new. Prior to this he had owned two 250 GTOs, the second one of which was extensively modified by him to keep it competitive. Likewise with chassis No. 8165, he carried out extensive modifications to maintain its competitiveness while he was racing it internationally, and continued to run it in historic racing until recently. As noted previously, the FIA refused to homologate the 250 LM as a GT car, and therefore it had to compete against larger-capacity sports cars, like the 4.7-litre Ford GT40, in the over-3.0-litre prototype GT class. The Ford

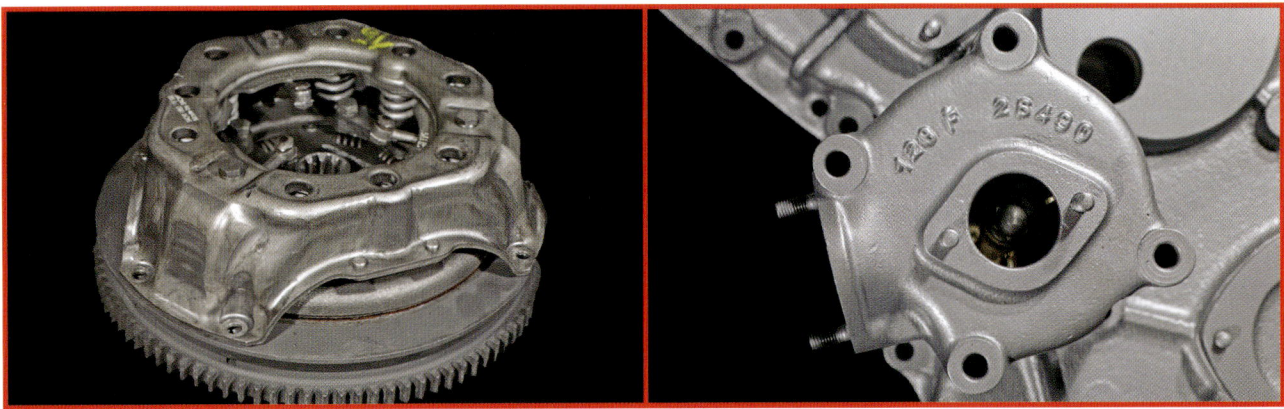

GT40 had come into being as a response to Enzo Ferrari's decision not to pursue a deal that was almost done with Henry Ford II, to sell his company to Ford, who wanted to use racing as a marketing tool. The failure of the deal at the eleventh hour was said to be due to Ferrari not being able to maintain independent control over the racing department, and he refused to sign the contract. This rebuff prompted Henry Ford II to instigate his own sports-racing programme, initially with Lola in the UK, which eventually led to the production of the GT40 to take on Ferrari on the race tracks of the world.

It was a pity that the 250 Le Mans was not developed and updated, other than by private clients, because it had the potential to be a successful weapon. Even so, it had numerous successes driven by many of the top drivers of the period, such as Lorenzo Bandini, John Surtees, Jackie Stewart, Graham Hill, Denny Hulme and Jochen Rindt, to name but a few. The car's first major race victory was in the 12 Hours of Reims in July 1964, where Graham Hill and Joakim Bonnier won, driving the Maranello Concessionaires-entered example, with the NART entry of John Surtees and Lorenzo Bandini finishing second. The model's most prestigious win came in the 1965 Le Mans 24 Hours, where Jochen Rindt and Masten Gregory steered their NART entry to victory, after a late-race puncture relegated the Ecurie Francorchamps entry, driven by Pierre Dumay and Gustave 'Taff' Gosselin, to second overall, with all six of the Ford GT40s being early retirements. To date, this is still the last overall win for Ferrari in the Le Mans 24 Hours.

↖ **The dry, single-plate clutch, shown here with the flywheel and clutch pressure plate, is manufactured by Fichtel & Sachs.**

↑ **The timing cover casting is marked with the enginee code from the previous 128 F engine.**

→ **A light-hearted photograph representing a face, composed by laying out the connecting rod, bearing shells, piston, valves, springs, washers and valve caps.**

↓ **The three inlet manifolds, viewed here upside down. Two carburettors were fitted to each manifold.**

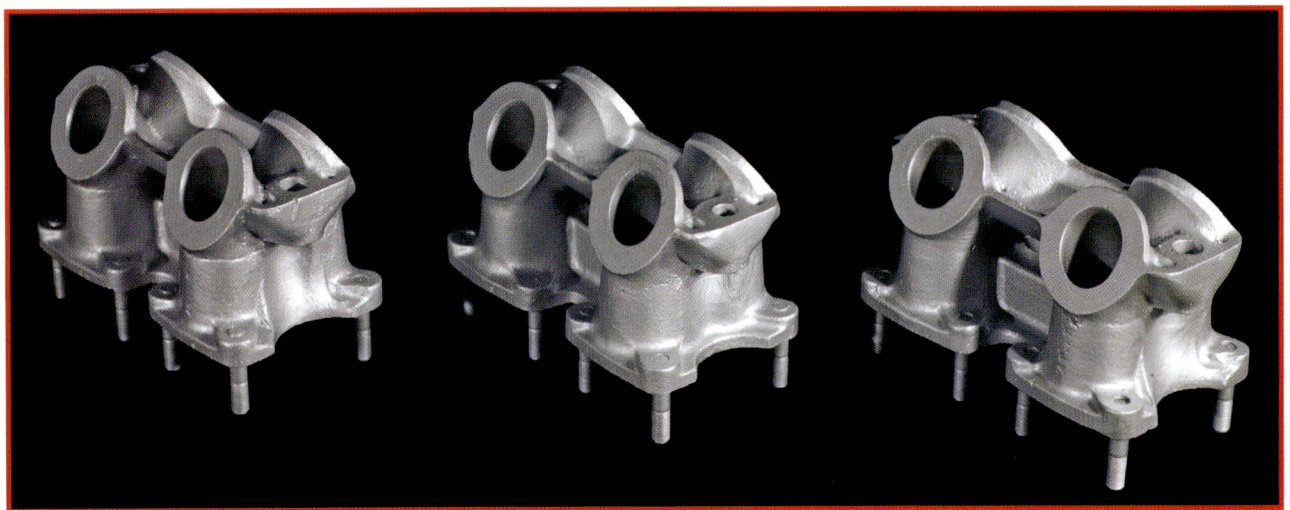

↑ The aerodynamic shape of the 250 LM – destined for the race track – was styled by Pininfarinai making use of a wind tunnel.

↑ The rear view of chassis No. 5995 shows the road modifications including the bumper and long, sloping screen.

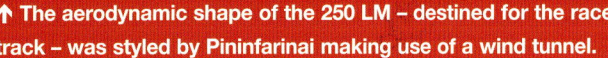

➔ A side view of the curved windscreen with a single rear-view mirror on the left-hand side.

↘ The oval air intakes in the rear wings feed air to cool the inboard disc brakes.

↘↘ The Plexiglas inlets on the bonnet provide air to cool the compact and warm cockpit.

↘↘↘ The headlights have Plexiglas covers to improve the aerodynamics of the 250 LM nose.

↓ This LM, chassis No. 5995, was modified for Count Volpi for road use, with a Plexiglas rear window, electric windows, air conditioning, and chrome bumpers.

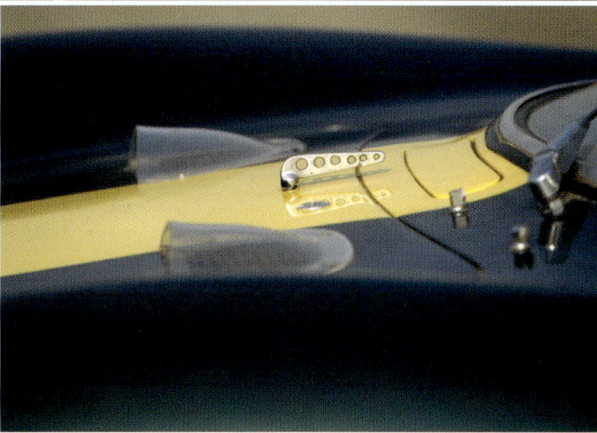

73

250 LM: The first rear-engined Ferrari 'road car' (1963)

275 GTB
The transaxle arrives (1964)

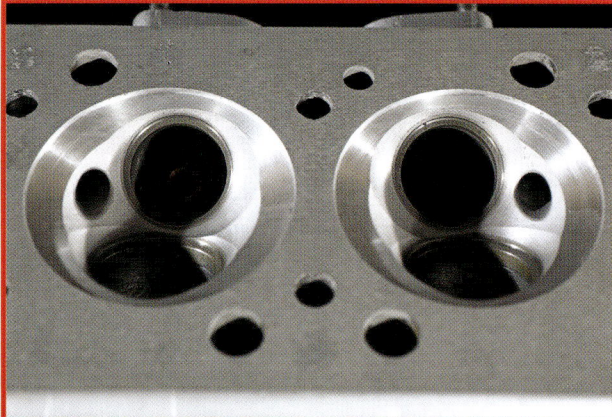

← A close-up view of two of the combustion chambers, showing the valve seats and spark-plug holes.

↙ The engine code number 213 appears on the right side of the cylinder block casting, with the 'internal number' below, used by the factory to identify the individual engine.

The Ferrari 275 GTB Berlinetta, which replaced the 250 GT Lusso model, introduced new technology on a Ferrari road car, namely the use of a combined gearbox and differential unit in a transaxle assembly, and concurrently the provision of independent rear suspension. With the presentation of this berlinetta at the 1964 Paris Motor Show (chassis No. 06449), Enzo Ferrari wanted to emphasise once more his ability to produce a Gran Turismo car that could easily double up as a 'ready-to-race' berlinetta.

The new 275 GTB featured a body style from the pen of Battista Pininfarina, and was reminiscent of the 1962 250 GTO, with more bulbous curves. It featured Plexiglas-covered headlights in the front-wing extremities, bounding a long bonnet that led into a set-back cabin, the roof line of which ran through the rear screen into a recessed Kamm tail. There were further references to the GTO in the vertical cooling air outlet slots in the front wings, which were mirrored in smaller form on the sail panels for cabin ventilation. It was also the first Ferrari road car to feature cast-alloy wheels as standard, although the traditional Borrani wire wheels were available as an option. Whilst Pininfarina constructed the bodies for the 275 GTS model at their plant in Turin, the bodies for the 275 GTB were built at the Scaglietti facility in Modena.

The new model also featured a new 60° V12 275 'short block' engine, type 213. This engine was a larger-capacity derivation of the previous 128 F, 168, and 168 U units, which themselves were derivatives of the Maranello factory's first V12 engine – Gioachino Colombo's project, the 125. The new 275 unit, which had a total capacity of 3,285.72cc, supplied an impressive power output of 280bhp (209kW) at 7,600rpm, with a maximum torque of 294Nm (217lb ft) at 5,000rpm. In fact, the bore and stroke (and thus the single-cylinder capacity – 273.81cc – of this engine), was the same as the previous 250 LM model, whose model-number designation, normally denoting the approximate single-cylinder capacity, was at odds with the true capacity, as explained on page 12. As

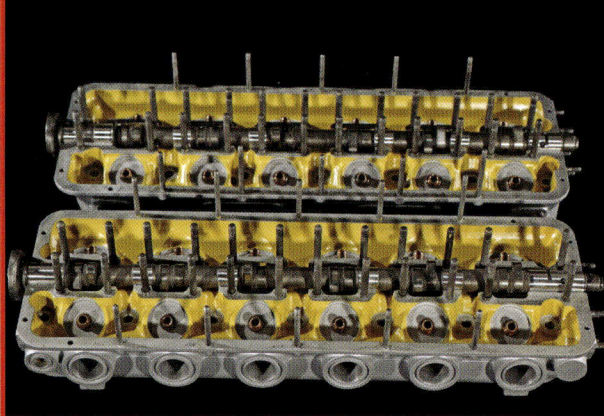

↖ The single overhead camshafts in place in the cylinder heads.

← The lower rear engine cover, which bolts to the cylinder block, behind the flywheel/clutch assembly.

noted there, the 250 LM had a 3.3-litre engine – only the first Pininfarina prototype initially had a 3.0-litre engine, which was updated to a 3.3-litre unit following a crash in which the car caught fire – and was essentially a competition car. Therefore, as the 275 GTB engine was built after the LM, it was a straight heir to the more powerful competition unit of that car. The 213 engine was also the motive force for the less-overtly sporting 275 GTS Spider, which was presented on the same occasion as the 275 GTB, during the Paris Motor Show in 1964.

The 275 GTB played its winning card with its transmission, introducing, for the first time in the history of Ferrari road cars, a transaxle. The five-speed transaxle unit featured a lightweight alloy casing as standard, although some competition versions featured a magnesium casing. This layout, where the gearbox and differential are combined as a single assembly in a casing as part of the rear axle, was a revolutionary development and technological advance, which derived from the Maranello factory's experiences with their racing cars. The transaxle, built entirely at Ferrari, was connected to the engine by a driveshaft that rotated at engine speed. On the first series of the GTB, the engine was secured by four mountings, whilst the transaxle had three. The driveshaft was 16.5mm in diameter, splined at each end, with a central support bearing mounted on the chassis. It was designed to have some degree of flex to counteract any misalignment between

↑ **The differential crownwheel, complete with roller bearing, which was incorporated in the rear transaxle assembly.**

the engine and transaxle. This arrangement proved difficult to set up and maintain in equilibrium, causing rapid wear on the central bearing, which resulted in vibration problems. This was addressed in late 1965 by providing a larger,

↓ **Every component a work of art! The aluminium pistons and steel connecting rods, with horizontally split big-ends.**

18.5mm diameter, shaft with the splines at each end running into universal joints mounted on flanges to the engine and transaxle, which was a major improvement over the original layout, but still not perfect. In early 1966 a third and final layout was introduced, with the engine and transaxle each now having only two mounting points, joined by a rigid torque tube flanged to each unit, within which the driveshaft ran. The result was a rigid torsion-proof configuration. The clutch of the type 213, mounted on the engine flywheel, was initially a single dry-plate unit supplied by Fichtel & Sachs, but this was replaced by a Borg & Beck clutch in late 1965, which gave a smoother, more progressive take-up.

Returning to the engine, the bore and stroke were 58.8mm and 77mm respectively, and the single-cylinder capacity was 273.81cc. The cylinder block, cylinder heads, pistons (manufactured by Borgo), sump, timing covers, camshaft covers and transmission casing were all cast in light alloy. The crankshaft was machined from a solid billet of forged steel, running in seven main bearings. The firing order was 1–7–5–11–3–9–6–12–2–8–4–10. The connecting rods were steel, with a horizontal split to the big-ends.

The ignition system comprised twin distributors and coils, one for each cylinder bank, with the distributors driven off the rear of each camshaft. The single overhead camshaft

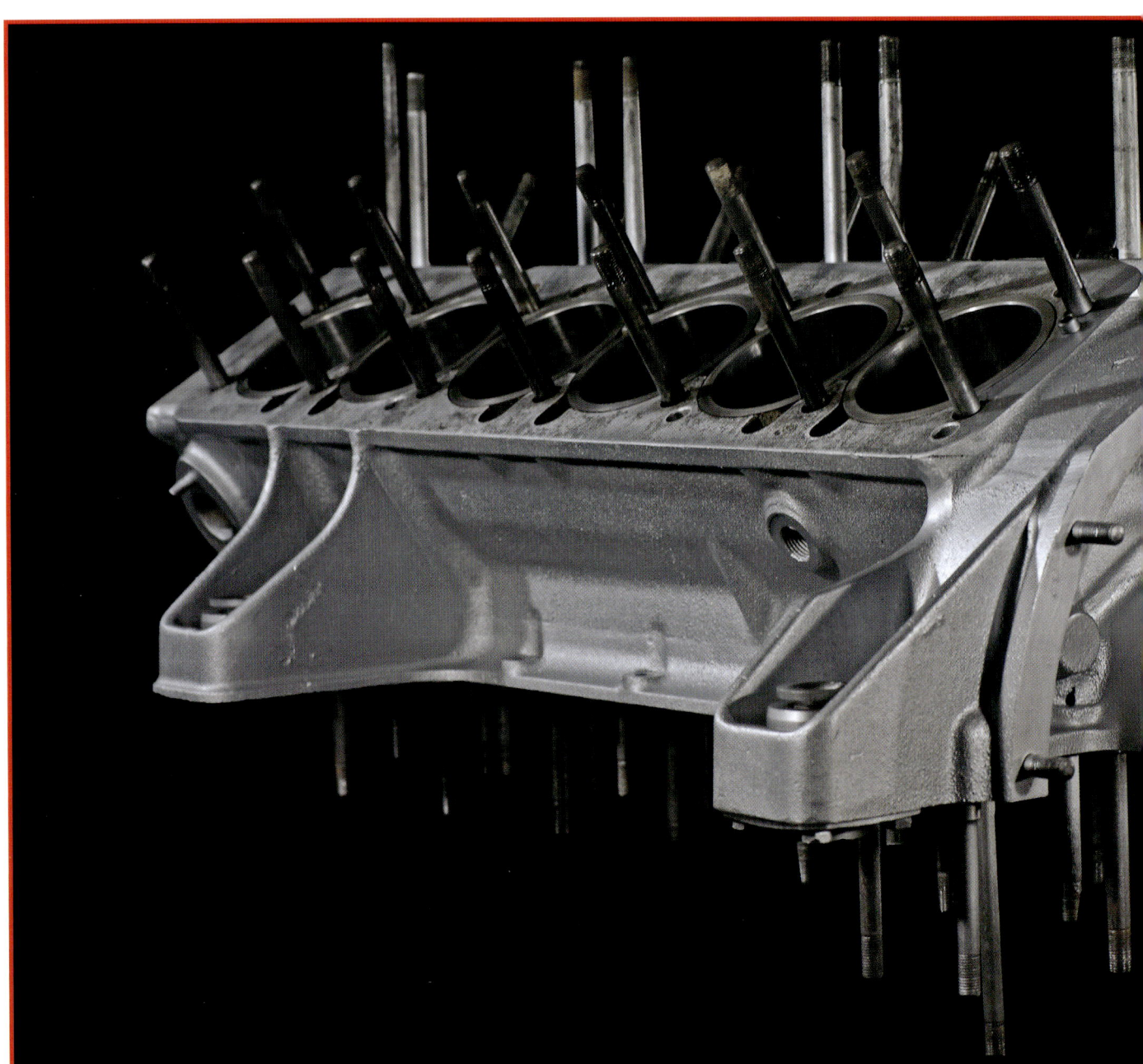

per bank was chain-driven from the crankshaft, with two valves per cylinder. The valves, with helical springs, were actuated by steel rocker arms with screw adjustment of valve clearances. The spark plugs were located outside the vee of the cylinder heads, as with the immediately preceding 250 series engines. Fuel was fed to the carburettors – normally triple twin-choke Weber 40 DCZ/6 or 40 DFI/1 – from the fuel tank via a filter and an electric pump. As an option, for customers who may want to use their 275 GTB for racing, a six Weber 40 DCN/3 carburettor set-up was also available, which increased both the power and the torque of the engine.

Another very important innovation on this Ferrari berlinetta, which also derived (as did the transaxle) from the company's competition cars, was the independent rear-suspension layout. This featured pressed-steel, unequal-length upper and lower wishbones, with a coil spring encircling a hydraulic shock absorber, mounted between the top wishbone and a bracket on the chassis. This virtually mirrored the layout used for the front suspension, apart from the location of the spring/shock absorber assembly, which at the front was mounted between the upper and lower wishbones. Anti-roll bars were fitted front and rear.

The single-overhead-camshaft-per-bank 275 engine was only built for two years. It did not undergo any significant changes to the mechanical layout, apart from the already mentioned changes to the torque-tube assembly, resulting in alterations to the number of engine and transaxle mounts. However, there were some small but visible changes to the bodywork during the course of production, which were presented on a revised model shown at the 1965 Paris Salon. The most obvious difference was in the shape of the radiator opening and grille, which protruded further, and was shallower and wider, with the quarter-bumpers now running into the extremities, instead of stopping at the edge of the opening. The egg-crate grille was also further recessed into the aperture. Not so apparent was a change to the size of the rear screen, which was enlarged, and to accommodate this, the previously internal boot-lid hinges became external elegant chrome-plated items. This also gave a little more space in the boot, as there was no internal hinge arc. There was also a change to the dashboard layout, with the earlier cars having a one-piece top section featuring a hump over the instrument nacelle in front of the driver, whilst the new model featured a separate instrument nacelle set into the dash top. With the arrival of the new model, the 'old' and 'new' models came to be referred to as 'short'- and 'long'-nose respectively to differentiate them, although this is an unofficial term. The reason for the change of the shape of the nose was to combat high-speed lift of the nose to which the original design was susceptible.

The number of type 213 'short block' engines produced by the Maranello factory was not officially stated, but at the very least 466 engines were produced, of which 235 were fitted in the 'short-nose' version (the first series), and 231 in the 'long-nose' version (the second series). Undoubtedly, there were also spare replacement units manufactured, although the quantity is unknown. The chassis number range of the 275 GTB SOHC models produced went from chassis No. 06003 (the first prototype; Ferrari records list chassis No. 06021 as the first

← A view of the light alloy type 213 'short block' cylinder block with cylinder liners in place.

↑ The three twin-port inlet manifolds – shown inverted – on to which the Weber twin-choke carburettors bolted.

FERRARI 275 GTB – TECHNICAL DATA

Engine code	213
Engine type	Front, longitudinal, V12, 60°
Bore and stroke	77 x 58.8mm (3.03 x 2.31in)
Total capacity	3,285.72cc (200.50cu in)
Unitary capacity	273.81cc (16.70cu in)
Compression ratio	9.2:1
Maximum power	276bhp (206kW) at 7,600rpm
Power per litre	84bhp/litre (62kW/litre)
Valve operation	Single overhead camshaft per bank, two valves per cylinder
Fuel feed	Three or six double-choke Weber 40 DCN/3 carburettors
Ignition	Single spark plug per cylinder, twin distributors, twin coils
Lubrication	Wet sump
Clutch	Dry, single plate
Maximum torque	294Nm (216.8lb ft) at 5,000rpm
Firing order	1–7–5–11–3–9–6–12–2–8–4–10

production car) to chassis No. 09085 (the last 275 GTB/C – C = 'Competizione'), with cars produced in both left- and right-hand-drive form. The 275 GTB, beyond the technological and mechanical improvements already mentioned, called for a redesign of the chassis, due to the transaxle and independent rear suspension layout. It maintained the 2,400mm wheelbase of its predecessor, and was still constructed from the traditional oval main longitudinal tubes with cross-bracing, plus body-support framework. However, towards the rear, the main tubes swept inwards, instead of carrying on straight as on the 250 series, to support the transaxle. The transaxle layout was also beneficial in terms of weight distribution, which in turn improved the handling and roadholding when compared to its predecessor, and would continue to be used in the succeeding 365 GTB4 model – the last of Ferrari's front-engined V12 cars of the period. A front-engined V12 model came back into the Ferrari range in 1995 with the 550 Maranello, and that also featured a transaxle layout.

The SOHC-per-bank type 213 engine was succeeded by the DOHC-per-bank type 226 version in the 275 GTB4 model, which was presented, like its predecessors, at the Paris Motor Show, this time in October 1966, with chassis No. 09021. Visually, it was almost identical to the 'long nose' SOHC model, the most obvious distinguishing feature being a longitudinal central bonnet bulge. The engine type

↑↑ The underside of the wet-sump pan, heavily 'winged' to increase the oil capacity while keeping the sump shallow.

↑ The single friction plate of the dry clutch locates between the flywheel and the clutch pressure plate.

↑↑ One of the 12 pistons, showing the two compression rings and the single oil-control ring.

↑ The sping-loaded clutch pressure plate, complete with appropriately coloured springs!

number for the DOHC model was 226, and it was the first Ferrari road car to be fitted with this arrangement, where the camshafts ran directly above the inlet and exhaust valves, with their lobes bearing directly on to the bucket cam followers, instead of rocker arms as on the previous SOHC examples. This DOHC arrangement was another case of racing improving the breed, as Ferrari had used four-cam engines in competition cars on and off since the mid-fifties. The upgraded engine was provided with dry-sump lubrication, and fitted with six carburettors as standard, to produce a claimed 300bhp (224kW). Despite the power increase, the DOHC engine was generally thought to provide a more linear power and torque curve, making it more user friendly, while it also benefitted from the rigid torque-tube layout introduced on late-series SOHC examples.

The 275 GTB went into production just after Ferrari and the FIA had fallen out over trying to get the 250 LM homologated as a development of the 250 GT series. In late 1964, Ferrari decided to produce a competition version of the 275 GTB, and between then and early 1965, they produced three examples, chassis Nos. 06701, 06885 and 07217, and these 'Speciales' are often referred to as the 1965 GTO. In April 1965, the FIA refused Ferrari's 275 GTB homologation submission, as the example submitted was way below the weight quoted in the sales literature. Ferrari offered to increase the weight of the car to the specified value, but the FIA turned this offer down. Enzo Ferrari was enraged and said that his cars would not participate in the 1965 GT Championship. This brought the FIA back to the negotiating table, and eventually an agreement was reached and the 275 GTB was homologated in June 1965. Due to all this political bickering, only one of the three cars produced saw any race action that year. This was chassis No. 06885, which was a Ferrari works entry in the Targa Florio on 6 May, running in the prototype class, where it was driven by Giampiero Biscaldi and Bruno Deserti. It was unclassified in the results, and it then appeared in the Nürburgring 1,000km

on 23 May, again as a works entry, where it finished second in class and 13th overall, driven by Giampiero Biscaldi and Giancarlo Baghetti. It was then sold to Belgium's Ecurie Francorchamps and repainted in yellow. In this livery, it ran in the 1965 Le Mans 24 Hours where it finished first in class and third overall (behind two 250 LMs), driven by Willy Mairesse and 'Beurlys' (Jean Blaton).

On the subject of competition variants, Ferrari built two series of competition-orientated 275 GTBs. The first series comprised ten cars with the 'short-nose' configuration, and the second series was of 12 cars with the 'long-nose' body style. All these cars featured alloy bodies, those on the second

↖ A side view of the sump, showing one of the 'winged' sections extending from the side to increase the oil capacity.

↑ The insides of the bare aluminium cylinder heads are coated with yellow sealing paint to seal the tiny pores often present after castings have been cleaned by bead-blasting.

→ The car photographed for this book was fitted with three Weber 40 DCZ/6 twin-choke carburettors.

↓ The black crackle-painted camshaft cover has the Ferrari logo incorporated into the casting.

series being of a lighter gauge with the bumpers fixed directly to the body rather than to the chassis. To further reduce weight, the transmission casing and some engine covers were cast in a magnesium alloy. All were provided with dry-sump lubrication, and the first series had a six-carburettor set-up, whilst the second series had a triple-carburettor arrangement featuring swept-back intake trumpets, sometimes within a gauze cage to catch 'rocks'! It is believed that the triple-carburettor assembly came about through a mistake when the homologation papers were submitted. These cars were sold to private clients or teams who wished to go GT racing, but none were entered in competition directly by the factory. They acquitted themselves quite well, with numerous class wins in the late sixties. After 06885's class success at Le Mans in 1965, there were further class wins there in 1966 and 1967 for 275 GTB/C models, the 'C' being an official suffix only added to the second series of cars.

The great success and wide appreciation of this beautiful and powerful berlinetta was a further step in the technological evolution of series-production Ferraris, which were becoming more and more popular, as the ultimate statement of a GT road car with competition heritage. Battista Pininfarina himself, the 'creator' of this design masterpiece, owned, as a personal car, a first-series 275 GTB 'Speciale' (chassis No. 06437), painted Acqua Verde Metallizzato (Sea Green Metallic), with the six-carburettor set-up, together with some special personal features, including the omission of the quarter light on the driver's door, which allowed him to experience the delights of his masterpiece.

➔ **A view of the gear clusters, showing the helical gear teeth, the synchromesh components and one of the roller bearings.**

↘ **The alloy transaxle casing. Some competition cars featured a magnesium casing. This was Ferrari's first transaxle.**

↓ **The front timing cover assembly, with the left-hand oil-filter mounting and cooling-fan mounting in place.**

↓↓ **The two cylinder heads, showing the polished inlet ports in the foreground, with recesses for the manifold sealing O-rings.**

↓ **A side view of the forged-steel crankshaft, showing the main journals, shared crankpins and counterweights.**

↓↓ **On the top of the timing cover, in the centre of the vee, a riveted plate shows the cylinder firing order.**

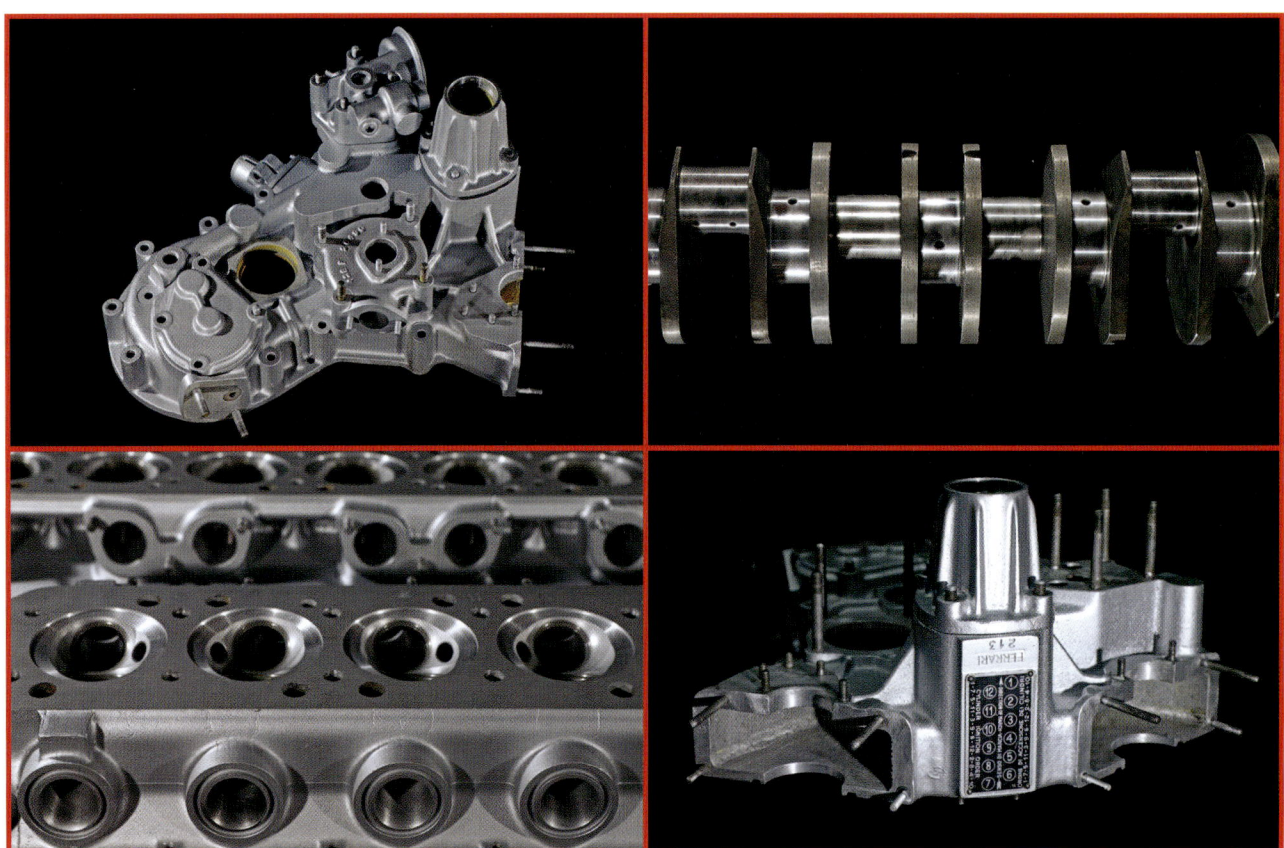

275 GTB: The transaxle arrives (1964)

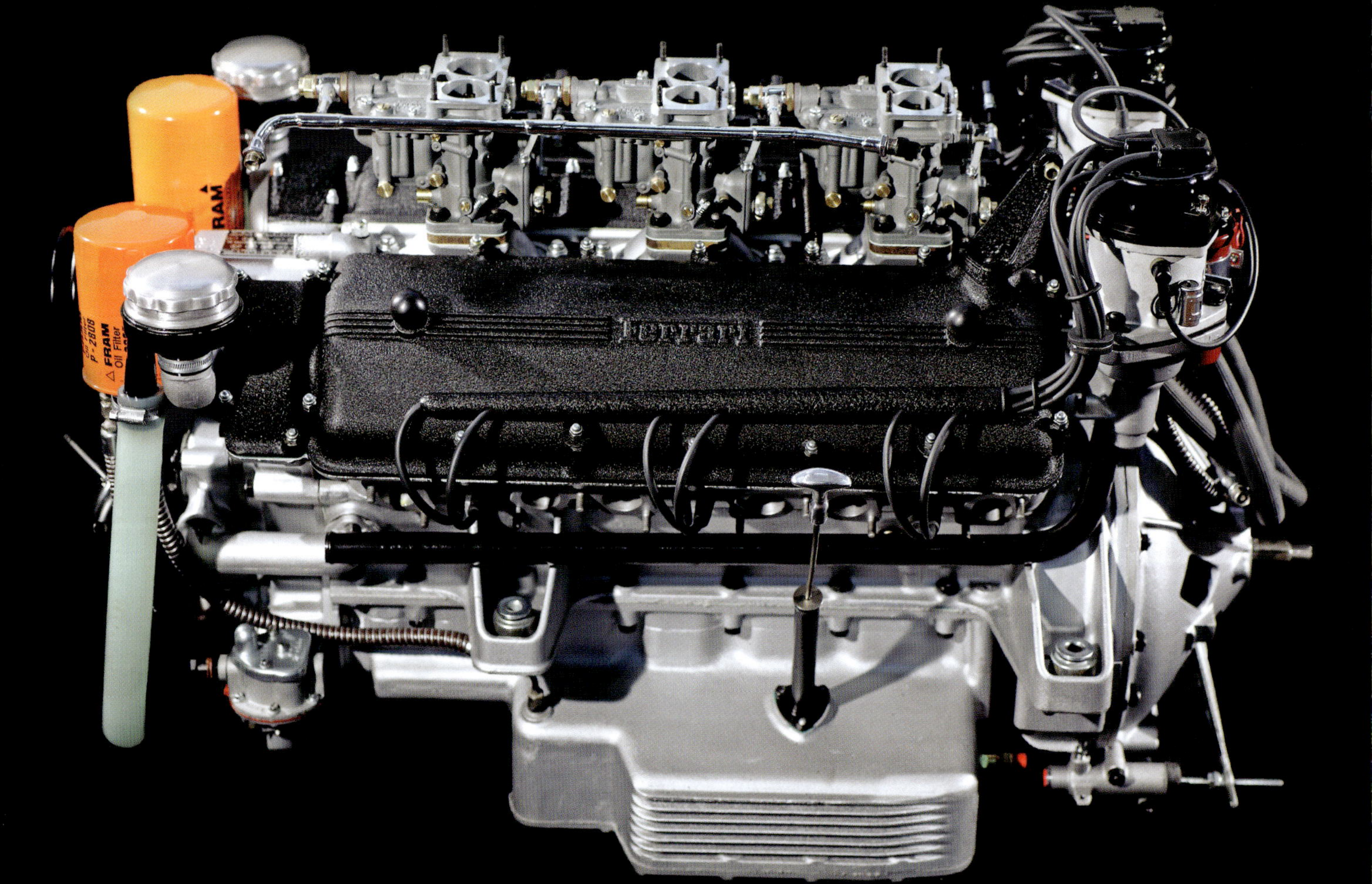
FRAM
Oil Filter
P-2808

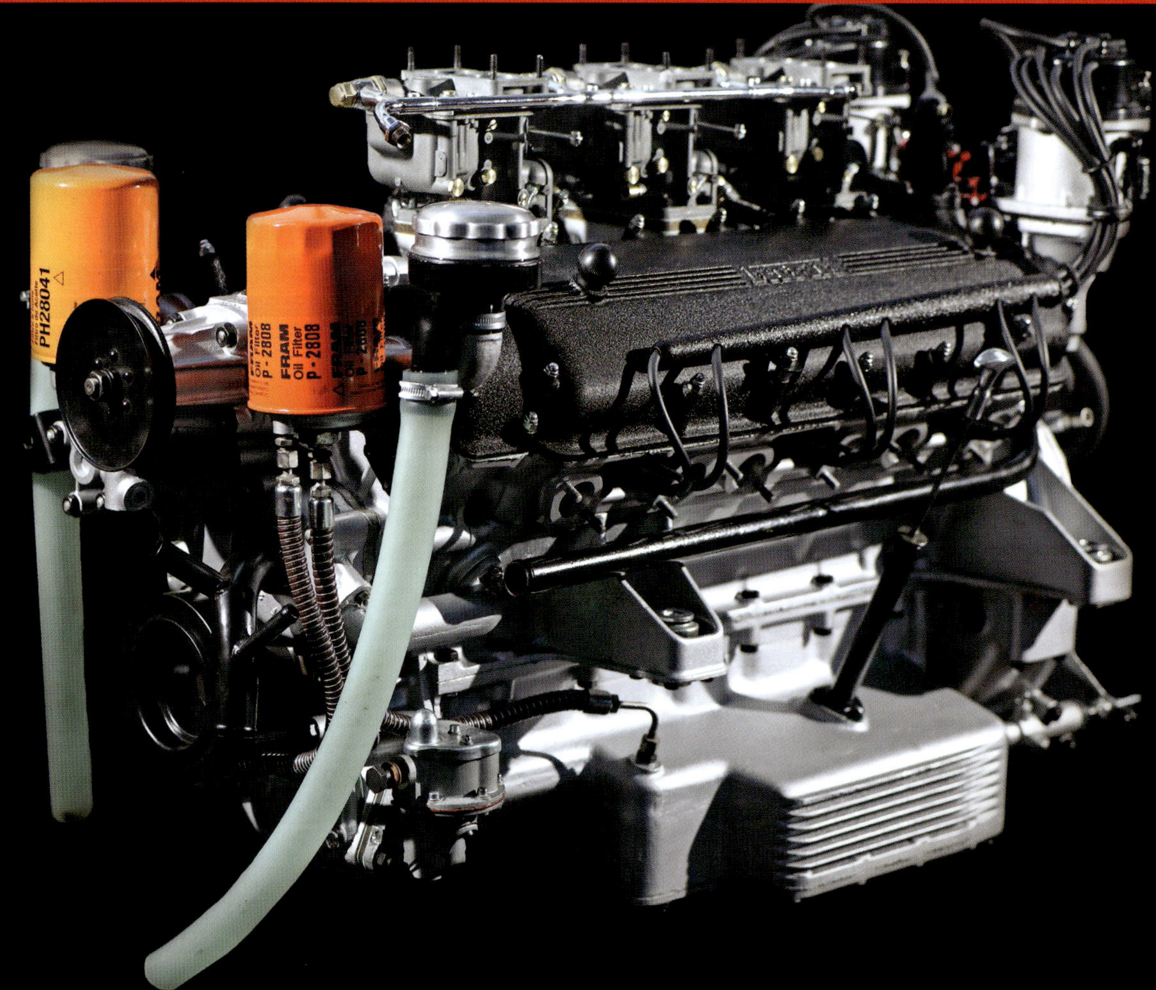
PH28041
FRAM
Oil Filter
P-2808

↑ The 275 GTB 'long nose' has a slimmer and prettier front grille compared to the wider 'mouth' of the 'short nose'.

↑ The Kamm tail, with single tail-light assemblies and chrome number-plate surround. Note also the chrome boot hinges.

➔ Both the Prancing Horse emblem and the Ferrari script are chromed, along with the boot lock recessed into the spoiler.

↘ The rounded tail-lights and integrated rear spoiler underline the sporty nature of this 'ready to race' road car.

↘↘ The Plexiglas-covered headlights, recessed sidelights and teardrop indicator lights emphasise the streamlined styling.

↘↘↘ The curvacious rear wheel arches and the three cooling gills on the rear flanks leave no doubt as to the sporting nature of this beautiful berlinetta.

↓ This low three-quarter view emphasises the powerful, voluptuous curves of Pininfarina's masterpiece.

330 GTS
Increasing the capacity (1966)

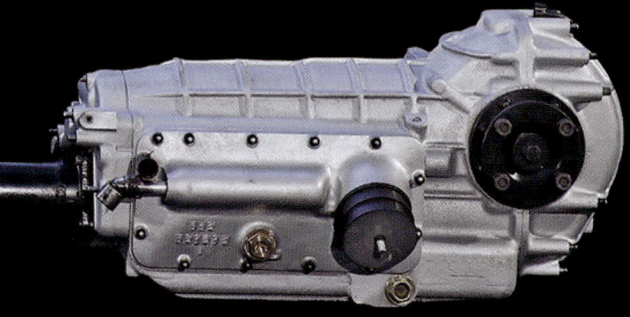

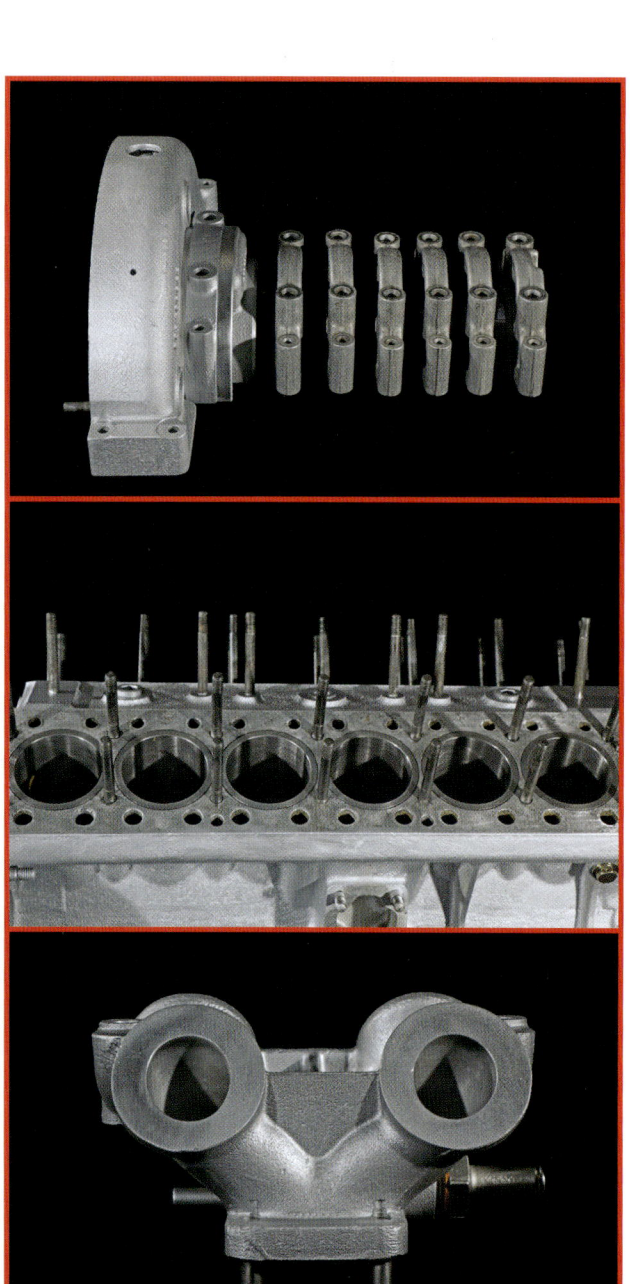

← The seven crankshaft main-bearing caps, and the lower flywheel cover (left).

↙ A view of one side of the cylinder block on this 'short block' engine. Note the narrow gaps between the cylinder liners.

In 1959, a revised 'short block' 4.0-litre engine was born, based on the earlier V12 designed by Gioachino Colombo, as Ferrari finally abandoned the 'long block' design, with screwed-in cylinder liners, created by Aurelio Lampredi. This new engine featured wider cylinder-bore spacing, and was an update of the original Colombo engine with the goal of increased performance. The new engine featured a light alloy cylinder block, with a distance of 94mm between the bore centres, rather than the previous 90mm. This new engine first appeared in 47 examples of the 400 SuperAmerica model, which replaced the 410 SuperAmerica series, which had been fitted with the last of the 'long block' engines. The type code for the engine was 163, and derivatives of it also appeared in the 330 TRI/LM, 330 LM Berlinetta and the 4.0-litre GTO. This engine was then further developed into the type 209, maintaining the same overall capacity of 3,967.44cc. Almost 1,800 type 209 engines were built during the sixties. Power was around 300bhp (224kW) at 6,600rpm, with a torque of 406Nm (300lb ft) at 5,000rpm. Specific power was 75bhp/litre (56kW/litre), and the compression ratio was 8.8:1. In order to increase the capacity of the 'short block' engine used in the 250 series, the cylinder bore and the stroke were increased to 77mm and 71mm respectively, making it necessary to modify the cylinder block to provide larger water ways to ensure adequate cooling.

This user-friendly and reliable engine was designed for use in various road-going Ferrari models, from the early 250 GTE-based 330 America, then its replacement, the 330 GT 2+2, to the sportier GTC and GTS models. Ferrari also developed this powerful engine for competition use, developing the unit through several evolutions (330 P, 330 P2, 330 P3 and 412 P). In 1967, the legendary 330 P4 appeared, taking Lorenzo Bandini and Chris Amon to victory in the Daytona 24 Hours race.

The first car to be fitted with the type 163 engine was a Ferrari 400 SuperAmerica PF Coupé Speciale, chassis number 1517SA – built for Gianni Agnelli. This was the car

↖ One of the three inlet manifolds (shown inverted). The manifolds fit between the cylinder heads within the engine vee.

← One of the lightly domed alloy pistons, viewed with inlet and exhaust valve. The valves were operated by roller cam followers.

→ A view of the clutch bellhousing. The four studs (at the top in this view) secure the propeller-shaft torque tube.

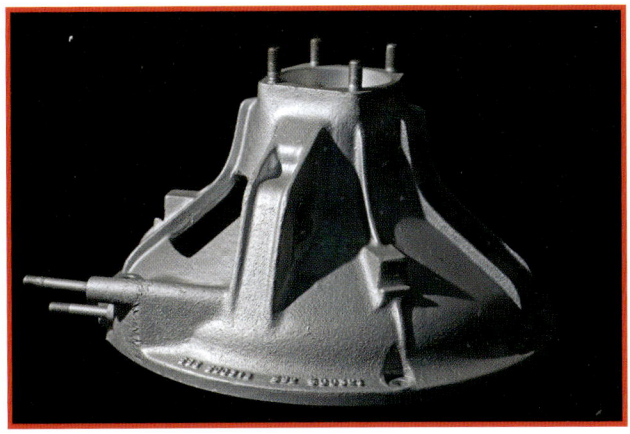

shown at 1959 Turin Motor Show and 1960 Geneva Salon. Initially, it is said that designer Pinin Farina and, also Agnelli, did not like the frontal design, and Agnelli sent the car back to the coachbuilder to modify the shape of the radiator opening and nose details to lighten what had appeared quite cumbersome for a Ferrari.

As mentioned previously, alongside 330 road-car production, Enzo Ferrari developed special competition versions of the engine, which featured significant detail differences to the road engines. These engines were fitted in the legendary sports prototypes with the suffix 'P' – cars that have featured heavily in the story of Maranello's racing history. The first car in this series – the 330 P Spider – was built in 1963, with a body designed by Carrozzeria Fantuzzi in Modena, and equipped with an engine of identical capacity to that used in the road cars. The 330 P featured a rear, longitudinally mounted engine, and differed from the type 209 engine, as it was fitted with dry-sump lubrication, a dry twin-plate clutch, located behind the longitudinal gearbox, six Weber carburettors and race camshafts. This engine produced 370bhp (276kW) – an increase of 70bhp (52kW) over the road cars.

Between 1963 and 1967, a number of other competition evolutions of the engine were developed, all carrying the suffix 'P'. The last and most famous of these 330 prototypes was the P4 – the car with which Enzo Ferrari planned to

↓ The cast-aluminium cylinder block. On this engine, the distance between bore centres increased to 94mm (from 90mm for previous 'short block' engines).

have his revenge on Ford. This mid-longitudinal 330 V12 – type 237 – was heavily modified by Franco Rocchi, who designed new, lighter DOHC cylinder heads which featured an innovative three-valves-per-cylinder layout (two intake valves and one exhaust). The power rose to 450bhp (336kW) at 8,000rpm, with fuelling provided via an updated Lucas fuel-injection system (used for the first time in 1966 on the P3). The thunderous noise produced by this incredible twin-overhead-camshaft, 36-valve V12 power unit was almost comparable to that of a jet fighter! In 1967, Ferrari reached the peak of success for the 330 prototype series, with victory on Ford's home turf in the Daytona 24 Hours race. P4s finished first and second, Chris Amon and Lorenzo Bandini taking victory ahead of Mike Parkes and Ludovico Scarfiotti, with a NART-entered 412 P driven by Pedro Rodriguez and Jean Guiche finishing third, providing Ferrari with a clean sweep of the podium.

In parallel to the competition exploits, the 4.0-litre type 209 Ferrari engine was a remarkable success in production form. It powered 50 examples of the 330 America (these cars featured 250 GTE 2+2 bodywork, but with a 4.0-litre engine), 1,099 examples of the 330 GT 2+2 (series I, Interim and series II), 598 examples of the 330 GTC, plus four Speciale examples and just 100 examples of the 330 GTS.

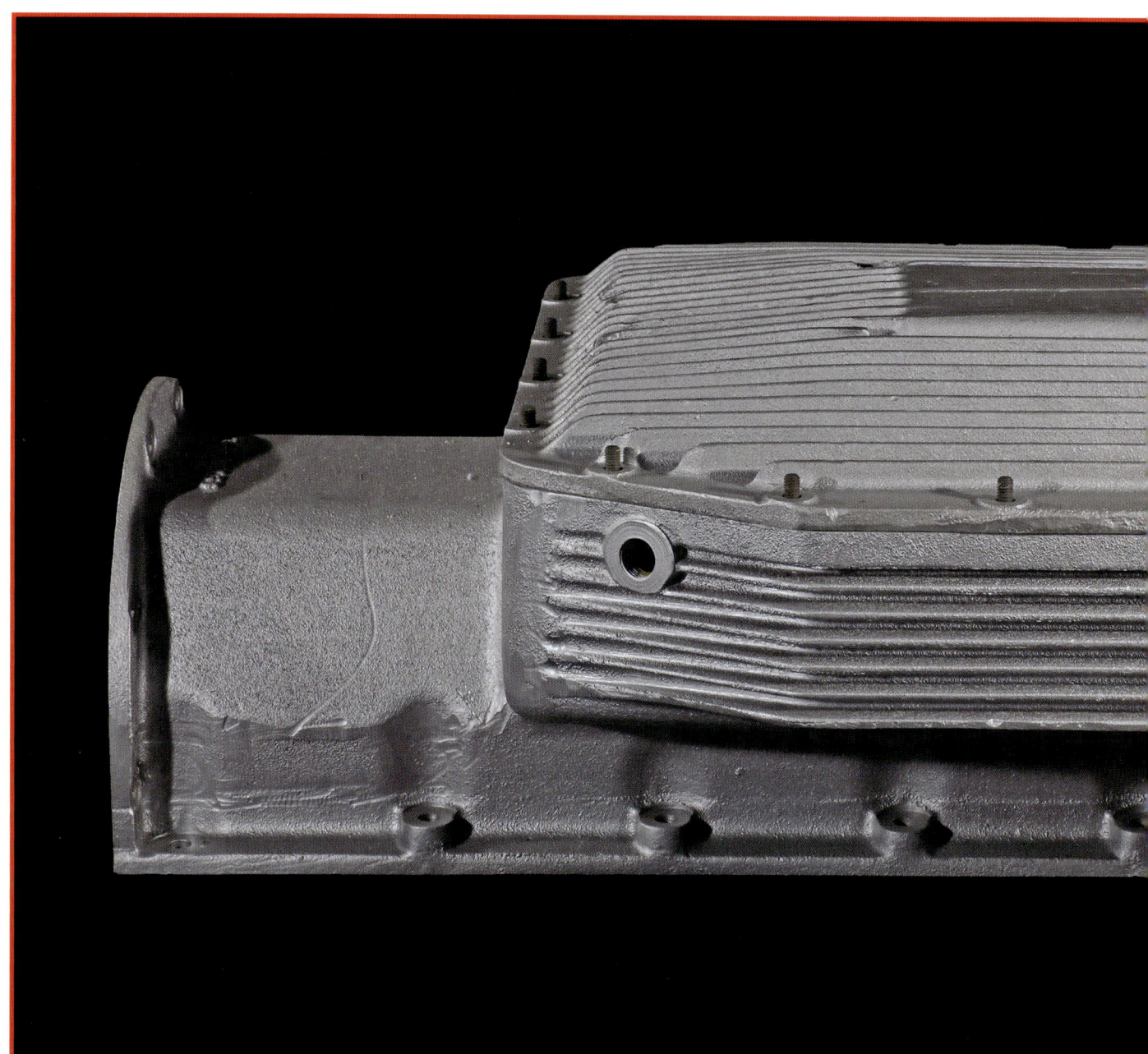

The 330 GTC/GTS models featured a transaxle, which had been adopted for the first time on the 1964 275 GTB. The 330 America and 330 GT 2+2 models used a conventional gearbox location to the rear of the engine, with a prop shaft to a rigid rear axle. The 50 cars which featured the 250 GTE 2+2 bodywork were fitted with a four-speed overdrive gearbox, as were the first series of 330 GT 2+2 models.

Before 330 GT 2+2 series II went into production, 125 Interim cars were built, as was the Ferrari tradition (the Interim cars introduced some of the changes between the different series). These cars were fitted with a five-speed gearbox that eliminated the Laycock overdrive, and at the same time a change was made from a mechanically operated clutch to a twin-plate hydraulic clutch by Borg & Beck. From 1965, the series II was introduced, with the new five-speed gearbox and a modified nose with a single headlight layout replacing the 'Chinese' twin-headlight arrangement of the Series I car. For 330 GT 2+2 cars built after chassis No. 08729 (in 1966), engines with type number 209/66 were used, and the engine block was modified, with only one engine mounting per side, instead of two, although the model still retained the conventional gearbox/rigid rear-axle layout.

The 330 GTC/GTS models were unveiled in 1966, in March at the Geneva Motor Show and in October at the Paris Motor Show respectively. Both shared the engine/transmission mounting system (one engine mounting on either side and two transmission mountings) with the 275 built from April 1966. As with the 275 (see 275 GTB chapter), the revolutionary transaxle was connected to the engine via a driveshaft running in a rigid torque tube flanged to each unit.

The engine featured a light alloy cylinder block, and a single camshaft per bank. At the time Ferrari was working on a twin-overhead-camshaft layout, which from 1966 was fitted in the 275 GTB/4 Berlinetta, whilst the 365 GTC/GTS models, with their less overtly sporty nature, retained the SOHC layout. The camshafts were triplex chain-driven via gears from the crankshaft, and the valves were operated by roller cam followers actuating the rocker arms. The pistons were lightly domed in a hemispherical combustion chamber, and were manufactured by Borgo, with two compression rings and an oil-control ring. The crankshaft, connecting roads and cylinder liners were steel. Lubrication was via a wet sump, with an alloy sump casing. Timing and camshaft covers were also alloy. The ignition system featured twin coils and distributors, with the spark plugs located outside the engine vee. Fuel was supplied from the tank via an electric pump, with a separate filter sited adjacent to the fuel tank, to a mechanical pump and filter assembly in the engine bay, then to triple Weber 40 DCZ/6 or 40 DFI/2 carburettors mounted in the centre of the vee. The firing order was 1–7–5–11–3–9–6–12–2–8–4–10.

The 330 type 209 engine was considered to be a great compromise between reliability, driving pleasure (despite the high performance) and straightforward maintenance. This engine brought Maranello closer to customers who appreciated refinement in addition to the Ferrari tradition for speed. The considerable torque that this V12 was capable of producing was part of the new 'user-friendly' trend that

← The wet sump is very similar to that shown previously for the 275 GTB. The timing cover bolts to the flange at the front.

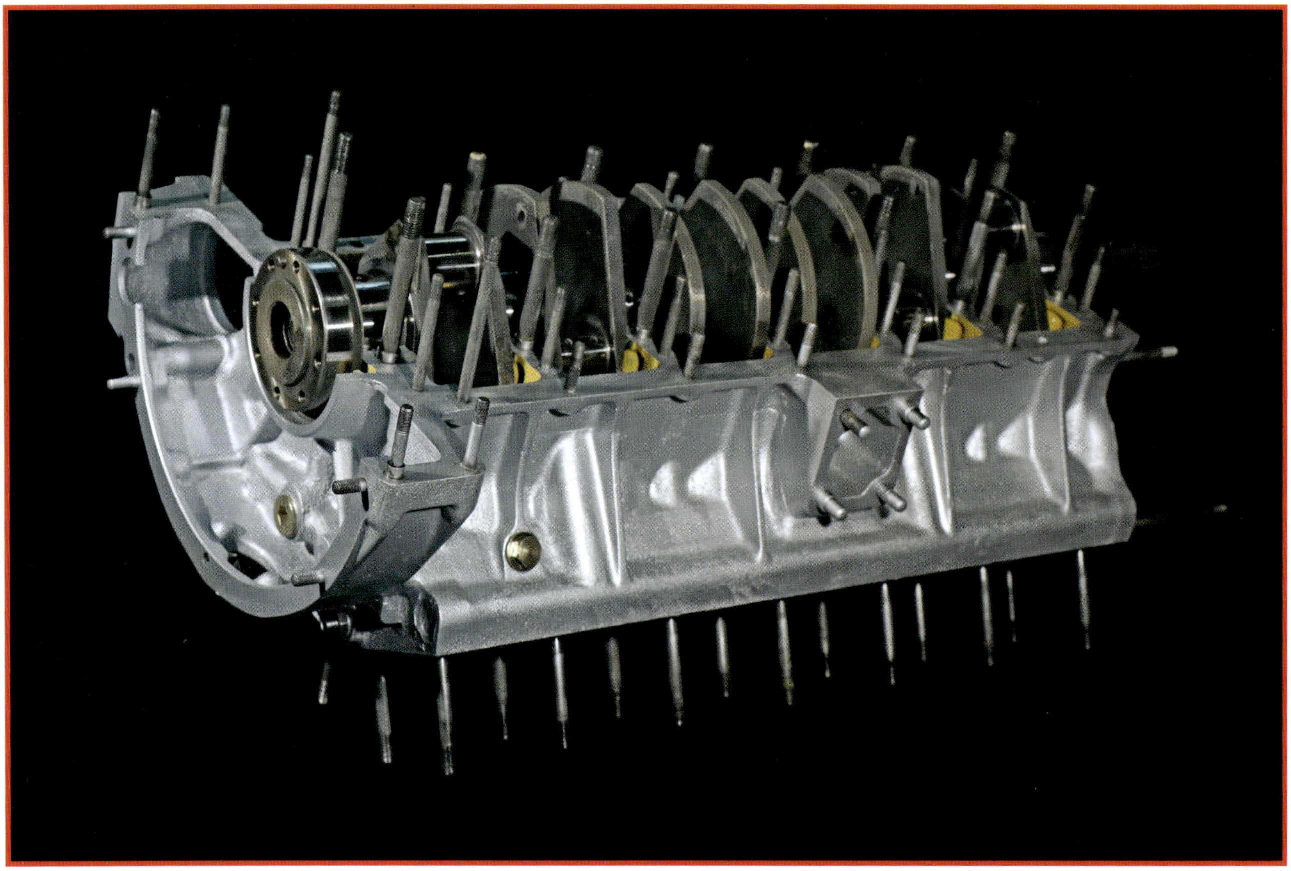

↑ **A view of the cylinder block inverted, with the steel crankshaft resting in position without the main bearing caps fitted.**

enabled the *Cavallino Rampante* to embrace its customers. Today, the rarest cars fitted with this refined engine are the 330 America and the 330 GTS – the only spider fitted with this engine. Auction prices for the 330 GTS have reached over 2 million Euros, as the cars become increasingly more sought-after by Ferrari collectors.

During the sixties, Sergio Pininfarina took control of his father's design house, introducing his own ideas into the DNA of the company, keen to make his mark. The 330 GTS would be Sergio's first Ferrari design (with the exception of the unusual and underappreciated 400 SuperAmerica Speciale of 1959). Taking cues from the nose of the 500 Superfast and the tail of the 275 GTS, Sergio designed the 330 GTS – the supremely elegant spider that we have chosen to illustrate

↓ **A view of one of the cylinder heads, with the inlet ports closest to the camera. The protruding studs secure the camshaft cover.**

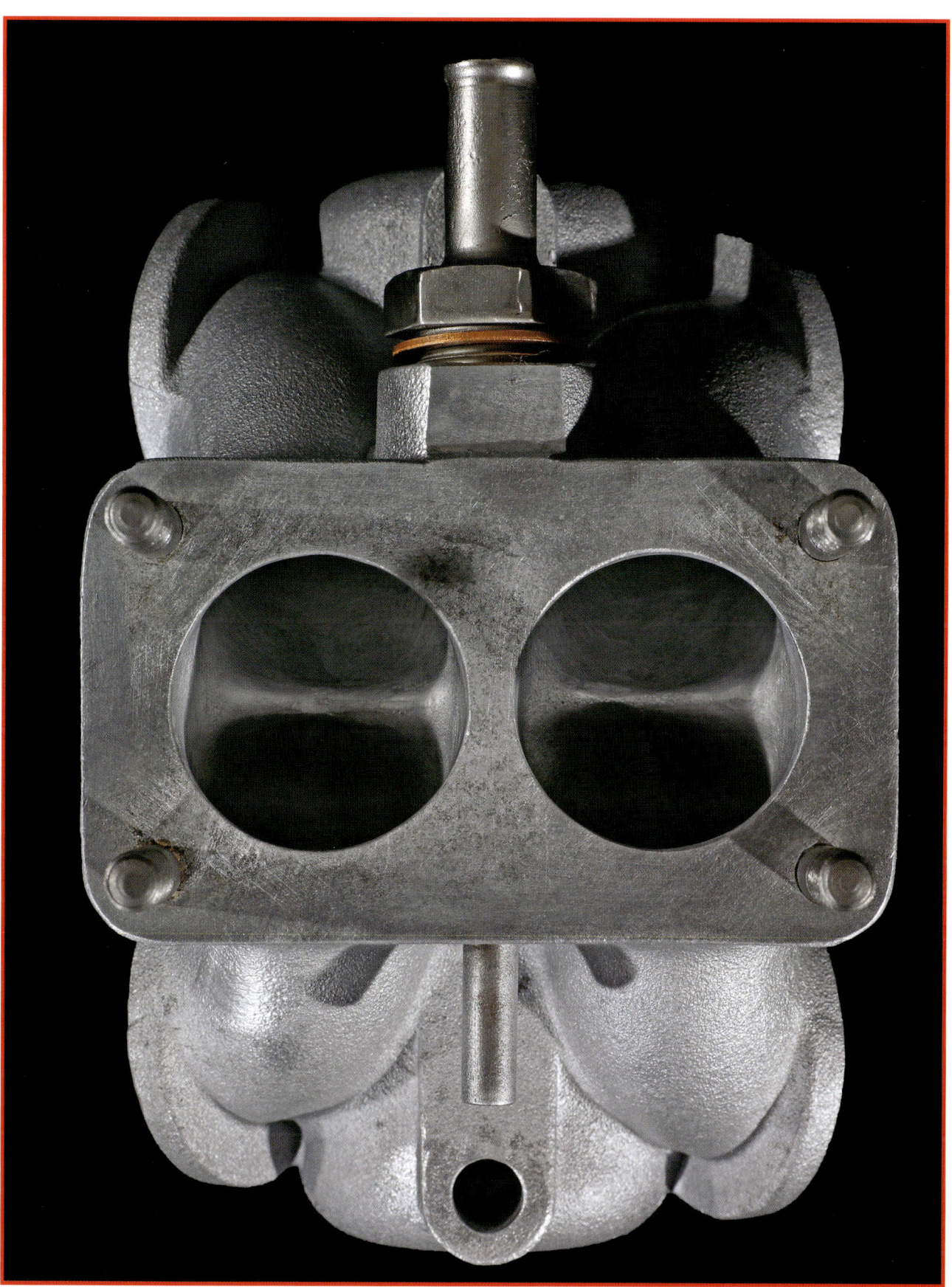

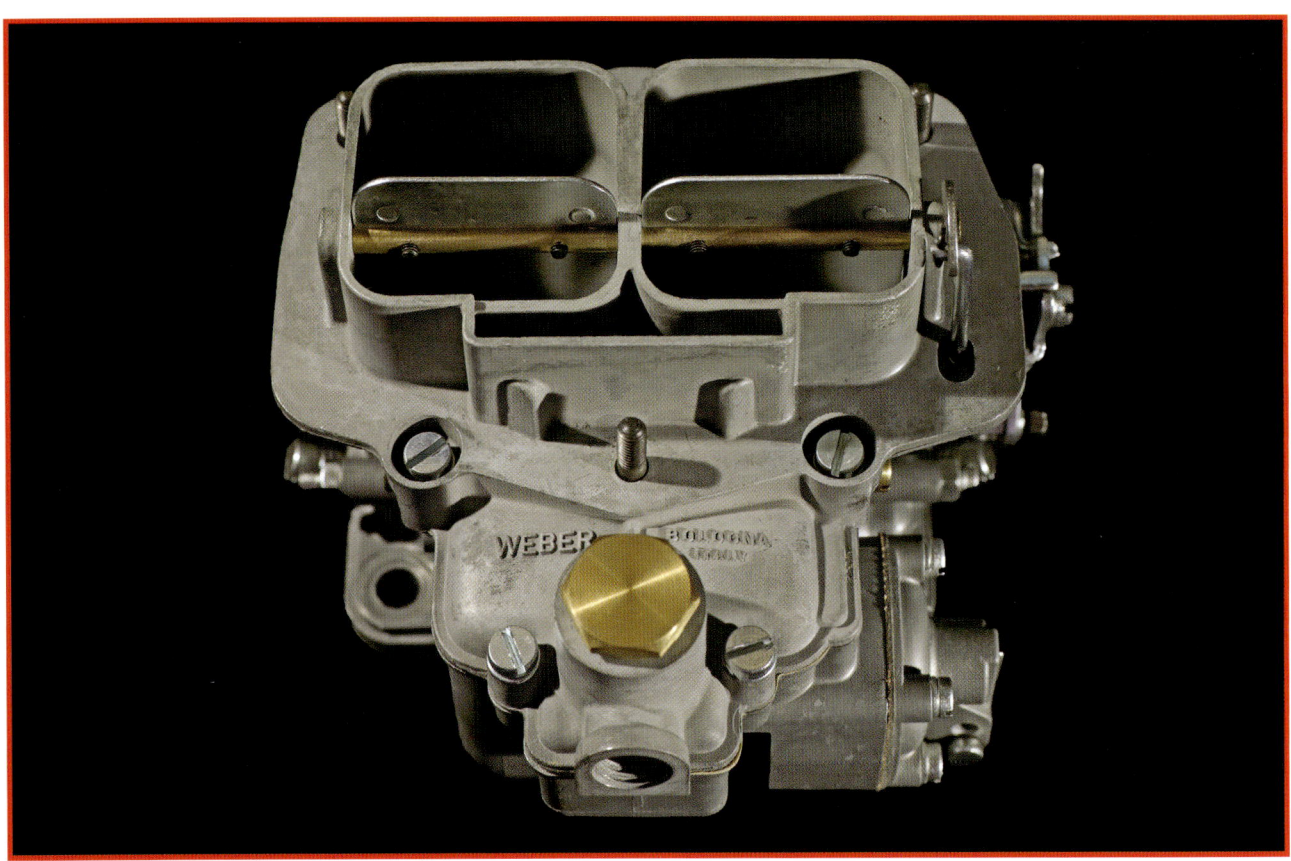

↑ One of the twin-choke Weber 40 DFI/2 carburettors fitted to the car photographed for this book.

FERRARI 330 GT – TECHNICAL DATA

Engine code	209
Engine type	Front, longitudinal, V12, 60°
Bore and stroke	77 x 71mm (3.03 x 2.79in)
Total capacity	3,967.44cc (242.10cu in)
Unitary capacity	330.62cc (20.17cu in)
Compression ratio	8.8:1
Maximum power	296bhp (221kW) at 7,000rpm
Power per litre	75bhp/litre (56kW/litre)
Valve operation	Single overhead camshaft per bank, two valves per cylinder
Fuel feed	Three twin-choke Weber 40 DCZ/6 or 40 DFI/2 carburettors
Ignition	Single spark plug per cylinder, twin distributor, twin coils
Lubrication	Wet sump
Clutch	Dry, single plate
Maximum torque	406Nm (299.4lb ft) at 5,000rpm
Firing order	1–7–5–11–3–9–6–12–2–8–4–10

were then introduced on the replacement 365 GTC and 365 GTS; for example, the provision of exhaust air grilles in the rear corners of the bonnet replaced the triple louvre assembly on the front wings.

Additionally, Pininfarina trialled retractable headlights, derived from the idea adopted for the rare 365 California Spider (14 cars built). The philosophy for the 4.0-litre coupé and spider was a compromise between the more sporty 275 GTB and the touring-orientated 330 GT 2+2.

Towards the end of 330 production, just as the V6 Dino was introduced, Ferrari decided to increase the capacity of the 4.0-litre V12 to 4,390.35cc. With an increased bore of 81mm, while the stroke remained at 71mm, the engine type 245 was born in 1967. This engine equipped the 365 GT 2+2, nicknamed 'Queen Mary'. This car was the heir to the 500 Superfast and 330 GT 2+2, and shared the SOHC V12 engine layout.

In 1968, a new generation of 4.4-litre cars appeared. There were actually two different cars, one of these, the 365 GTC, as noted was very similar to the 330 GTC, both in terms of its shape and the SOHC engine layout. The second car, the 365 GTB4, featured a twin-overhead-camshafts-per-bank configuration, developed from that of 275 GTB4. The engine type used in the 365 GTB4 was the 251, and the nickname attributed to this streamlined new car was 'Daytona' – a tribute to the glorious 1–2–3 finish achieved

↑ A close-up view of the details of the forged-steel crankshaft – a work of art in itself.

by Ferrari at Daytona in 1967. At the end of the sixties, there was also a short production run of the final SOHC Ferrari engine (type 245/C) which was fitted to a small production run of 20 365 GTS cars. This car signified the end of the Ferrari single-overhead-camshaft era, as the Maranello factory progressed to a future featuring more and more technological advances.

↑↑ The three Weber 40 DFI/2 carburettors assembled on their inlet manifolds, complete with beautifully made fuel-supply pipe.

↑ A view inside the top of one of the cylinder heads, showing the camshaft laid in position with the cam lobes visible.

↙ The friction disc from the dry single-plate clutch, manufactured by Fichtel & Sachs.

↓ The clutch pressure-plate assembly, with the diaphragm spring visible in the centre.

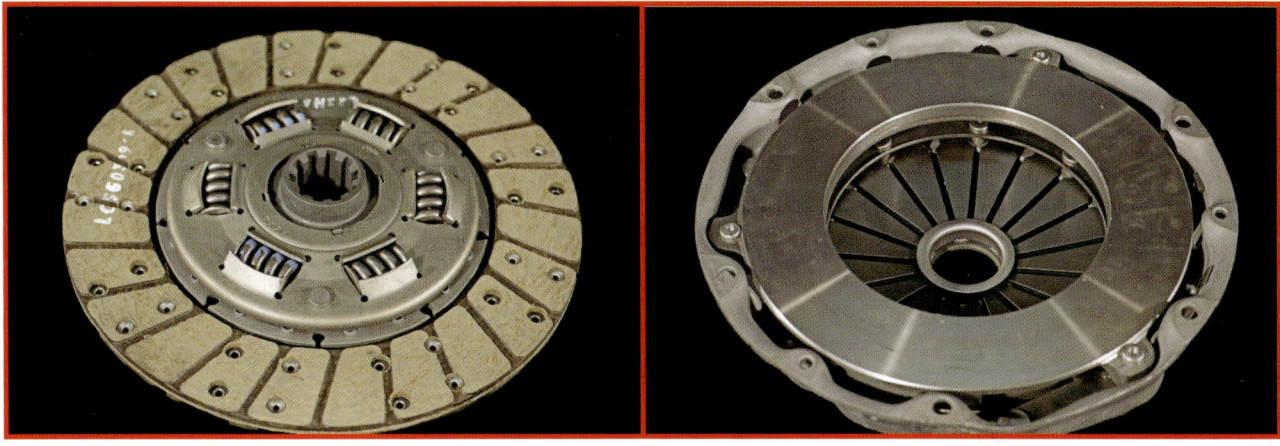

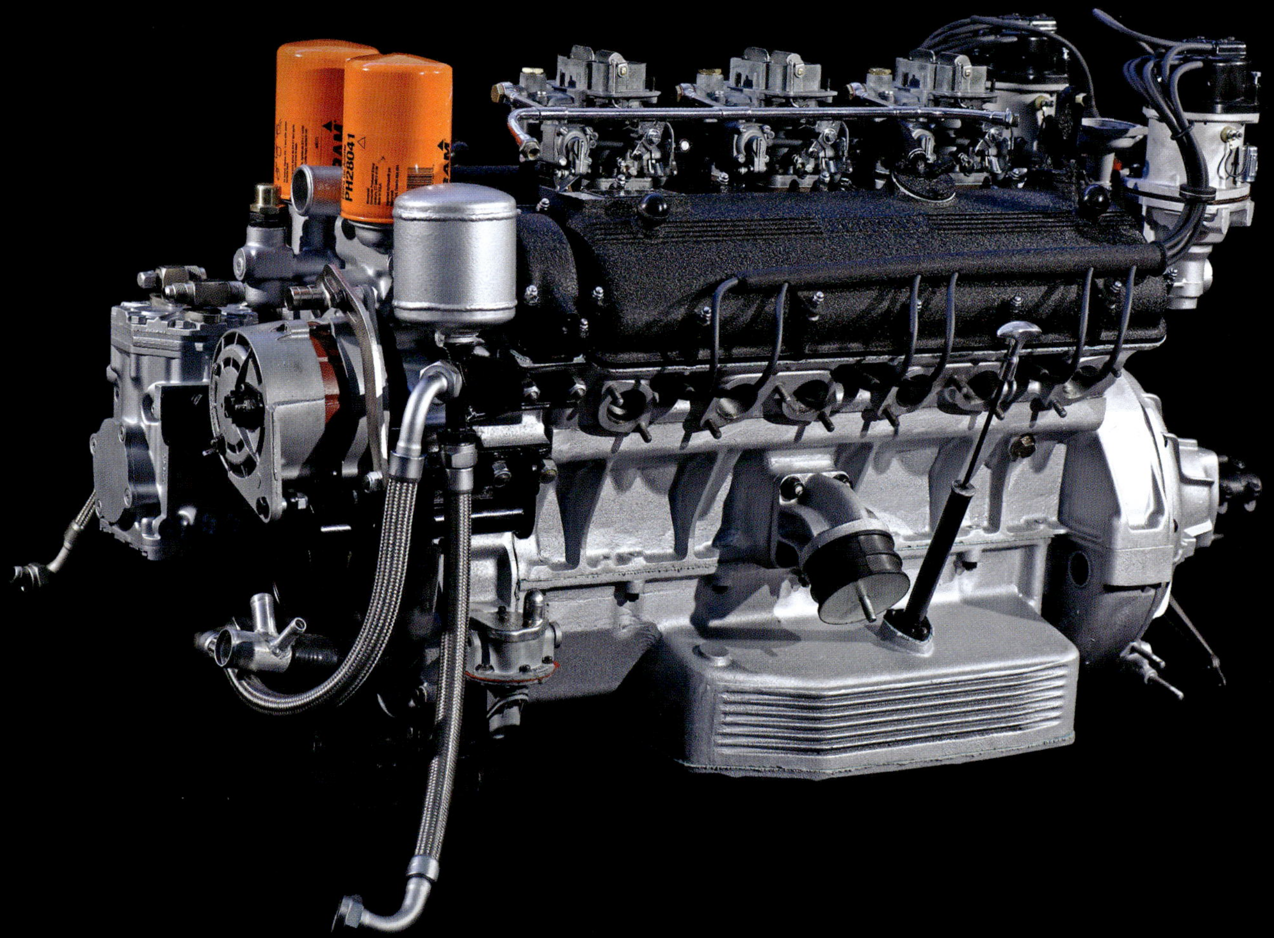

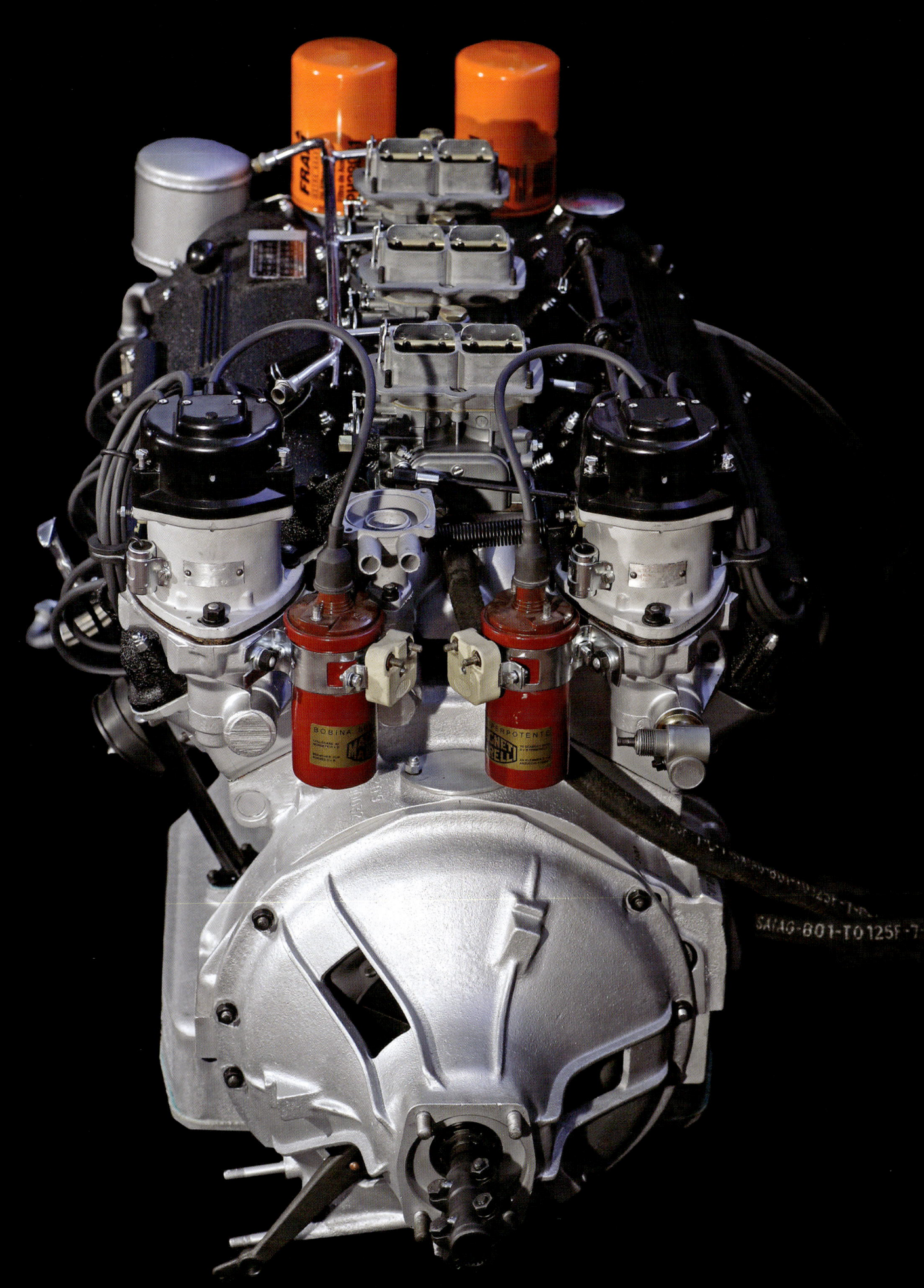

↑ The tapered nose of the 330 GTS was the work of Pininfarina, and was an evolution of the shape of the previous 275 GTS.

↑ Apart from a 330 script badge, the rear of the 330 GTS was identical to the preceding 275 GTS model.

➜ The tail-lights have chrome frames in keeping with the class and style of this elegant Ferrari.

↘ Three air outlet gills, an evolution of those fitted to the 500 Superfast, are fitted to extract air from the engine bay.

↘↘ The recessed chrome-trimmed headlights and 'teardrop' indicator lights complement the luxurious styling.

↘↘↘ A close-up view of one of the chromed Borrani wire wheels, with central 'knock off' retaining nut.

↓ The 330 GTS was the epitome of open-air motoring elegance of the period.

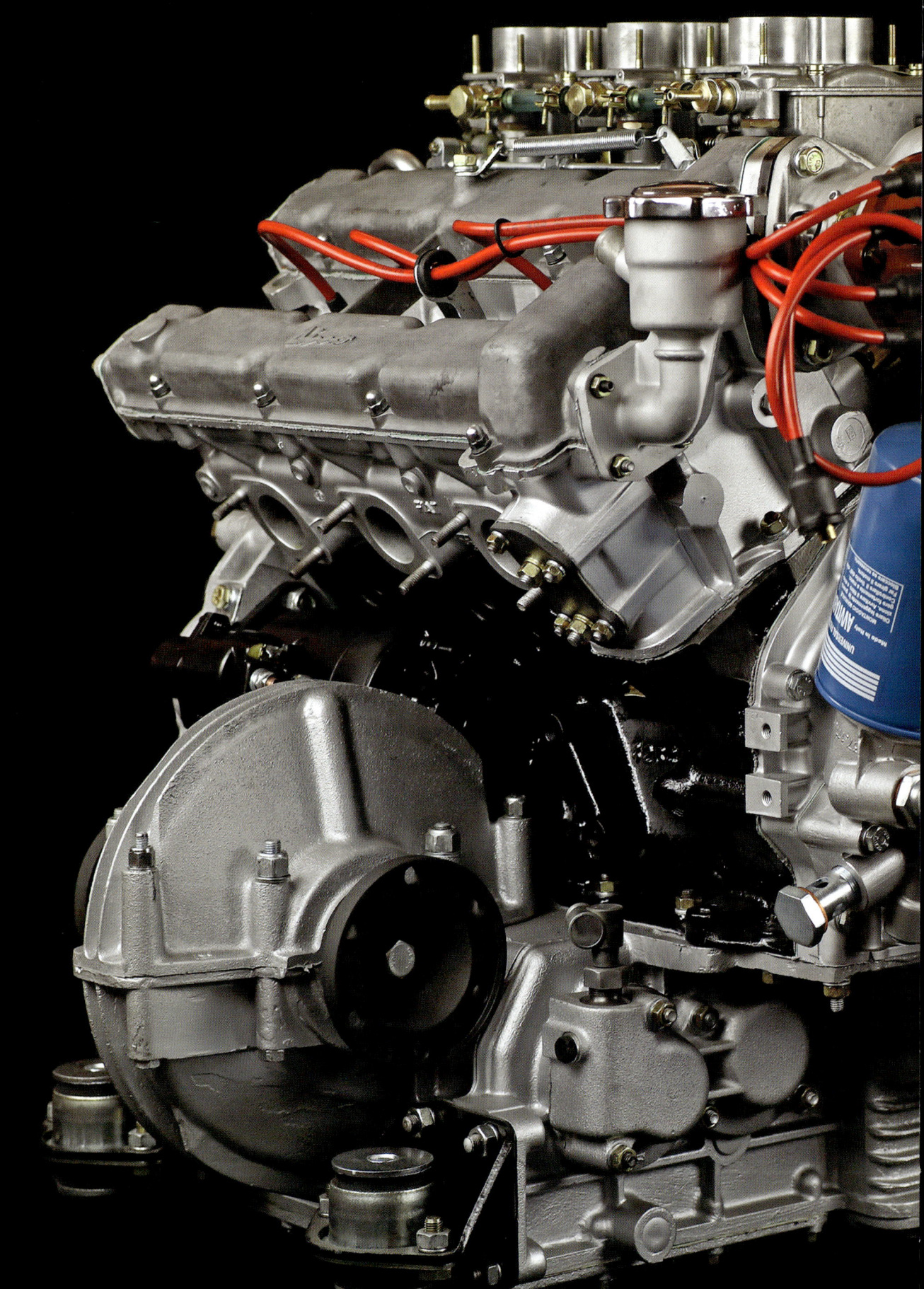

Dino 246
The Fiat partnership (1972)

← The aluminium pistons were manufactured by Borgo, and featured cut-outs in the skirts on either side to reduce weight and aid cooling.

↙ Each piston has two compression rings and one oil-control ring.

The arrival of the six-cylinder Dino road car engine was the beginning of a period of change and innovation at Ferrari, both technical (with the introduction of a series production engine other than the classic V12) and also regarding the shareholding structure of the brand. Indeed, the 1967 Dino 206 model was the first car built as a result of an agreement between Ferrari and Fiat, which heralded the later arrival of Fabbrica Italiana Automobili Torino (Fiat), as a purchaser of 50 per cent of the Ferrari shares in early 1969. The Dino also heralded the introduction of a new style of Ferrari road-car model designation, by combining the total engine capacity (cc) with the number of cylinders, instead of the classic single-cylinder capacity (cc) model notation generally previously used for their road cars. Ferrari had actually already been using this 'new' designation system for their monoposto cars for a number of years, starting with the 156 F2 in 1957 and then the 246 F1 model in 1958. Therefore, the '246' model designation equates to 2.4 litres and six cylinders. The most important technical innovation introduced on the Dino was the mid-mounted transverse engine layout with a unitary transmission – a layout that was maintained by Ferrari for over 20 years through the succeeding eight-cylinder models, only reverting to a longitudinal layout when the 348 model was introduced in 1989.

The V6 Dino engine highlighted an important turning point in the Maranello factory's history: it was the power unit that brought Ferrari and Fiat together and pointed the way to the future marriage in 1969. Indeed, it was with this revolutionary V6 engine, initially in 2.0-litre form, and then upgraded to 2.4-litre capacity in 1969, that Ferrari started the partnership with Fiat in 1965. The reasoning behind this was that the regulations for the 1967 Formula 2 World Championship deemed that the engines had to be production-based, with a minimum of 500 cars produced per year. This was an impossible number for Ferrari at that time, but an alliance with Fiat, so that both companies produced cars with the

↖ Engine lubrication is via wet sump, with a mechanical oil pump driven by reduction gears from the crankshaft.

← Another first for Ferrari on this engine was the use of sodium-filled hollow-stem valves, to improve heat dissipation.

same engine, meant that this figure was achievable. Thus the Fiat Dino Coupé and Spider models came into being in 1966, albeit with a traditional front-mounted engine, but like their siblings from Maranello, bearing a 'Dino' script badge. The Fiat cars preceded the Ferrari-built Dino – which was established as a marque in its own right – by two years.

The basis for the project was the 1,500cc 65° V6 engine envisaged by Enzo Ferrari's beloved son Alfredino (more widely known as Dino), in cooperation with the famous engine designer Vittorio Jano, father of exceptional Fiat and Alfa Romeo competition engines and the V8 Lancia D50 F1 engine, which propelled Juan Manuel Fangio to the 1956 World Drivers' Championship in its Ferrari guise. In an interview, Enzo Ferrari recalled: 'In the long snowy winter in which nephritis kept Alfredino in bed, me and my friend Jano passed long hours by his sickbed discussing engine projects of four- or six-cylinder inline, but also of V6 and V8 layouts. Every day, Vittorio and I took the notes from Maranello to Alfredino, and I remember with how much knowledge and certainty he discussed the projects. For reasons of mechanical performance and efficiency, Dino reached the conclusion that we should adopt a V6 layout, so Jano and I stood by his decision.' Thus the first Ferrari V6 65° engine – the famous 156 – was born, which would burst into life in November 1956,

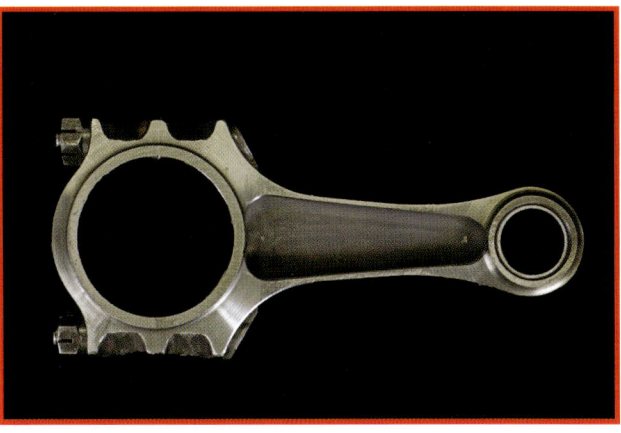

→ The connecting rods each have their own crankshaft journal, and feature white-metal big-end bearings.

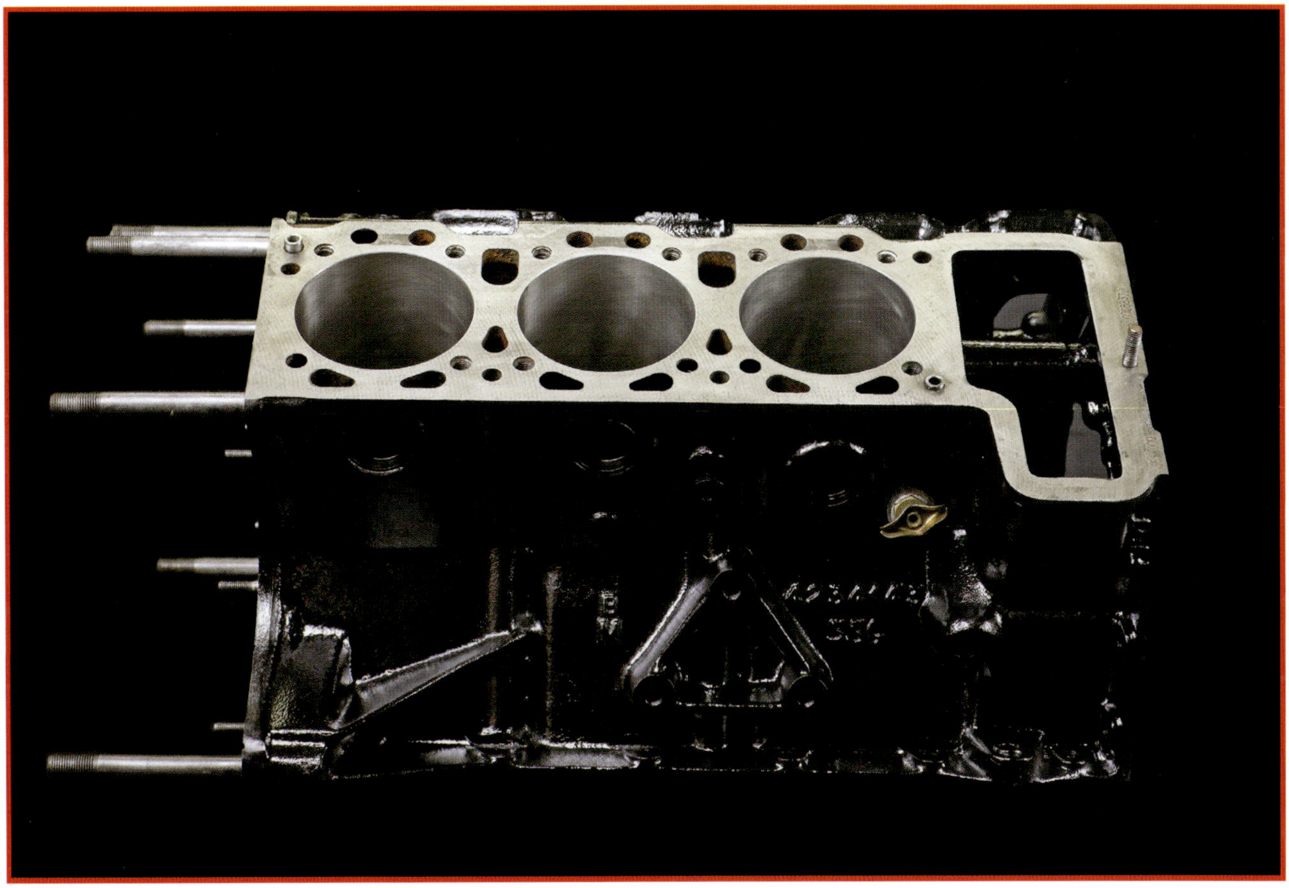

just five months after Dino passed away. This 1,500cc engine made its debut in the Napoli Grand Prix in April 1957, powering a 156 F2 driven by Luigi Musso. He finished third overall. In

↓ A move to cast iron for the cylinder block reduced costs and provided room for the larger bores of the 2.4-litre engine.

2.4-litre form, this V6 engine powered Mike Hawthorn to the 1958 F1 Drivers' World Championship.

Following the collaboration with Fiat to produce the requisite number of road-car engines, the 166 F2 made its race debut in 1967, but it wasn't until 1968 that Enzo Ferrari would gain any real satisfaction from the project. This came through two race wins courtesy of Tino Brambilla – one at Hockenheim in Germany, where Derek Bell finished third in a sister car, and then again in the Rome Grand Prix. This was run in two heats, with Brambilla winning both, and team-mate Andrea de Adamich finishing second on aggregate, to close the season on a winning note. At the end of the European season the cars were used in the Temporada Series in Argentina, where de Adamich won the series championship for Ferrari. The V6 had been used in 2.4-litre form earlier in 1968 in the Tasman Series in Australia and New Zealand, where Chris Amon finished as runner-up in the series to the Lotus of Jim Clark. Amon went one better in the 1969 series to win the championship for Ferrari, while Graeme Lawrence repeated Amon's feat in 1970, using the same car that Amon had steered to victory in 1969.

As previously mentioned, the birth of the Dino brand goes back to the passing of Alfredino at a young age, and his father's decision to dedicate to his memory the generation of

six-cylinder competition cars (166 P, 166 F2, 246 F1, 196 S, 206 P, 206 S and 246 Tasman), naming them Dino. Almost without exception, the V6 race- and road-car engines which were fitted in Ferrari and Fiat Dino cars, had Dino Ferrari's script signature cast on their cam covers. The development of the Ferrari (Dino) six-cylinder engine for road use was carried out at the Fiat Reparto Studio Motori by Aurelio Lampredi, the engineer who had previously been responsible for the V12 Ferrari 'long block' engines at the beginning of the fifties. He had moved to Fiat in 1956, and remained there until 1982. Re-examining the V6 Ferrari project for road-car use, Lampredi cooperated with Fiat engineer Franco Rocchi and decided to design an engine block with the crankshaft centreline positioned 85mm above the base of the crankcase, to make it stronger and more reliable for road use. The revised V6 by Lampredi and Rocchi had an alloy block for the initial 2.0-litre version, but with the increase in engine capacity to 2.4 litres the material was changed to cast iron, which is the example that is featured in this chapter.

Both the 2.0-litre and 2.4-litre engines were fitted to the (Ferrari) Dino models and the Fiat Dino Spiders and coupés. Before arriving at the final Dino body style as we know it today, Ferrari and Pininfarina produced five prototypes. The first and second prototypes – the Dino 206 GT Speciale and Dino Berlinetta GT – were presented at the 1965 Paris Auto Show and the 1966 Turin Auto Show respectively. Both cars were designed by Pininfarina's Aldo Brovarone and were equipped with a 2.0-litre longitudinally mid-mounted V6 engine. It was not until the third prototype (produced in 1967), which was never shown officially at any motor show, that the definitive transverse mid-engine layout was used. At the 1967 Turin Motor Show, the fourth prototype – again featuring the transverse mid-engine layout of 2.0-litre capacity – was shown. This had an oval front radiator grille, which was modified for the production model, reportedly due to aerodynamic problems. The last of the five prototypes, which was very close to the form of the production car, was unveiled at the 1968 Turin Motor Show. The definitive Dino shape, evolving from Aldo Brovarone's original sketches, became reality when designer Leonardo Fioravanti added his touches following his arrival at Pininfarina, where in 1972 he would become the director of the research centre.

The (Ferrari) Dino's series production commenced in April 1968 with the 206 GT, and just 152 examples were built in total. The chassis had a wheelbase of 2,280mm, and was clothed in an alloy body constructed by Carrozzeria Scaglietti in Modena, featuring the 2.0-litre alloy engine with Fiat code number 135 B (Ferrari code 246 B). To establish Dino as a separate marque, the cars were given their own unique even chassis number sequence, whereas traditionally Ferrari road cars of that period had an odd chassis number sequence, with their even number sequence being used for competition cars. The revolutionary (for Ferrari) and much discussed decision to fit a mid-mounted transverse engine in the Dino made it possible to lower the centre of gravity compared to a front-engined layout. Moreover, the engine and transmission were almost directly above the driven wheels, providing a low polar moment of inertia, and thus excellent handling characteristics.

← **The clutch bellhousing with the clutch-release fork and boot in the foreground. The clutch cable connects to the bellcrank to the left of the fork and operates the fork via an adjustable rod.**

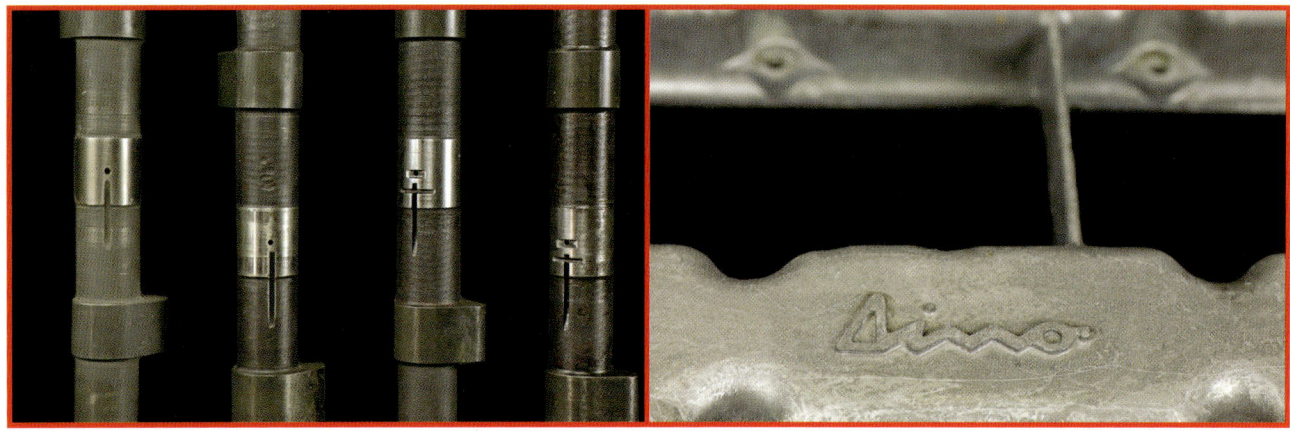

The total capacity of the 2.4 Dino engine, produced from 1969 (the same year in which Ferrari sold 50 per cent of the company to Fiat), was 2,419.20cc, with a unitary capacity of 403.20cc, a bore of 92.5mm and a stroke of 60.0mm. This 'little' but powerful 65° V6 engine produced 195bhp (145kW) at 7,500rpm, with a maximum torque of 166lb ft (225Nm) at 5,500rpm, a specific power of 81hp/litre (60kW/litre), and a weight/power ratio of 5.5kg/hp (12lb/hp) – absolutely worthy of any car from Maranello. With a weight of 1,080kg (2,381lb), this aerodynamic and compact berlinetta reached a top speed of around 146mph (235kmh), accelerating from 0–62mph (0–100kmh) in around six seconds. This new engine, built

↖ **A close-up view of the four forged-steel nitrided camshafts.**

↑ **The Dino script is cast into the alloy cam covers of the six-cylinder, 2.4-litre engine.**

→ **The solid forged-steel crankshaft runs in four main bearings – one at each end and one between each pair of connecting-rod journals.**

↓ **A view of one of the alloy cylinder heads showing the combustion chambers and valve seats, and the three exhaust ports.**

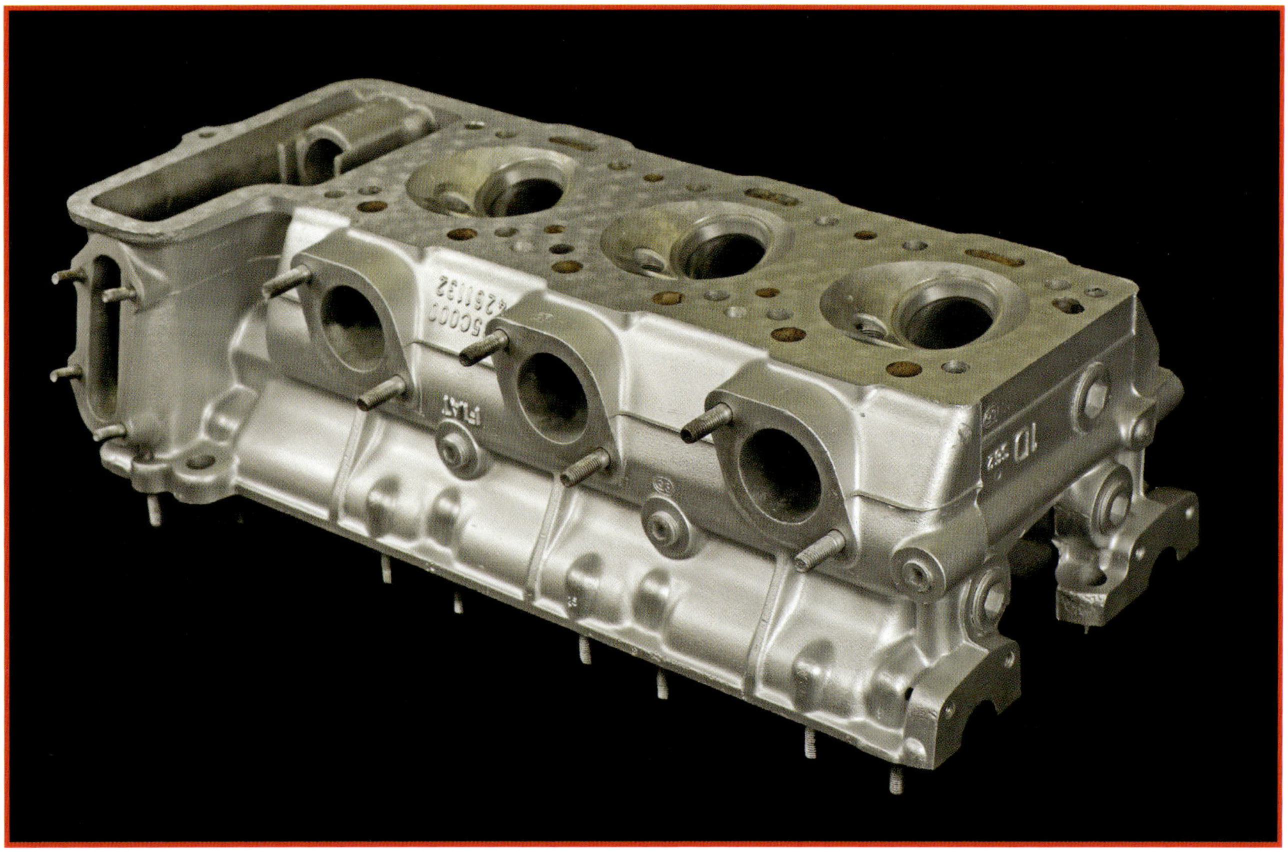

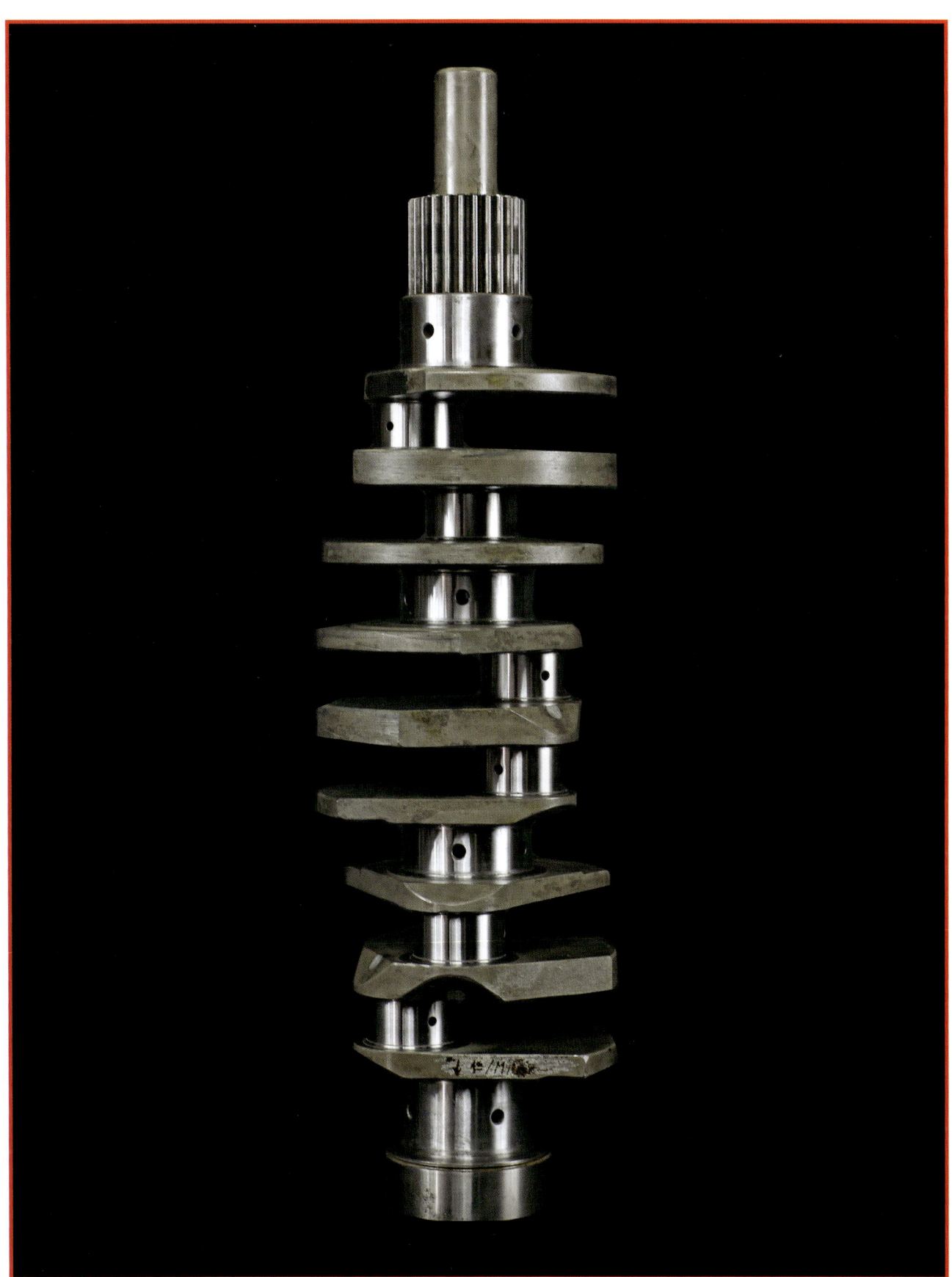

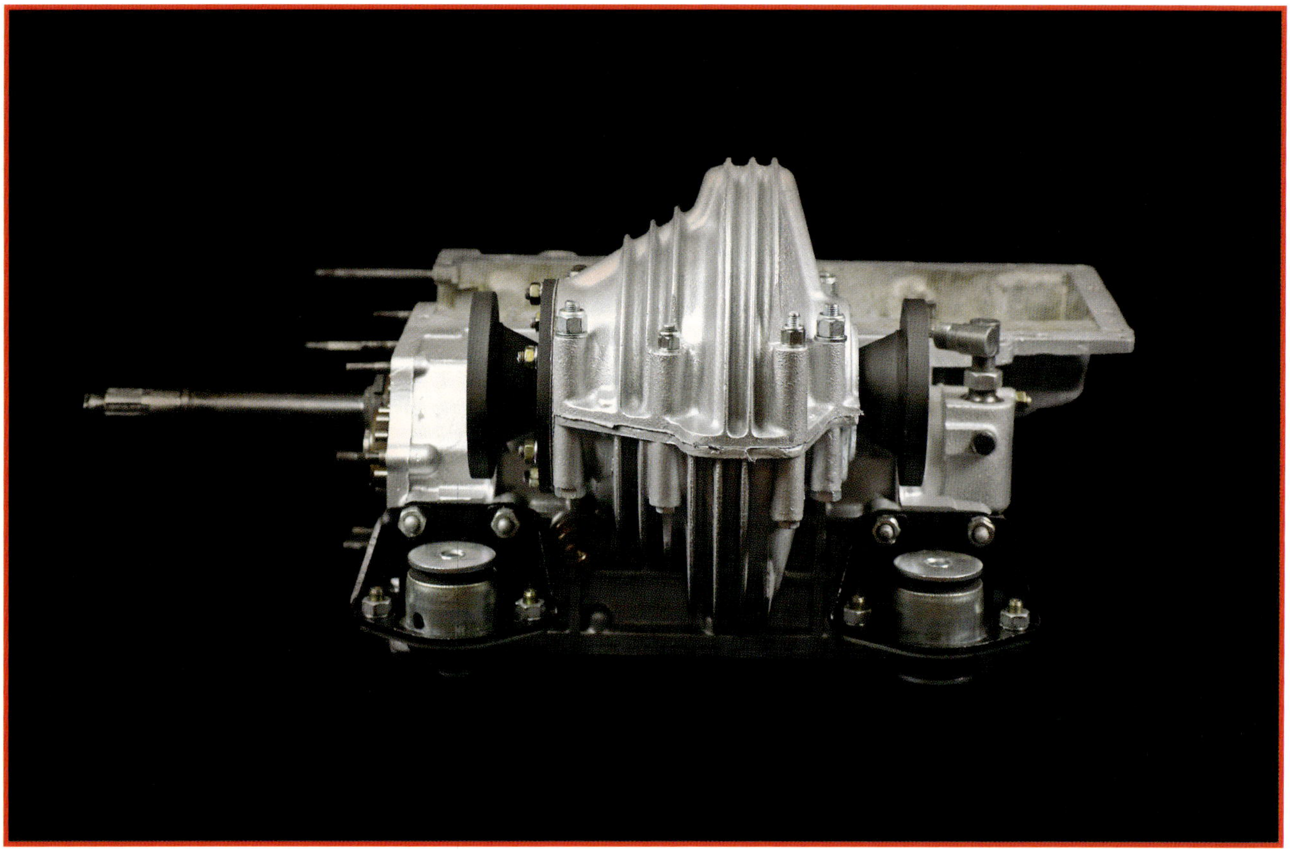

↑ The Dino's revolutionary transmission, with five forward speeds and reverse, is fitted beneath and to the side of the engine block.

↓ The water pump and thermostat are incorporated in a housing at the timing-chain end of the engine.

FERRARI DINO 246 GTS – TECHNICAL DATA

Engine code	135 CS
Engine type	Mid, transverse, V6, 65°
Bore and stroke	92.5 x 60.0mm (3.64 x 2.36in)
Total capacity	2,419.20cc (147.62cu in)
Unitary capacity	403.20cc (24.60cu in)
Compression ratio	9:1
Maximum power	195bhp (143kW) at 7,600rpm
Power per litre	81bhp/litre (60kW/litre)
Valve operation	Double overhead camshafts per bank, two valves per cylinder
Fuel feed	Three twin-choke Weber 40 DCN F/7 carburettors
Ignition	Single spark plug per cylinder, single distributor, single coil
Lubrication	Wet sump
Clutch	Dry, single plate
Maximum torque	225Nm (166lb ft) at 5,500rpm
Firing order	1–4–2–5–3–6

↑↑ Looking down on one of the three twin-choke Weber 40 DCN F/7 carburettors.

↑ A view of the gear clusters inside the five-speed gearbox.

↑↑ Fiat branding appears on the inlet manifold.

↑ The Dino was the first road car to use the Magneti Marelli Dinoplex AEC 101 DA capacitive-discharge ignition system, and featured a single distributor.

between 1969 and 1974, was mounted in 2,487 246 GT models and 1,274 246 GTS models (the engine featured in this chapter was mounted in a 246 GTS series E model, and has the Fiat code number 135 CS, and Ferrari code number 246 L). As with the first 2.0-litre models in the series, it featured a real treasure trove of innovations in Ferrari road car production. Perhaps the most important innovation was the revolutionary five-speed transmission, incorporated beneath and to the side of the engine block, with a dry, single-plate clutch mounted on the flywheel, and the differential housing positioned to the rear of the engine. The transmission was designed and built by Ferrari, and was completely different to the unit used in the front-engined Fiat Dinos.

As previously noted, the cylinder-block material was changed from light alloy to cast iron for the 2.4-litre unit. The reasons for this were that, without losing rigidity, there was no room to enlarge the bore of the cylinder liners in the 2.0-litre aluminium block in order to accommodate the larger-diameter pistons required to provide the increased capacity, and also, maybe more significantly, the cast-iron block was more economical to produce. On the 2.0-litre version, the chains driving the camshafts were a weak point, so heavier-duty chains were used on the 2.4-litre version. While the engine block was cast iron, the cylinder heads, cam covers, sump, and transmission casing were all special Silumin alloy castings. The engine featured a solid forged-steel crankshaft, weighing 17kg (37lb), well supported by four main bearings, one at each end and one between each pair of opposed-cylinder connecting rods, to minimise vibration and to provide good reliability. The pistons were aluminium, made by Borgo (each weighing 440g/0.97lb), and for the first time on a Ferrari road car (after the previous 206), the pistons featured cut-outs in the skirts on both sides, with a slight 'T' configuration, to reduce weight and also to aid cooling. Hereafter, this 'T' solution (even more pronounced) would become the 'rule'

↖ A sump baffle, designed to avoid oil surge when cornering.

↙ A single oil filter is used, located at the timing-chain end of the engine. With the engine in the car, the filter is on the right-hand side of the engine compartment.

for most future Ferrari models. The short-stroke connecting rods (each weighing 520g/1.15lb) each had their own crankshaft journal, and featured white-metal big-end bearings with bolted bearing caps. Ahead of its time, Ferrari used the first definitive electronic capacitive-discharge ignition system (derived from its competition programme) – the Magneti Marelli Dinoplex AEC 101 DA system. This controlled the ignition via distributor impulses to the spark plugs, with the six cylinders firing at equal intervals during two rotations of the crankshaft, in the firing order: 1–4–2–5–3–6. A further new development introduced for this engine was the use of sodium-filled hollow-stem inlet and exhaust valves, as this provided improved heat dissipation. As noted previously, the camshafts were chain driven, with one

↓ The three twin-choke Weber 40 DNC F/7 carburettors are mounted on a single manifold located in the vee of the engine.

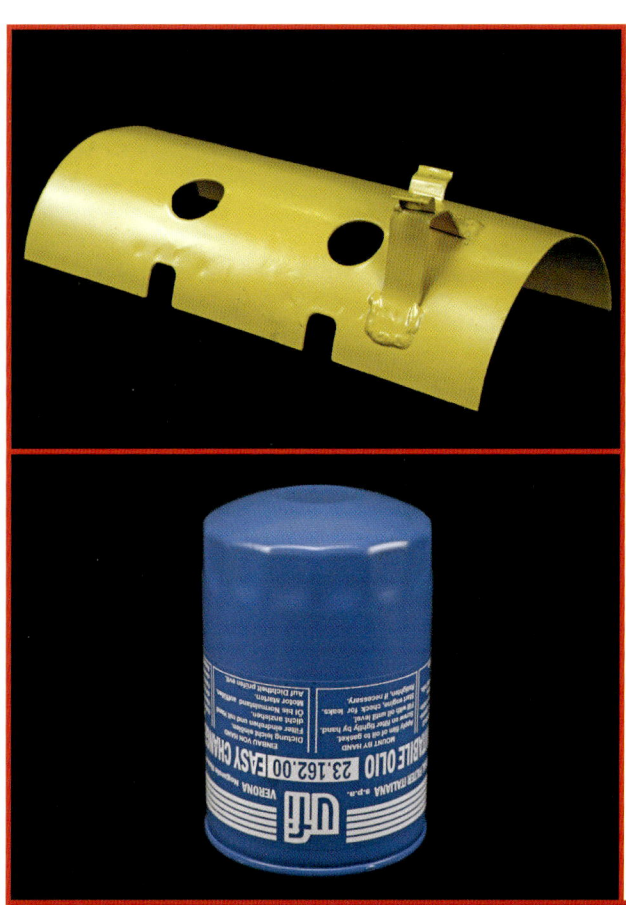

chain per bank of cylinders, driven via reduction gears from the crankshaft, each chain with its own tensioner.

Engine lubrication was via a wet sump, with a mechanical oil pump driven by reduction gears from the crankshaft. A cartridge-type oil filter was used, and a cylindrical oil cooler was fitted in the engine compartment. Engine cooling was via a belt-driven water pump driven from the crankshaft. A front-mounted radiator was fitted, with twin thermostatically controlled electric fans. The cooling system also incorporated a circuit to the oil cooler in the engine compartment. Fuel was supplied from twin tanks, with the outlet in the base of the left tank, via twin Bendix electric fuel pumps (and a filter) which fed three twin-choke Weber 40 DNC F/7 carburettors mounted in the vee of the engine. A steel filter box was mounted on the carburettor inlets.

The innovative use of twin fuel tanks, situated either side of the engine, was a design feature first used on the company's sports-racing cars of the period. This improved weight distribution for balanced handling characteristics, while a change to a flatter nose profile on the production cars, compared to the prototypes, reduced front-end lift at high speed. A highlight of the Dino body styling was the bulbous front wings, which was another reflection of the period sports prototypes. These blended into the door lines, which had tapered, scalloped sections leading into intakes on the rear wings, feeding air to the engine bay. The cockpit had buttresses bounding the curved vertical rear screen, which ran gracefully down to the Kamm tail panel, which featured the traditional-for-the-period Ferrari paired twin light assemblies. As the Dino was marketed as a separate marque, no Ferrari badging was fitted at the factory, and all examples carried only the stylised Dino signature – in blue on a yellow-background rectangular nose badge, and in chrome script on the tail panel. However, some dealers fitted Ferrari script badges and a *Cavallino Rampante* to the tail, to provide an analogy with the parent company as a promotional sales tool. Due to the close proximity of the engine to the cabin firewall, the engine-cooling-water tubes running beneath the cabin, and the car's large windscreen, air conditioning became available as a desirable option in late 1971. This was at the same time that a US-market version of the model was announced, and that is a market where air conditioning is de rigueur.

Following the end of Dino 246-series production in 1974, the V6 engine layout has since only been used by Ferrari in F1 cars, which is essentially where the story started. Indeed, from 1980 to 1988 Ferrari competed in F1 with a turbocharged V6 turbo engine, with a 120° configuration between 1980 and 1986, then a 90° vee angle for the final two years. From the 2014 F1 World Championship season to date, the F1 governing body has mandated the turbocharged V6 layout as standard, so once again Ferrari is using a V6, albeit featuring modern materials and hybrid technology for energy recovery. However, 1974 did not see the death of the Dino brand, as a second model was introduced that year – the 2+2 Dino 308 GT4, with a 3.0-litre, 90° V8 engine. This model was initially badged only as a Dino, but was later badged as a Ferrari to try and boost sales, particularly in the USA, although the Dino name remained on the script badge on the boot lid. This was the first car produced by Ferrari with a mid-mounted V8 engine, and as with the Dino 246, the engine was transversely located. The 308 GT4 and its sibling 208 GT4 (introduced in 1975, featuring a 2.0-litre V8 engine for fiscal purposes in the Italian market, where cars exceeding 2.0-litres capacity attracted much higher tax rates) continued in production until 1980. The mid-mounted V8 engine has been the backbone of Ferrari production in various models ever since, with a transverse layout up to 1989, and with a longitudinal layout since the introduction of the 348 model in that year.

So it can be seen that the Ferrari–Fiat engine alliance that started in the mid-sixties still bears fruit with the V8 road cars and V6 F1 cars of today.

↓ **The cylinder block is designed with the crankshaft centreline 85mm above the base of the crankcase, providing improved strength and reliability for road use.**

↑ The compact, tapered shape of the Dino paved the way for future mid-engined Ferrari berlinetta designs.

↑ The round tail-lights add to the sporty rear view of this revolutionary berlinetta.

➜ The fuel filler cap for the Dino sits behind a cover on the left sail panel.

↘ The 'Dino' script also appeared on the front-engined Fiat Dino, albeit not with the 'gt' suffix appearing on the Dino 246.

↘↘ The side air intakes became a trademark Ferrari feature and were used on later berlinetta designs.

↘↘↘ The rectangular yellow badge with the 'Dino' script started a successful series of entry-level Ferraris.

↓ The aerodynamic shape of this beautiful berlinetta was designed for Pininfarina by Aldo Brovarone.

Dino 246: The Fiat partnership (1972)

365 GT4 BB
The first flat-12-engined Ferrari road car (1973)

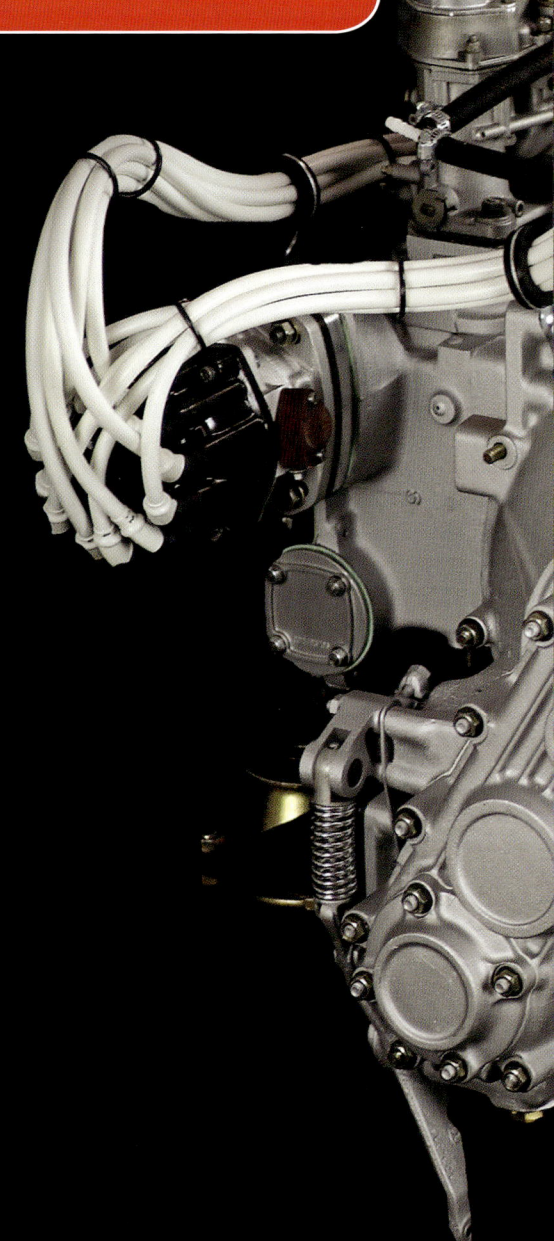

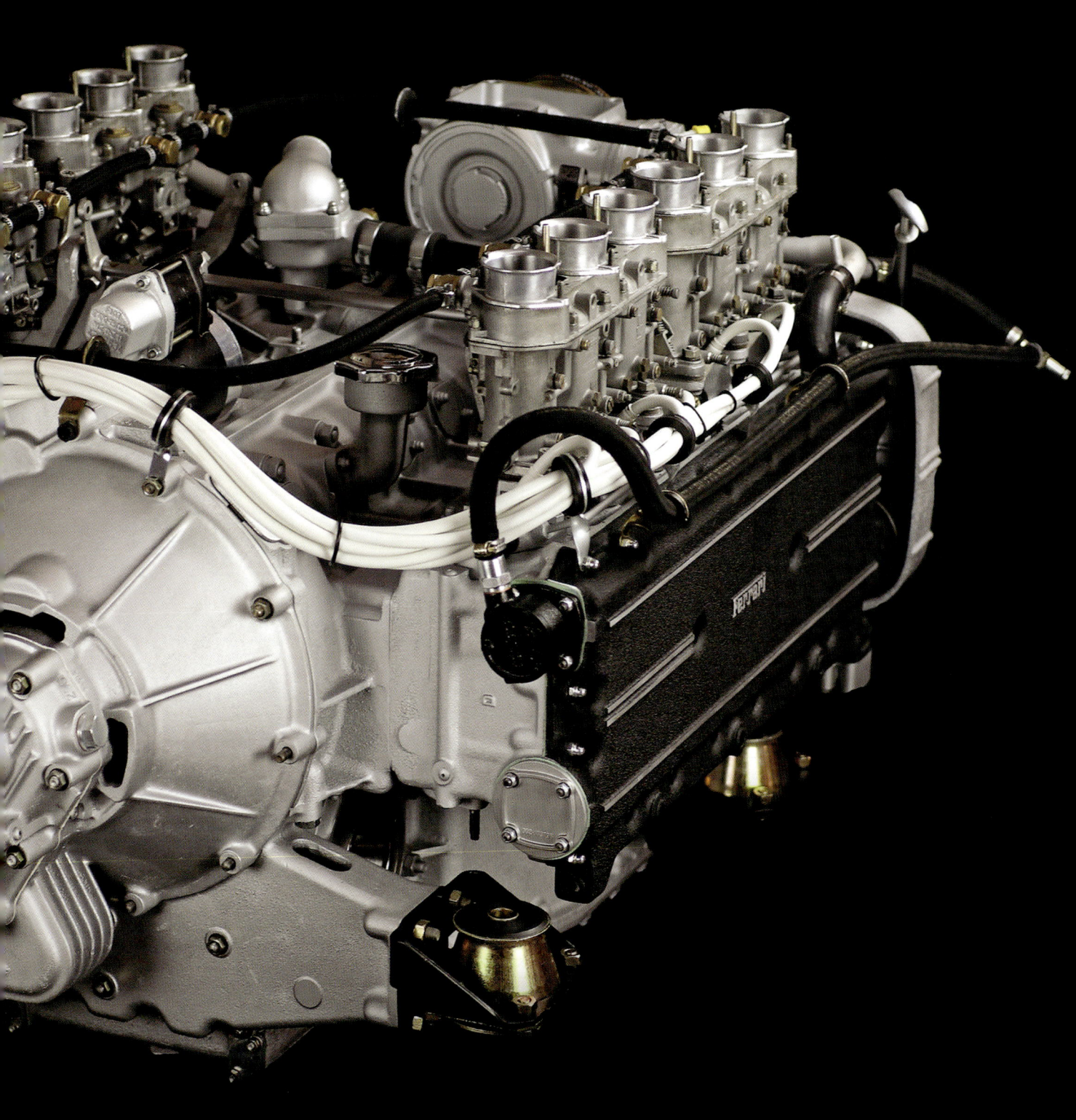

← A view of the drop-gear casing. The gearbox was mounted below the crankshaft and took drive to the differential, integrated with the sump.

↙ Following Ferrari tradition, the unmistakable logo was cast into the camshaft covers.

In the wake of the great innovations introduced by Mauro Forghieri on F1 Ferraris, at the 1971 Turin Motor Show, Maranello unveiled a then-in-vogue wedge-shaped berlinetta fitted with a mid-mounted, longitudinal 'flat-12' 180° V12 engine. The flat-12 engine, designed in 1970 for the single-seater 312 B, aimed to close the gap to Ferrari's rival F1 teams, and Maranello wanted to use a flat-12 derivation in its road cars. It may be recalled that Lamborghini had stolen the thunder with their transverse V12 engine layout Miura, which was shown as a rolling chassis at the 1965 Turin Salon and then in completed form at the 1966 Geneva Motor Show, and had proved a great success with its garish range of colours. The 365 GT4 BB was Ferrari's response, using this innovative engine design to position the brand at the forefront of the sports-car market. Enzo Ferrari had resisted the idea of mounting the engine behind the shoulders of the driver, as he believed 'you never put the cart before the horse!', but as in F1 a decade earlier, followed by the sports prototypes, and then more recently with the Dino series of road cars, he could see that it was time to introduce a revolutionary change for Ferrari V12 berlinettas. Following the prototype berlinetta's debut at the 1971 Turin show, it would be another two years before the 365 GT4 BB reached production. This delay was needed both to refine the tuning and handling of the new configuration, and also to provide the 'grande Enzo' with time to determine whether his customers would react favourably to such a radical change. To hedge his bets, the 365 GTB4 'Daytona' continued in production alongside the 365 GT4 BB for a few months.

The 365 engine, code number F102 A, (also known as the 'Boxer') was also one of the most revolutionary engines in the Ferrari road-car story. The technology used for this engine was derived directly from the experience gained in Formula 1 competition. Indeed, a flat-12 engine was fitted to the 1970 Ferrari 312 B F1 car, driven by Jacky Ickx, the poor Ignazio Giunti (who was killed driving a Ferrari 312 P

↖ A side view of one of the domed alloy pistons, shown here with the piston rings and gudgeon pin removed.

← The code number F102 AB stamped into this engine casting denotes the chassis type to which the engine is fitted.

→ Pistons for cylinders 3 and 4 fitted into their respective cylinder liners in the cylinder block.

(B) in 1971), Clay Regazzoni and Mario Andretti, and on the following 312 B2 that raced in 1971 and 1972. In reality, this innovative 12-cylinder F1 engine, conceived with the aim of lowering the centre of gravity of the racing cars in which it was fitted, was not a 'boxer'. Indeed, designer Mauro Forghieri, who was very precise, commented: 'Please, don't call it boxer.' He went on to say: 'Technically, it is correct to say that this engine is a flat-12, or has 12 cylinders with the heads at a vee angle of 180°. The difference between this engine and a true 'boxer' is that on the Ferrari engine the corresponding connecting rods of each bank are coupled on the same crankpin, so the two pistons move in the same direction, whereas in a true boxer engine (for example the flat-six Porsche engine) the pistons move in opposite directions.' Despite this, the suffix 'B' for the 312 F1 car was linked (incorrectly) to the word boxer.

This innovative engine configuration, developed by Ferrari, brought a breath of fresh air to the F1 world, in which more traditional engines had prevailed, notably the Ford Cosworth DFV V8, which had remained fundamentally unchanged since its introduction in 1967, and was enormously successful. The new 'flat-12' was Maranello's hope to take it back to the front of the F1 grid, and although it was not immediately a championship winner, Ferrari took four grand prix victories in the second half of the 1970 season (three

↓ A view from above of the cylinder block assembled (split along the crankshaft centreline). Note the cast-in cylinder numbers.

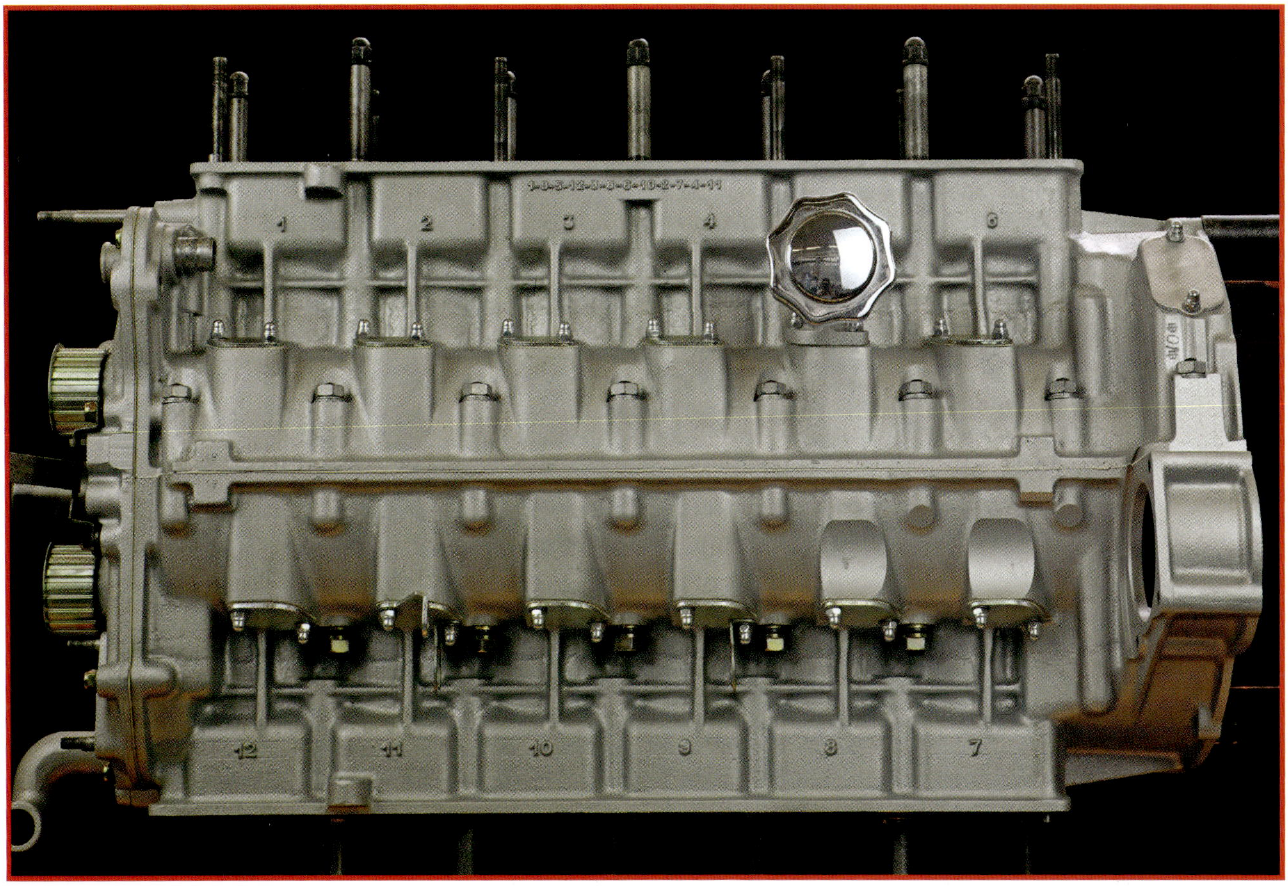

for Ickx and one for Clay Regazzoni), taking Ickx to second place in the drivers' championship and Ferrari to second place in the constructors' championship. This was the year that Jochen Rindt became the first posthumous F1 World Champion Driver, after his fatal accident at Monza. The story of Ferrari flat-12 engines in F1 continued for a decade until 1980, and along the way, the engines took Ferrari to three Drivers' World Championships (Niki Lauda in 1975 and 1977 and Jody Scheckter in 1979) and four Constructors' World Championships (1975, 1976, 1977 and 1979), with a certain 'novice' driver, Gilles Villeneuve, contributing to the title in 1979. Between 1970 and 1980, Ferrari took 37 F1 victories.

The 365 GT4 BB Berlinetta car appeared on the Pininfarina stand at the 1971 Turin Motor Show, and was designed by Filippo Sapino, under the supervision of Leonardo Fioravanti. Aesthetically the front of the car was very similar to the Pininfarina P6 mid-engine concept car, presented at the Turin Salon in 1968. The lower section of the nose featured a full-width aluminium egg-crate radiator grille, with driving lights behind it, from the top edge of which an indent line ran around the body perimeter, visually creating an upper and lower half to the body. This was made even more evident, as the standard paint finish below this line was satin black. This satin black bottom body section subsequently became an option on other models, and was referred to as the 'Boxer' paint finish. Above the nose was a one-piece, forward-hinged, front lid/wing assembly featuring flush-mounted turn indicator light panels close to the forward edge. Behind these were twin retractable headlights in rectangular pods, either side of the plain-aluminium-finished

radiator-outlet air-louvre panel. The cabin had a steeply raked screen with a teardrop-shaped side-window profile, and the rear screen was a shallow vertical flat panel, bounded by the buttresses of the one-piece, rear-hinged engine cover with an aerofoil bridging the sail-panel buttresses. The tail-light treatment followed that of the 365 GTC/4 model, with triple circular units, and this arrangement was echoed in the two banks of 'pea shooter' triple chrome-tipped exhaust tailpipes, projecting through either side of the lower tail panel. The doors, front and rear lids were constructed from aluminium, whilst the cabin frame was steel and the lower nose and tail sections were glassfibre mouldings. The chassis had a 2,500mm wheelbase with factory reference number F 102 AB 100. All were numbered in the odd chassis number road car sequence. The construction followed the Ferrari principle of a tubular steel chassis frame with cross-bracing and sub-structures to support the engine, suspension, and ancillary equipment. On this model a new dimension was added, in that the cockpit-section steel panels became an integral part of the structure, to form a rigid virtually monocoque central cell. The use of light alloy and glassfibre allowed the weight to be limited to 1,160kg (dry). Due to the close-fitting bodywork, and to provide a vestige of luggage space, a 'space-saver' spare wheel was used by Ferrari for the first time.

This revolutionary (for Ferrari) berlinetta entered production in late 1973 and was built through to 1976. In late 1973, the Maranello factory built just 24 examples of the 365 GT4 BB, followed by 229 in 1974, 119 in 1975 and, in 1976 only 15, as it was replaced by the 512 BB model with a 5.0-litre engine. Regarding the BB acronym (Berlinetta Boxer), which distinguished the new Ferrari, this was not entirely accurate, as explained by Mauro Forghieri's comments quoted previously, as the F102 A road-car engine used a crankshaft with a similar configuration to that used on the F1 engines, with a pair of connecting rods positioned on each crankpin.

The 365 BB engine was derived from the F1 engine (type 001), designed by Forghieri, which had a capacity of 2,991.01cc and powered the 1970 Ferrari 312 B. This 3.0-litre F1 engine was investigated by engineers Giuliano De Angelis and Angelo Bellei, who took many cues from it for the road-car engine. The 'BB' engine was also heavily influenced by the 'Daytona' 365 GTB4 (engine type 251), with which the 365 GTB4 BB shared the same bore and stroke dimensions (81mm x 71mm), even though the flat-12 did not use the same pistons and connecting rods as the Daytona V12. The type F 102 A flat-12 had the same overall capacity as the 'Daytona' V12, at 4,390.35cc.

The innovations introduced with this revolutionary engine were not confined to the vee-angle. Another first for a 12-cylinder engine was the positioning of the gearbox just below the crankshaft. The five-speed gearbox and differential were integrated with the alloy engine sump (a configuration continued for the subsequent 512 BB and 512 BBi models). Lubrication was via a wet sump, with a capacity of 12 litres. The original gearbox (derived from the V6 Dino 206 GT) resulted in a slightly higher centre of gravity for the BB, but allowed the overall length of the car to be reduced. This configuration made it possible to mount the engine between the car's axles (2,500mm wheelbase), providing optimum weight distribution and making the 365 GT4 BB more stable and precise in drive.

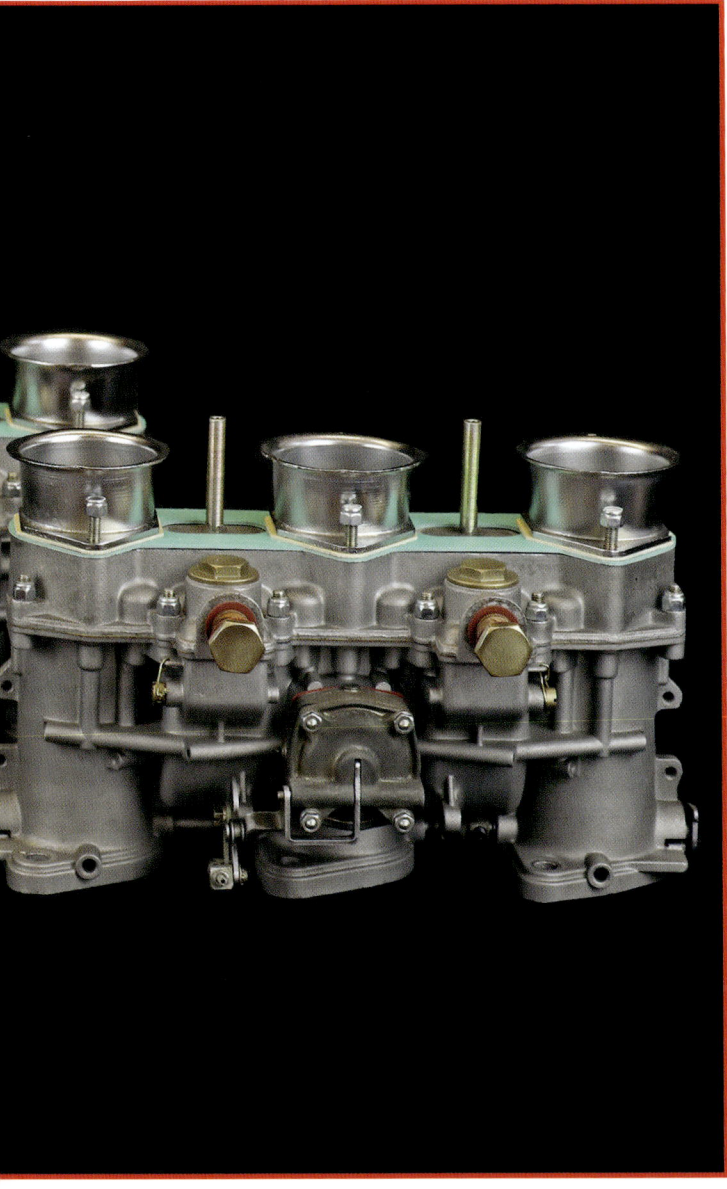

← **The four triple-choke Weber 40 IF3C carburettors – possibly the ultimate carburettor set-up, requiring skilled tuning.**

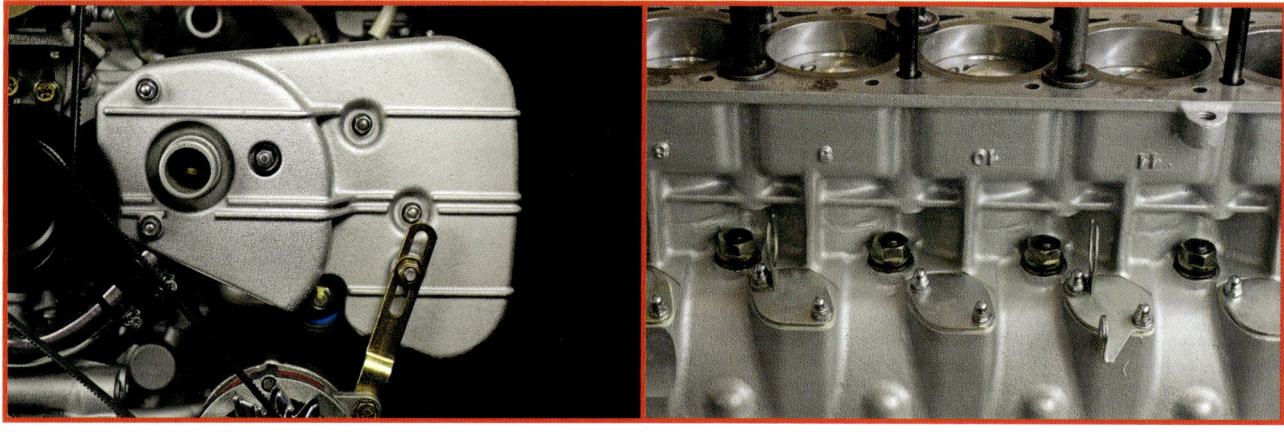

The five-speed transmission featured a limited-slip differential, integral with the rear part of the sump casting. The clutch was a dry, single-plate unit supplied by German company Fichtel & Sachs, and was located at the rear of the engine, with drop gears taking drive to the gearbox.

The F102 A engine fitted to the 387 examples of the 365 GT4 BB produced, in the chassis No. range 17187–19445, had steel crankshafts with a cross-plane configuration. The cylinder block and heads (DOHC configuration) were light alloy, and for the first time on a 12-cylinder Ferrari engine, the camshaft drive was provided by a timing belt, instead of the triplex chains used previously. The change from the

↖ The right-hand timing cover protects the camshaft drivebelt. Note the water pump inlet protruding through the cover.

↑ A close-up view of the cylinder block, with pistons fitted, also showing the cylinder numbers on the castings.

→ A view inside the sump casting. The oil-filter mounting can be seen at the top of the picture.

↓ A view into the bottom of the cylinder block shows the bolts connecting the two halves of the crankcase, and the crankshaft, with two connecting rods sharing each crankpin.

365 GT4 BB: The first flat-12-engined Ferrari road car (1973)

↑↑ One of the rear engine mountings bolted to the sump (viewed from above).

↑ A close-up view of the clutch bellhousing and drop-gear casing.

FERRARI 365 GT4 BB – TECHNICAL DATA

Engine code	F102 A
Engine type	Mid-rear, longitudinal, V12, 180°
Bore and stroke	81 x 71mm (3.18 x 2.79in)
Total capacity	4,390.35cc (267.91cu in)
Unitary capacity	365.86cc (22.32cu in)
Compression ratio	8.8:1
Maximum power	355bhp (265kW) at 7,500rpm
Power per litre	81bhp/litre (60kW/litre)
Valve operation	Double overhead camshaft per bank, two valves per cylinder
Fuel feed	Four Weber 40 IF3C carburettors
Ignition	Single spark plug per cylinder, single distributor, single coil
Lubrication	Wet sump
Clutch	Dry, single plate
Maximum torque	409Nm (301.6lb ft) at 3,900rpm
Firing order	1–9–5–12–3–8–6–10–2–7–4–11

Daytona's chain to the BB's timing belts was implemented both to reduce noise, as the engine was just behind the driver's ears, and to reduce weight. The light-alloy pistons were manufactured by Borgo, and featured conventional (non-cutaway) skirts. The twin overhead camshafts were forged steel, and the cam lobes actuated the valves directly via bucket tappets. Fuel was fed from twin tanks, mounted either side of the forward part of the engine bay, with a balance pipe between them, through a filter and electric fuel pump to four enormous triple-choke Weber 40 IF 3C carburettors, whilst the ignition system featured twin coils (one per bank) and a single Magneti Marelli distributor. The firing order of the cylinders was 1–9–5–12–3–8–6–10–2–7–4–11. The crankshaft, forged in steel, had a slightly different configuration to the 365 'Daytona' unit, due to the fact that in the BB higher stresses were involved because of the horizontally opposed cylinder-head positions. This 12-cylinder, 4.4-litre engine produced a maximum power of 360bhp (268kW) at 7,500rpm, with a specific power of 82bhp/litre (61kW/litre) and a maximum torque of 409Nm (302lb ft) at 3,900rpm. The excellent performances of this flat-12 Ferrari enabled the 365 GT4 BB to reach a top speed of 186mph (300kmh), covering 0–62mph (0–100kmh) in 5.3sec.

This first flat-12 road-car engine produced by Maranello was actually the most powerful of those fitted to the BB series. The 360bhp (268kW) of the F102 A, indeed, would never be equalled by its successors, the F102 B and F110 A, that equipped the evolutions of the 'BB'. Although the quad-carburettor 512 BB (929 examples built, from chassis No. 19677–38487) and the 512 BBi (injection) featured increased-capacity engines (4,943cc, instead of the 4,390.35cc of the F 102 A), these units were slightly 'detuned' to provide a more user-friendly driving experience than the cantankerous and aggressive 4.4-litre, which required expert driving skills. Indeed, the maximum power for the 512 BB and 512 BBi was reduced to 'only' 335bhp (250kW). The 512 BBi featured a mechanical Bosch K-Jetronic fuel-injection system in place of the quad triple-choke Weber carburettors (much to the disappointment of Ferrari enthusiasts!). 1,007 examples of the 512 BBi were produced, from chassis No. 38121– 52935.

Regarding the more user-friendly 512 BB, interestingly, despite the reduction in horsepower, Gilles Villeneuve, who received a 512 BB as a gift from Enzo Ferrari when he drove for Scuderia Ferrari for travelling from his home in Monaco to Maranello, preferred to use that car instead of his helicopter! Indeed, Villeneuve commented at the time that he preferred to 'fly close to the ground' with his berlinetta than with his helicopter! He took just 2 hours and 45 minutes to cover the 311 miles (500km)!

↑ A rear view of the water pump, showing the drive sprocket, driven by the left-hand timing belt.

↗ A front view of the water pump, showing the inlet which protrudes throught the left-hand timing cover.

→ The twin oil-filter mounting is bolted to the front of the sump casting, with an oil-pressure sensor screwed into the top.

Following the end of 365 GT4 BB production (1973–1976), the V12, 180° engine was developed and fitted into further Ferrari models, which adopted the mid-longitudinal engine configuration. After the already mentioned BB series, the flat-12 engine was used in the Testarossa, 512 TR and 512 M, which resulted in the engine configuration remaining in production at Maranello until 1996 – a run of 23 successful

→ The complete clutch bellhousing and drop-gear casing assembly, with the clutch-release and gearchange mechanisms.

↓ The aluminium timing covers positioned as they would be when fitted to the engine.

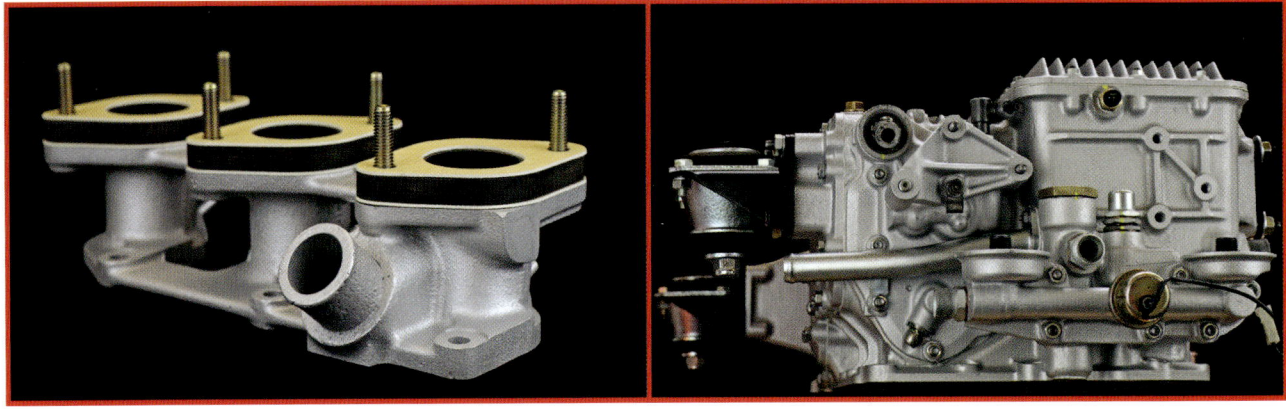

years. With the arrival of the 550 Maranello, the flat-12 era ended to make way for a return to front-engined V12 cars, resulting in a return to Enzo Ferrari's traditional idea of the 'horse that pulls the cart'. Fitting a V12, 65°, 5.5-litre engine under the front bonnet of the 550 Maranello Berlinetta was the start of a new era that continues today. It is a shame that the great Enzo was not there to see the return to his favourite and much-loved configuration. However, regarding the engine incorrectly referred to as a 'Boxer', the most fascinating, and rare incarnation remained the first F102 A, due to its brutal power delivery that made its potential fully accessible only to the experienced driver.

↖ One of the four intake manifolds used for the triple-choke Weber carburettors, with gaskets and rubber spacers in place.

↑ A view of the inverted sump/differential assembly. The twin oil-filter mounting can be seen on the right side of the photograph.

→ The inverted sump, showing the oil drain plug and the Italian wording 'OLIO MOTORE' (engine oil).

↓ The left-hand side of the crankcase, with numbered pistons in place in their liners. The sleeves and washers on alternate cylinder-head studs are fitted temporarily to retain the liners.

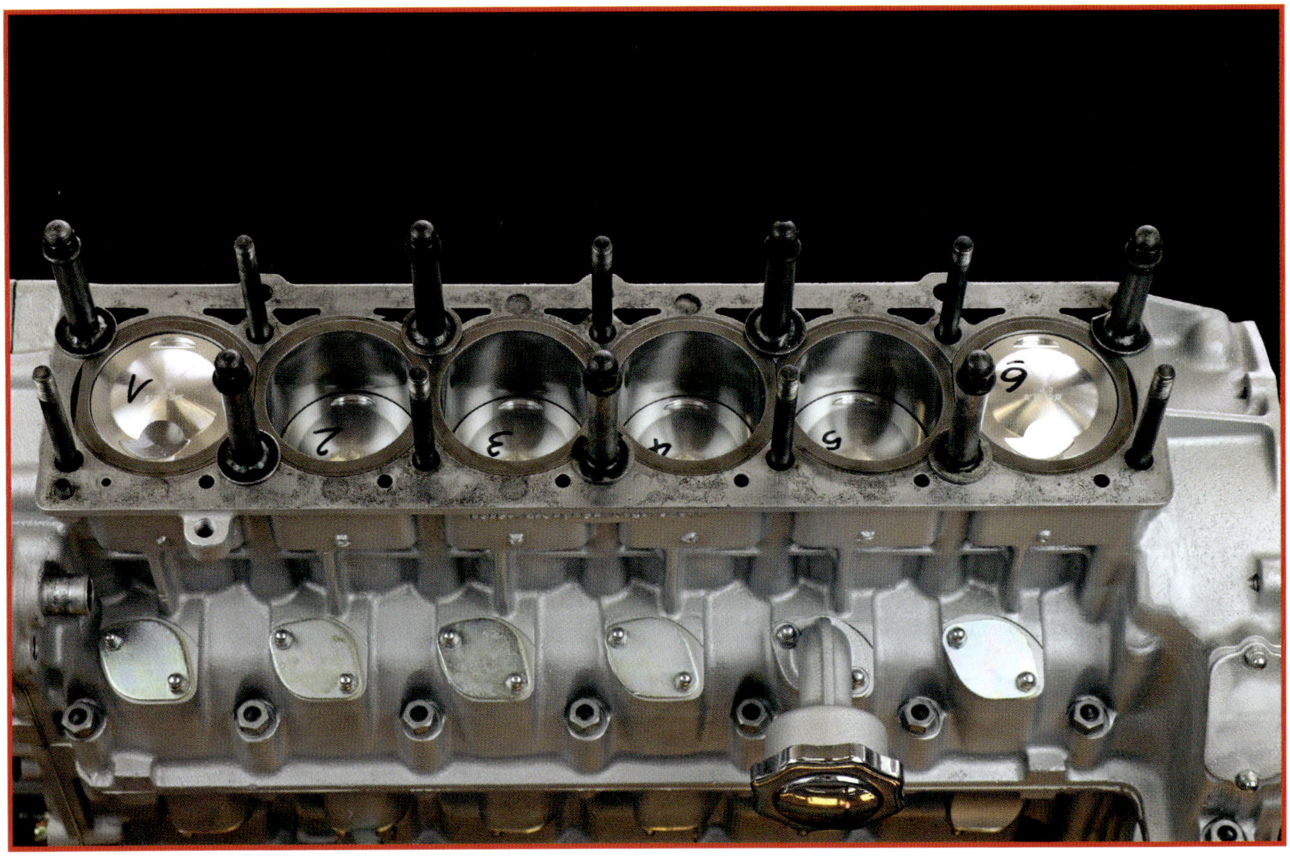

365 GT4 BB: The first flat-12-engined Ferrari road car (1973)

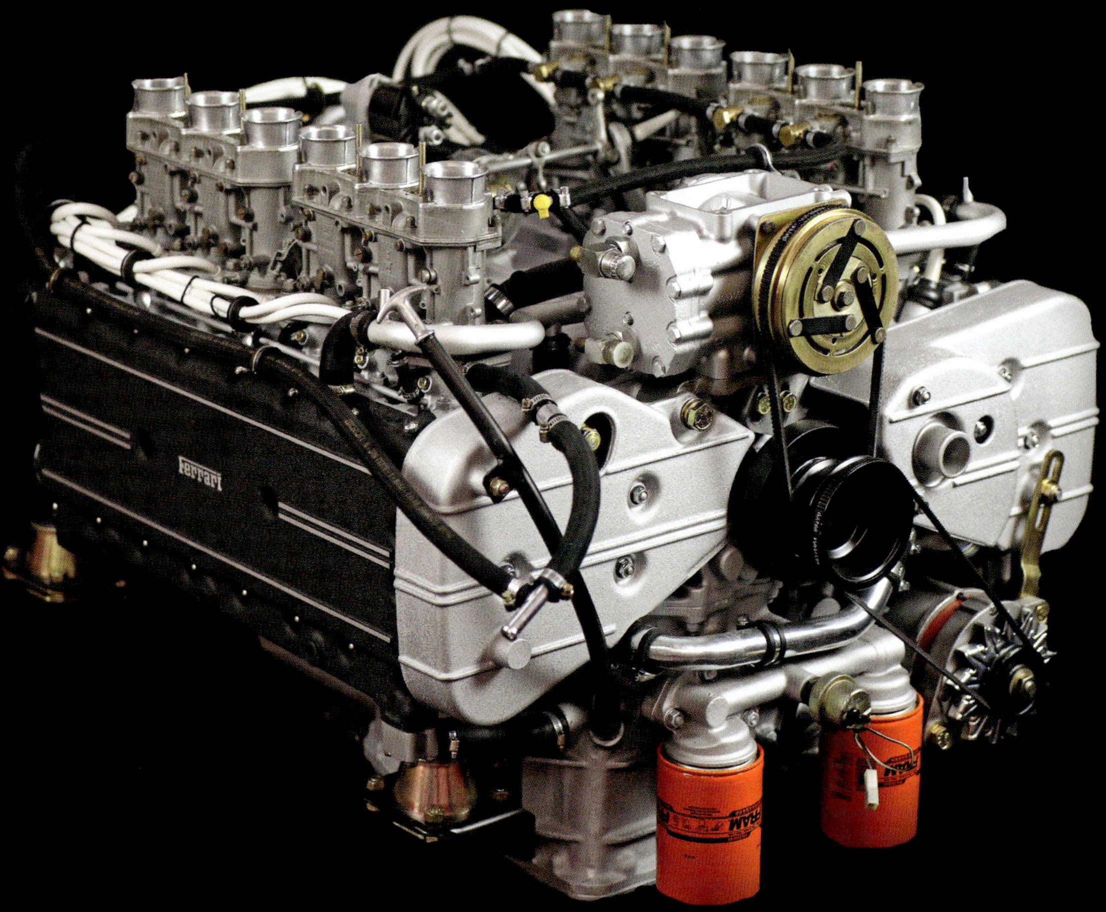

↑ With retractable headlights raised the 365 GT4 maintains its purposeful look. Note the single windscreen wiper.

↑ The perfect union of curves and straight lines adds to the powerful presence of the car thanks to Pininfarina's styling.

→ The retractable headlights were typical of the sports-car design trend at the time, aiding aerodynamic efficiency.

↘ Five-spoke light alloy Cromodora wheels with chrome knock-off nuts were similar to those used on the 365 GTB/4 Daytona.

↘↘ The one-piece hinged tail section allowed easy access to the engine compartment, and was reminiscent of a race car.

↘↘↘ The characteristic three round tail-lights on each side, with three chromed exhaust tailpipes, left no doubt as to the car's sporting heritage.

↓ Maranello's first flat-12-engined road car seems to be shaped to slide effortlessly through the air.

365 GT4 BB: The first flat-12-engined Ferrari road car (1973)

308 GTB
The arrival of the V8 (1975)

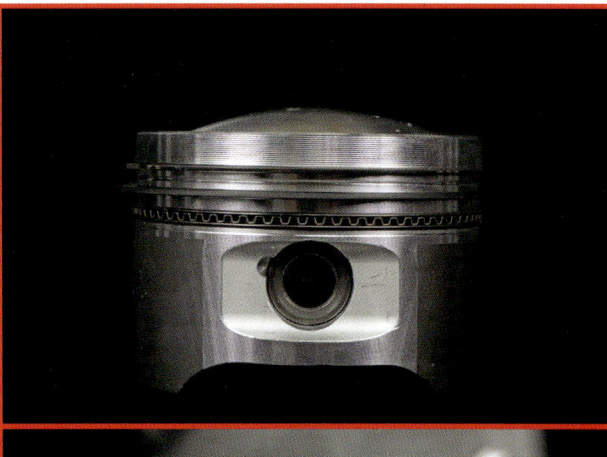

← Forged Borgo domed light-alloy piston, with oil-control ring and compression rings fitted.

↙ The classic Ferrari logo is cast into the top of each of the camshaft covers.

Following on from the big innovations and changes brought about by the revolutionary engines of the Dino 206 GT and the 365 GT4 BB, Ferrari decided to adopt a new engine configuration for their road cars: a 90° V8 unit. This motor appeared for the first time in the Dino 308 GT4 2+2 model, presented at the 1973 Paris Salon – the only series production 'Ferrari' (actually initially badged only as a Dino) designed by Bertone, who also designed the earlier Fiat Dino Coupé. The wedge shape of the car met with a mixed response, as it did not have the much-admired voluptuous curves of the Dino 246 models, although its performance and handling were praised. Thus, it did not have the anticipated success in the marketplace, particularly in the important US market, where it became the only 'Ferrari' model available, even though it was not badged as one! This led to the retro-fitment of Ferrari badges, in addition to the Dino badges, and the subsequent substitution of Dino badges for Ferrari ones in all markets.

The Dino 308 GT4 had been an addition to the Dino range, not a replacement for the beloved 246 model, which continued in production alongside it for a short time during 1974. Meanwhile, over at Pininfarina in Turin, design chief Leonardo Fioravanti was working on the two-seat replacement for the 246. The new model – the 308 GTB – was unveiled in October 1975 at the Paris Salon, and featured the then-popular wedge shape, but also carried over some of the design features of the Dino 246, notably the scalloped recesses through the doors, the curved vertical rear screen between buttresses running into the tail, and paired circular rear lights. This berlinetta was fitted with the same V8 engine used in the Dino 308 GT4, with one major difference – it was equipped with dry-sump lubrication instead of wet sump as in the GT4. The 308 engine provided a healthy 255bhp (190kW), and was the genesis of the V8 engines that have been the backbone of Ferrari production from then until today, in both the mid-mounted configuration, and in recent times also a front-mounted layout.

Ferrari's use of the 156 engine (1,500cc V6) in F1 in the

↖ One of the forged-steel, short-stroke connecting rods with the big-end bearing cap (and securing nuts) in place.

← Four of the eight steel cylinder liners, which form the cylinder bores in which the pistons slide.

early sixties, which took Phil Hill to the 1961 F1 World Drivers' Championship and Ferrari to the Constructors' title, led to the idea of developing a V8 version. Thus, in 1961, the renowned engineer Carlo Chiti designed a 90° V8 engine featuring a single overhead camshaft per bank of cylinders, and two different capacities which were used in sports racing cars – the 2.4-litre 248 SP model and the 2.6-litre 268 SP model, which used the same chassis and body layout as their V6 siblings the 196 SP and 246 SP. However, at the end of 1961 Chiti left Ferrari as part of the famous 'Palace Revolution', and the V8 sports-car engines were never fully developed, and thus met with little success. This project sowed the seed for an Angelo Bellei-designed F1 V8 engine, which made its debut in 1964, and although fragile in the early part of the season, gained reliability and propelled John Surtees to the F1 Drivers' World Championship and Ferrari to their second constructors' title. During the season the venerable 156 engine, together with a new Mauro Forghieri-designed 1512 (1,500cc, 12-cylinder) 180° V12 (or flat-12) engine, were also used by his team-mates.

The competition experience and success led to Ferrari considering the use of a V8 engine in a road car in the future. It took several years for the project to materialise – not the often rapid transition from race to road technology that one

↑ **A set of eight valves. The engine was fitted with one inlet and one exhaust valve per cylinder.**

might expect from Ferrari. The project eventually came to fruition in 1973 with the type F 106 AL 000 V8 engine, which powered the Dino 308 GT4 model, and which was created

↓ **A view of the V8 aluminium cylinder-block casting with the cylinder liners fitted.**

by Angelo Bellei (who had designed the 1964 F1 engine) and Franco Rocchi. However, as already mentioned, the styling of the Dino 308 GT4 did not meet with great acclaim from the clientele, who desired something more overtly sporting, which led to the birth of a two-seater berlinetta with a transverse mid-mounted V8 engine – the 308 GTB. This was the premise for the birth of a new series production model terminology for Ferrari, which would become the most successful format in the marque's history: a two-seater berlinetta with a 90° V8 mid-rear engine. The initials GTB (Gran Turismo Berlinetta) were adopted as part of the model designation, together with the total engine displacement and number of cylinders – three litres and eight cylinders – to produce the 308 part of the model name. The displacement/number of cylinders code was used on the previous Dino series, but prior to that had only previously been used on competition cars, such as F1 cars and the Dino 166 and 206 sports prototypes. Thus, the 308 GTB model and its engine – code number F 106 A 021, derived from that of the 308 GT4 – was born from the heartfelt request of the *Cavallino Rampante* customers.

The first mid-transverse V8 engine fitted in a two-seater was the brainchild of the marketing intuition of Enzo Ferrari. This engine had a displacement of 2,926.90cc, producing

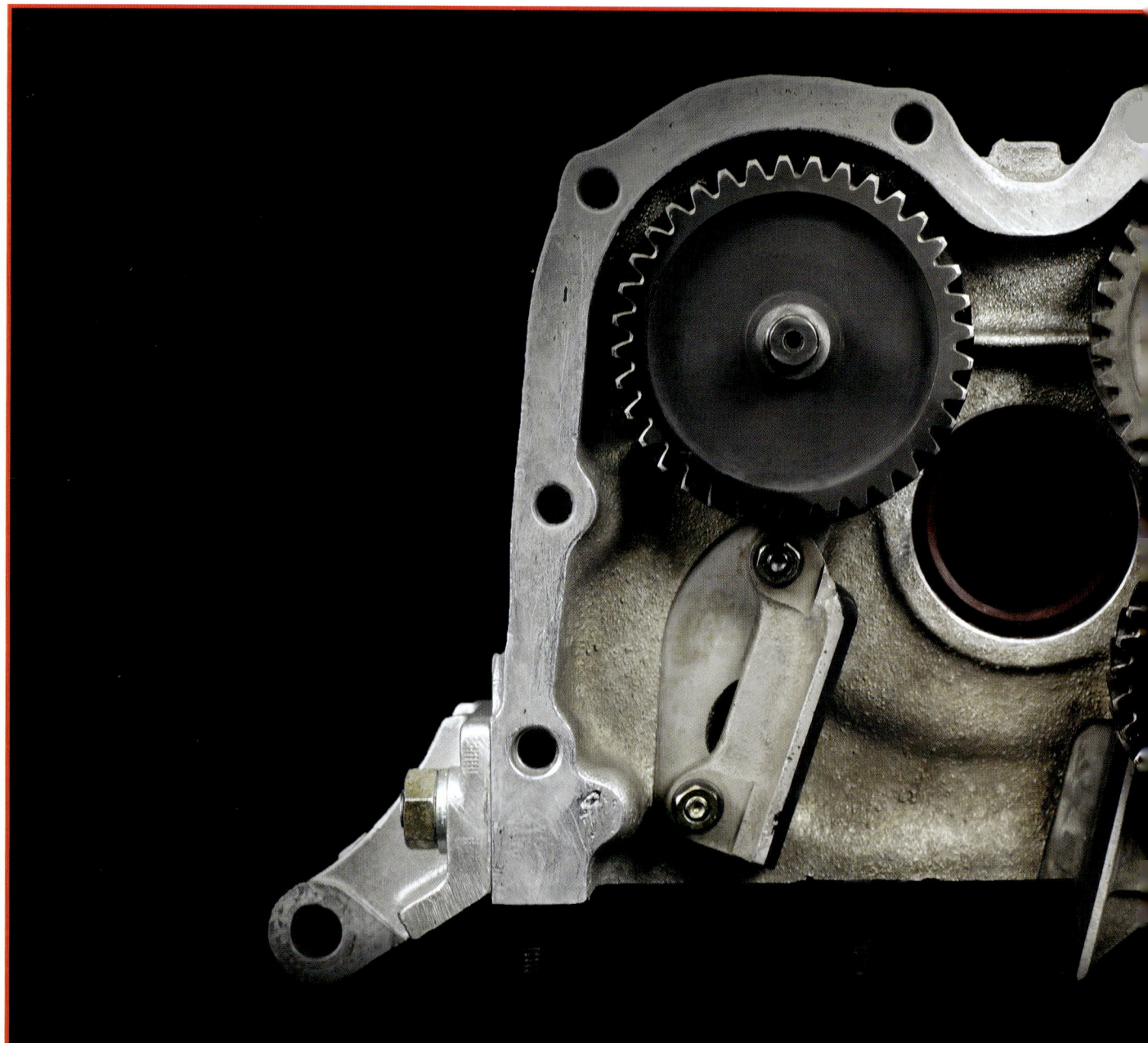

251bhp (187kW) at 7,700rpm, and was the most powerful of the V8 series until the arrival of the 328 GTB model in 1985, which produced 266bhp (198kW) at 7,000rpm; however, that was provided via an increased-capacity 3.2-litre engine. The 308's engine was capable of producing a maximum torque of 279Nm (206lb ft) at 5,000rpm, and, fitted in the first glassfibre versions of the car (the lighter model with a weight of only 1,050kg), had an impressive weight/power ratio of about 2.9kg/kW (8.8lb/bhp). From 1975 until 1980, this engine was equipped with a set of four Weber 40 DCNF twin-choke carburettors, fed by an electric fuel pump. In 1980, fuel injection was adopted, which resulted in a decrease in overall power output. This was addressed in 1982, with a change to four-valves-per-cylinder heads, although the original carburettor version still remained the most powerful.

The new V8 Ferrari 308 GTB was unveiled at the Paris Salon in October 1975, and was a break from Ferrari tradition in that it was fitted with a glassfibre body, which today are the rarest and most sought-after examples. There were two examples at the show, a yellow car on the Pozzi Ferrari France stand, chassis No. 18677, and a pale metallic blue example, chassis No. 18679, on the Pininfarina stand. It is said that the reason for using glassfibre was that it was quicker to have moulds made for fiberglass than dies for metal pressings, and due to slow sales of the 308 GT4 model, Ferrari wanted to get the new model on line as quickly as possible. During 1976–77, the models started to receive steel bodies, which were used for the remainder of the production period. The design of this sharp berlinetta, which featured retractable headlights to streamline the shape, as did Maranello's most ambitious cars of that period (365 GTB4 Daytona, 365 GT4 BB and 365 GT4 2+2), was the work of Leonardo Fioravanti (Pininfarina). He won the contract to design this car despite competition from Aldo Brovarone, the famous 'father' of the Dino Berlinetta Speciale prototype shapes and both 206 and 246 Dino models. The type F106 engine was fitted to more than 6,000 cars, comprising 712 308 GTB Vetroresina (fibreglass) cars, 2,185 steel-bodied 308 GTBs and 3,219 308 GTS 'Targa' (removable roof) models.

A feature of this V8 engine, which was first used in the 308 GT4 of 1974, was the use of cam belts instead of timing chains, which had featured on all Ferrari engines through to the 365 GTB4 'Daytona' model. Belts had first been introduced on the 365 GT4 BB model from its introduction in 1973. The light alloy cylinder heads featured steel double overhead camshafts for each bank, with the spark plugs located centrally between them. The other engine and transmission castings were also manufactured from light alloy, including the block, sump, timing casing and transaxle housing. In designing the block, the engineers Bellei and Rocchi took their cue from the layout of the Dino 206 and 246, positioning the crankshaft at a distance of 8cm from the base of the crankcase. This was done to create a rigid structure, resistant to twisting, with the crankshaft supported by five main bearings, which also minimised crankshaft vibration. An important characteristic of this engine was the flat-plane crankshaft, with the crank pins for alternate

← **A view looking into the rear of the engine front cover. The nose of the crankshaft fits through the hole in the centre of the cover, and a gear on the crankshaft drives the two upper gears shown, which drive the timing pulleys, fitted on the other side of the cover. The lower gear drives the oil pump.**

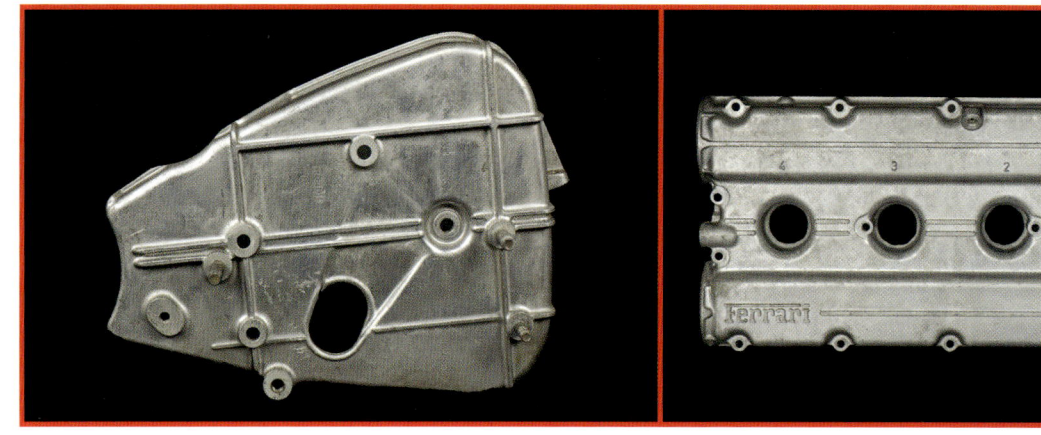

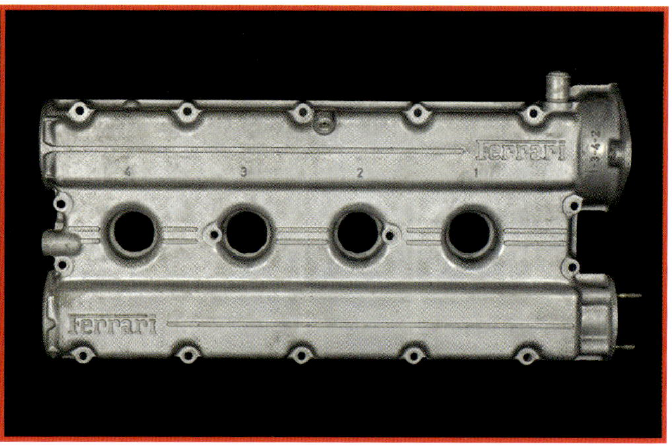

connecting rods laying at 180° to each other, which when viewed from the end appear in one plane. A V8 engine with a flat-plane crankshaft does not require counterbalance weights (a 'cross-plane' crankshaft, as used in American 'big-block' engines does) and is capable of higher revs, though a flat-plane V8 is more susceptible to vibration (hence the five main bearings). Also, the flat-plane configuration provides improved exhaust scavenging, improving the performance of the engine. The alternate movement of paired pistons together provides better torque at low revs and more power at high revs, while the flat-plane crankshaft is lighter than its cross-plane counterpart, which means that it can spin more freely and quickly.

↖ One of the two timing covers which protect the timing belts. The cut-out accommodates the timing belt tensioner.

↑ The forward camshaft cover, with the mounting flange for the distributor at the top right of the photograph.

→ The forged-steel flat-plane crankshaft, with the oil holes in the shared big-end-bearing journals visible.

↓ A cylinder head, shown inverted, with the inlet ports nearest the camera. The protruding studs locate the camshaft cover.

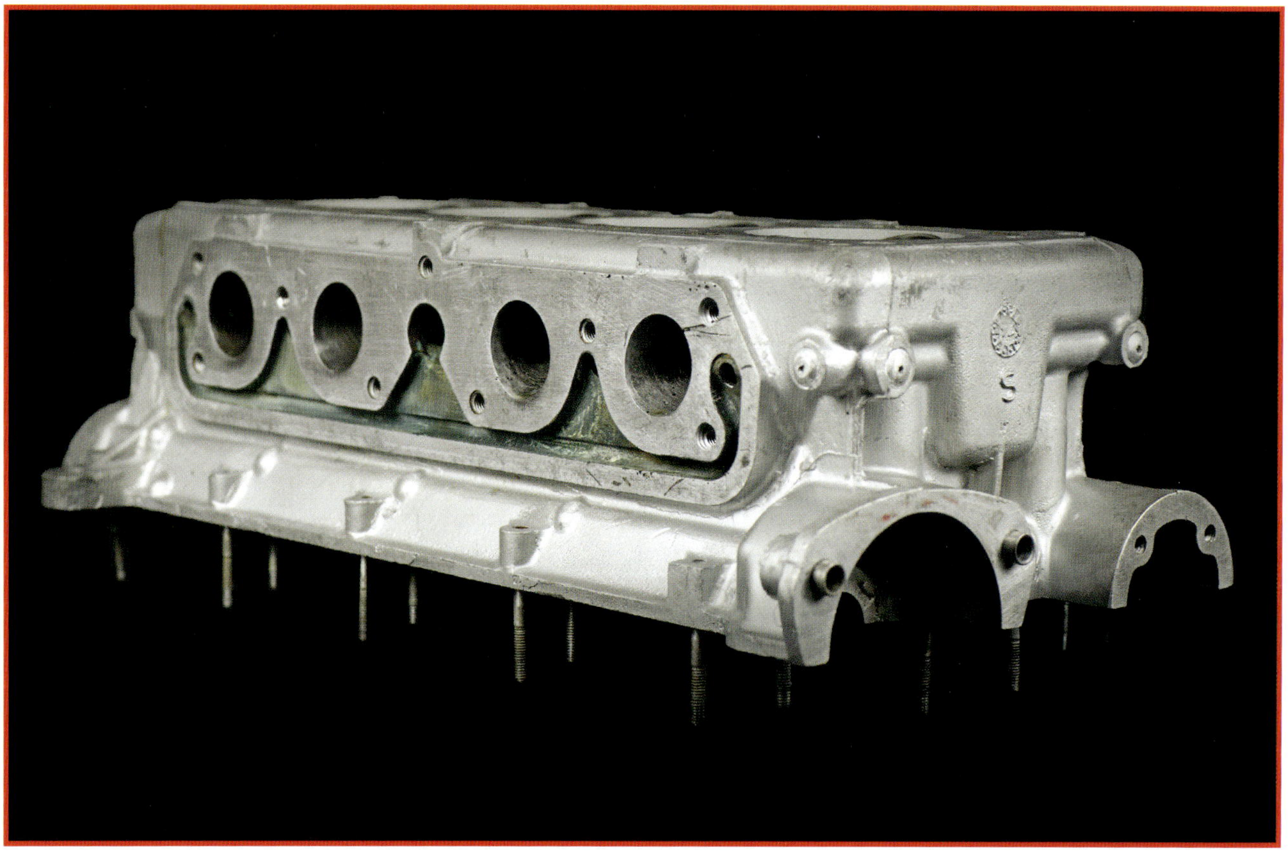

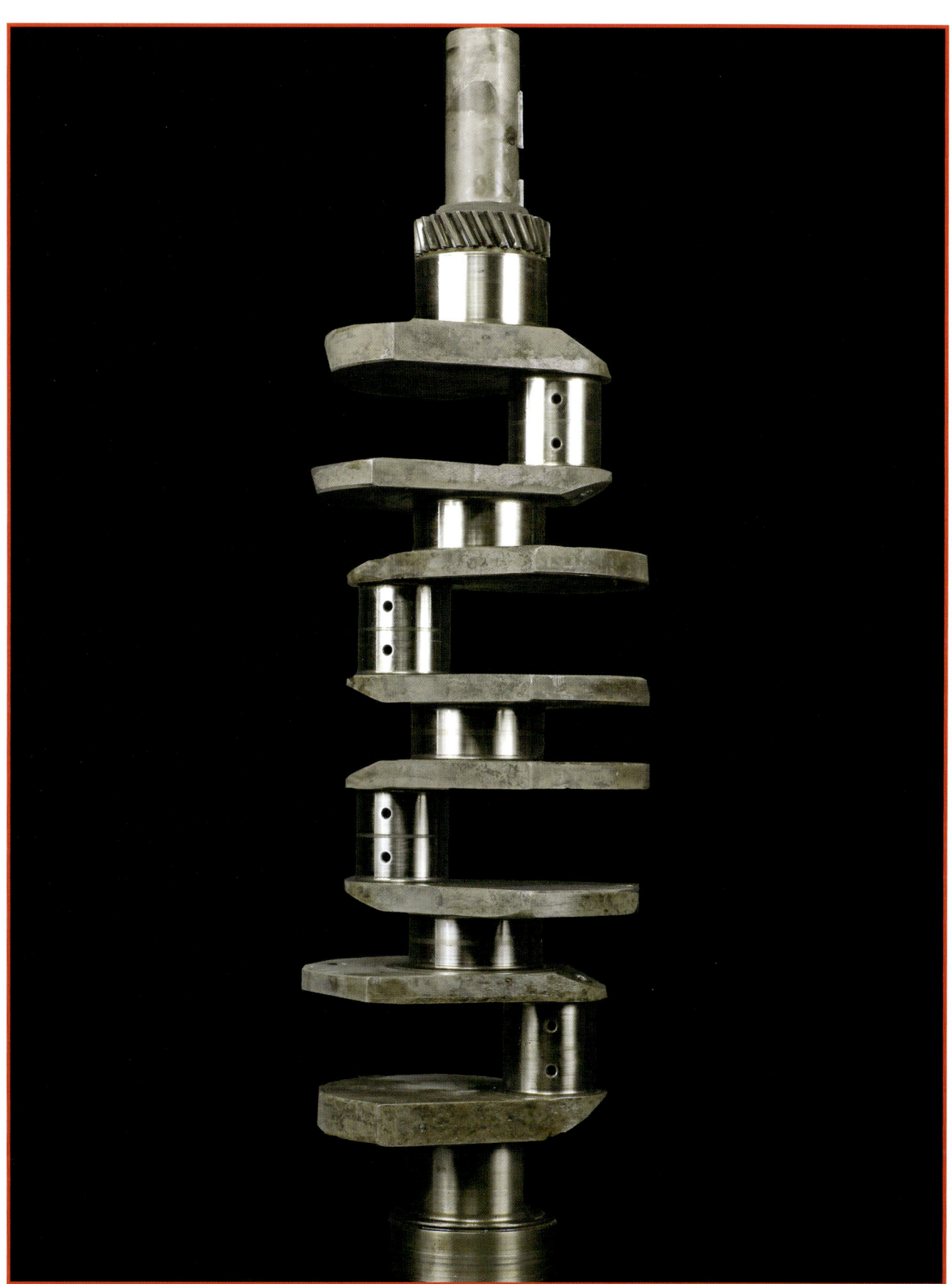
308 GTB: The arrival of the V8 (1975)

↑ A view of the transmission casing/sump casting inverted, showing the gearbox shafts and differential housing (right).

The initial specification of the F106 A 021 engine included a dry-sump lubrication system, provided by a pressure pump and scavenge pump system (instead of the wet sump of the Dino 308 GT4), with the oil tank in one rear corner of the engine bay and the oil-cooler radiator in the other. This technology, usually used on competition cars, provides consistent lubrication under the most extreme driving conditions, and more efficient cooling of the engine through the pressurised oil lines to the oil-cooler radiator. At the start of production for the 308 GTS, in 1977, a change was made to wet-sump lubrication, although the 308 GTB continued

↓ The four belt-driven forged-steel camshafts.

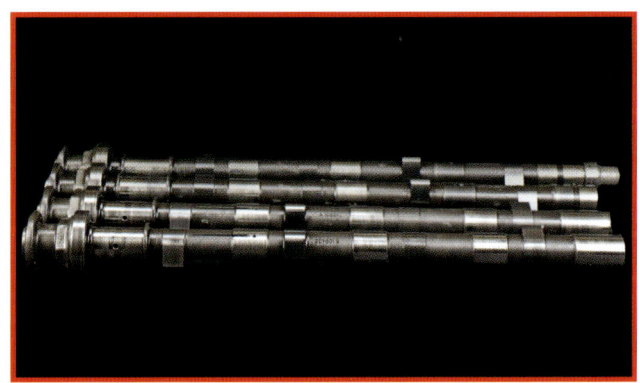

FERRARI 308 GTB – TECHNICAL DATA

Engine code	F106 A
Engine type	Mid, transverse, V8, 90°
Bore and stroke	81 x 71mm (3.18 x 2.79 in)
Total capacity	2,926.90cc (178.61cu in)
Unitary capacity	365.86cc (22.32cu in)
Compression ratio	8.8:1
Maximum power	251bhp (188kW) at 7,700rpm
Power per litre	86bhp/litre (64kW/litre)
Valve operation	Double overhead camshafts per bank, two valves per cylinder
Fuel feed	Four twin-choke Weber 40 DCNF carburettors
Ignition	Single spark plug per cylinder, single distributor, single coil
Lubrication	Dry sump
Clutch	Dry, single plate
Maximum torque	290Nm (213.8lb ft) at 5,000rpm
Firing order	1–5–3–7–4–8–2–6

↑↑ The two inlet manifolds, showing the inlet tracts. Two carburettors mount on each manifold.

↑ The five crankshaft main-bearing caps, which are dowelled and bolted to the cylinder block.

↑↑ The single oil filter, complete with mounting and oil-pressure sensor. The filter mounts in the vee at the rear of the engine.

↑ The five-speed gearbox is located below the engine, with drive to the mainshaft via triple transfer gears.

for a while with its dry-sump system. All US, Australian and Japanese-market cars had wet-sump lubrication from the beginning of production, and by the time the fuel-injected models appeared, in 1980, wet-sump lubrication was provided for all markets. The pistons for the 308 were forged in light alloy and supplied by AE Borgo, as were those of the Daytona and 365 GT4 BB, with a unitary displacement of 365.86cc – identical to those fitted to the two 12-cylinder Ferrari berlinettas. The connecting rods for the 308 engine were made from forged steel and had a short stroke of 71mm, while the bore of the steel cylinders liners was 81mm. The ignition system used twin coils and a single distributor, and the firing order was 1–5–3–7–4–8–2–6.

As on the Dino models which preceded it, the 308 engine/transmission featured a mechanically operated single dry-plate clutch on the flywheel, with triple transfer gears on the left side of the engine, dropping down to the gearbox main shaft. The five-speed gearbox was located below the engine, to the rear of the sump, with its own oil supply, and fed power to the rear wheels through a limited-slip differential and driveshafts with universal joints. Gear selection was controlled by a linkage running from the gearbox to the gear lever on the tunnel in the cabin. This compact engine/transmission arrangement provided optimum weight distribution for agile, secure handling, roadholding and traction. To aid high-speed handling, the car was provided with a small chin spoiler, with the option of a deeper one, and the engine cover featured a small lip to its trailing edge. The engine cover, between the buttresses that ran from the roof on each side, featured twin rows of black-painted air louvres to dissipate heat from the engine bay. The louvre layout changed during the course of production, depending on the model and market. To feed air to the filter box for the carburettors, and the oil-cooler radiator, Leonardo Fioravanti extended the door scoops used on the Dino, which also provided a family link with that much-loved model.

The cabin of the 308 was both compact and spacious, with two comfortable leather-upholstered sports seats, and three-point safety belts. The driver had the major instruments

↑ The four twin-choke Weber 40 DCNF carburettors which provide fuel to the 106 A engine.

→ The transmission/sump assembly, with the driveshaft flanges visible either side of the finned differential housing. Note also the gearbox input shaft protruding on the left of the photograph, and the two mountings (painted black) in the foreground.

↘ The clutch bellhousing and gearbox end casing. Transfer gears take the drive from the clutch down to the gearbox.

in an alloy-faced nacelle directly in his field of vision, forward of the leather-rim steering wheel, and the gear lever sprouted from the open-gate gearshift in the centre tunnel. The heat from the engine, mounted close to the rear bulkhead, filtered into the cabin, thus with this berlinetta, as on the previous Dino, it was recommended that air conditioning was fitted. The advantage of this layout, however, was the amazing symphony played by the engine, which, being close to the occupants' ears, provided an addictive soundtrack to complement the driving experience that the clients had been waiting for.

The great success of this V8 Ferrari is proven by the long production period, which lasted for ten years until the arrival of the face-lifted 328 GTB and GTS derivatives in 1985. The 308 sold in numerous variants: 308 GTB Vetroresina, 308 GTB, 308 GTS, 308 GTBi and 308 GTSi, and 308 GTB and 308 GTS Quattrovalvole. A total of 12,149 examples were built, without counting the 2.0-litre versions (normally aspirated and Turbo), setting a record at the time for Ferrari berlinettas. An adjunct to this was that in the USA, a successful TV series (*Magnum PI*, with the actor Tom Selleck) adopted a 308 GTS as the four-wheeled protagonist, providing the car with incredible international exposure and increasing the success of this Ferrari model even further. The GTS version was indeed the most popular 308, with 8,010 examples sold over the three versions – GTS, GTSi and GTS QV! One of the cars used in this American series (it is believed that there were about five cars used in each series, spanning GTS, GTSi and GTS QV) was sold in January 2017 at a Bonhams auction for US$181,500!

As mentioned earlier in this chapter, the V8 F106 AB is one of the Ferrari engines not strictly derived from competition, but Group 4 and Group B-specification competition versions were developed from this unit by Giuliano Michelotto's company – the famous engineer whose work on special Ferrari competition cars is renowned. Cars were modified by other workshops (such as Facetti and Finotto) for private customers. These competition 308 GTBs with glassfibre, and later composite, bodywork, featured enlarged wings and spoilers, wider wheels and other modifications, and were raced and rallied with success. The Michelotto 308s, with two and four valves per cylinder, were capable of producing 284bhp (212kW) at 7,000rpm (two valves) and 306bhp (228kW) at 7,500rpm (four valves). These cars were driven by drivers such as Jean-Claude Andruet and Tonino Tognana, and berlinettas (competing in Group 4) won the 1981 and 1982 Tour de France, two Targa Florios in the same years, one Italian Rally Championship and one Spanish Rally Championship. Moreover, in 1981, Carlo Facetti and Martino Finotto built a 308 Group 5 example, fitted with a twin-turbo engine that ran in a number of World Championship races, establishing a lap record at the 24 Hours of Daytona. Besides these competition developments and results, it should be mentioned that the F106 AB engine was also fitted to the prototype 308 Millechiodi, unveiled at the Geneva Motor Show in 1977 as an aerodynamic study by Pininfarina. This car was an early preview of the future GTO (288) Berlinetta that was presented at Geneva in 1984. Indeed, using the 308 engine as its basis, repositioning it longitudinally, reducing the displacement to 2,882cc and adding two IHI turbochargers, this became Ferrari's first supercar, which was capable of breaking the magic 300kmh (186mph) barrier. The incredible success of the 308 GTB and its derivatives was the light that lit the way for the Maranello factory in the direction of a V8 model range, which has been the backbone of the company's production ever since.

308 GTB: The arrival of the V8 (1975)

Ferrari
Ferrari

Ferrari
Ferrari

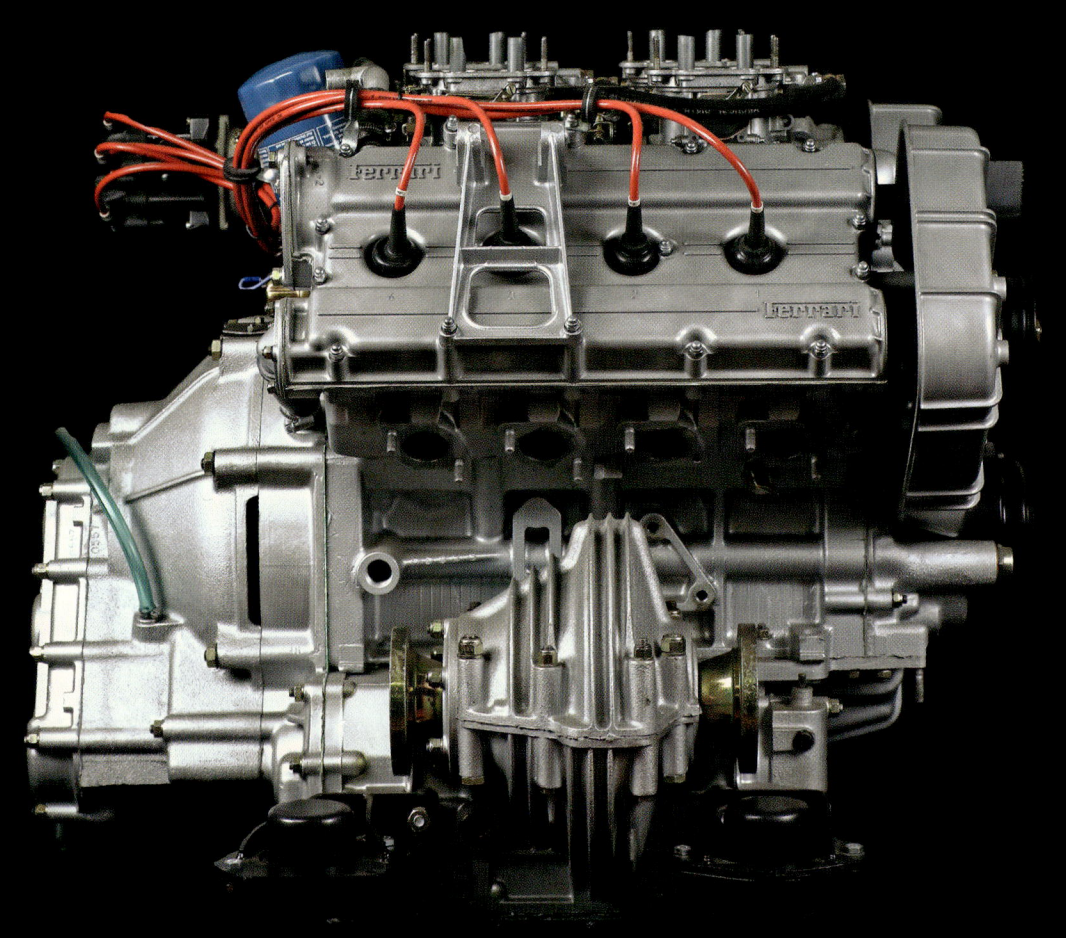

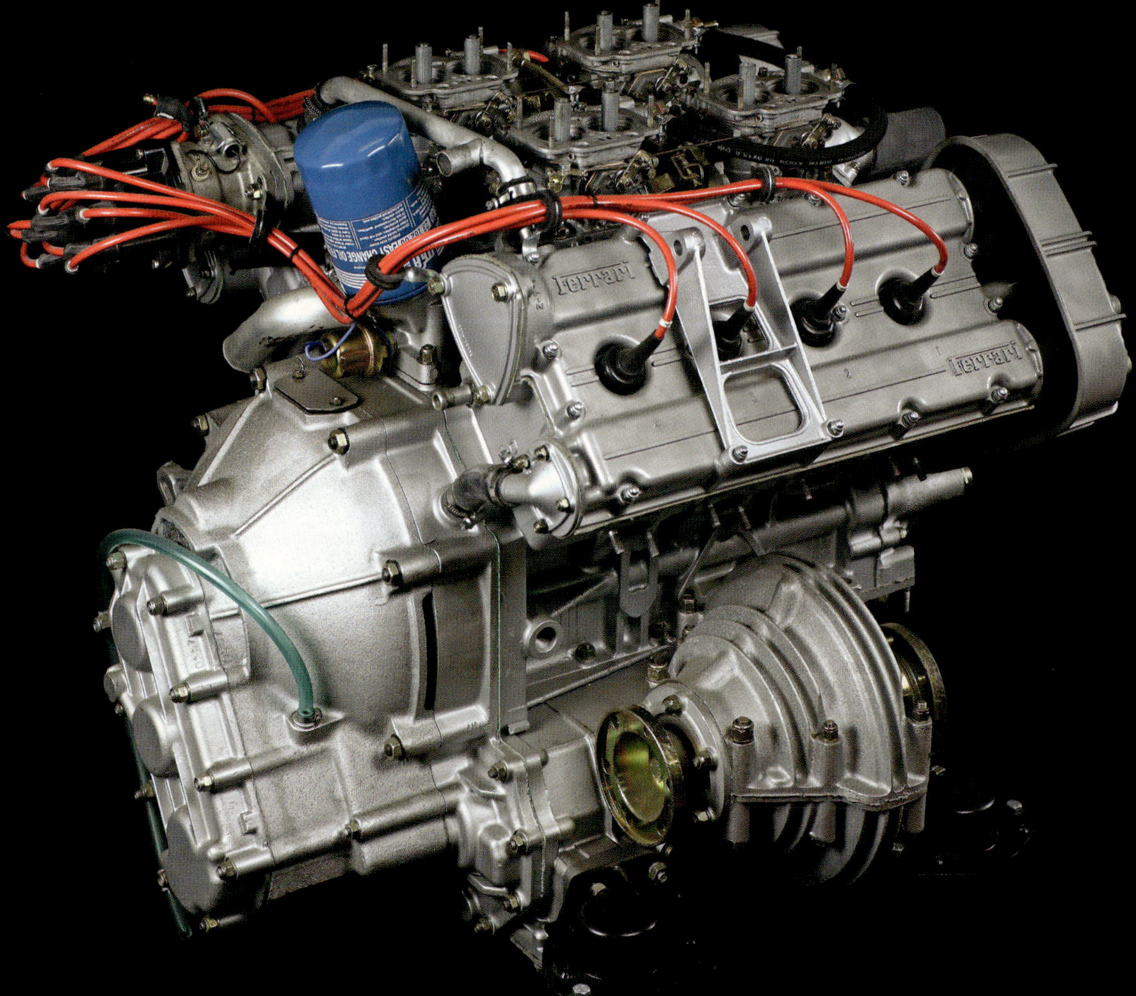

↑ The optional deep front spoiler, wide grille panel under the nose and muscular wheel arches add to the aggressive look of the car.

↑ The rear of the car features Ferrari's 'signature' round tail-lights, along with the model name.

➔ Alloy five-spoke wheels, with Ferrari logo centre-caps first featured on the 365 GTB4 in 1968.

↘ The cockpit featured buttresses, bounding the curved vertical rear screen, which ran gracefully down to the Kamm tail panel.

↘↘ The air intakes sculpted into the doors took inspiration from the much-loved 246 Dino.

↘↘↘ The 308 GTB features retractable headlights to streamline the shape of the car, as was typical for the Ferraris of the period.

↓ The fabulous profile of the Pininfarina-styled 308 GTB, unveiled at the Paris Motor Show in 1975, built on the strengths of the previous Dino 246.

208 Turbo
The first Ferrari turbo road car (1982)

At the beginning of the eighties, the engineer Mauro Forghieri, chief of the Ferrari Reparto Corse, designed and built the first turbocharged Ferrari engine (a V6, 120° 1,496.93cc unit, with a KKK turbocharger), which debuted in the 126 CK F1 car in 1980. Two years later, in 1982, Ferrari won the F1 Constructors' World Championship using a turbocharged car, the same year in which a turbocharged engine was first fitted in a Ferrari road car. Indeed, at the 1982 Turin Motor Show, Ferrari unveiled its 2.0-litre V8 90° F106 D engine, fitted in a mid-transverse position in the 208 Turbo model. This new approach, which enabled a reduction in engine capacity without losing the performance typical of all Ferraris, became an essential part of the Maranello factory's home market road-car programme. This was because of the very high 'luxury' taxes imposed on cars of over 2.0-litre engine capacity in Italy during a period of 'austerity'. Essentially this model was only sold in Italy, although some were also sold new in Portugal, which had similar tax laws. In F1, this turbo technology was necessary to produce an engine with less bulk than the previous naturally aspirated flat-12 'boxer' engine, used in the 312 T5 F1 car, which was rendered obsolete due to the ground-effect aerodynamic solutions of the day, which couldn't be incorporated with this engine layout. Maranello competed with a turbocharged engine in F1 from 1980 to 1988, winning two constructors' titles and many races. Following Ferrari tradition, many of the technological features employed in production cars derived from previous experiences in competition. In this case, the birth of the turbocharged Ferrari 208 was a result of the use of this technology in F1.

Prior to the 208 Turbo unit, Ferrari had produced a naturally aspirated 2.0-litre V8 engine, specifically for the Italian market, which was first installed in the Dino 208 GT4 model in 1975, which remained in production until 1980. This engine had code number F106 C, and Ferrari claimed a power output of 180bhp (134kW). A slightly revised version of this engine with the code F106 CB was used in the 208 GTB and GTS models introduced in 1980. Although by everyday car standards of the period both these cars had good performance, by Ferrari standards of the 3.0-litre cousins – the Dino 308 GT4 and 308 GTB and GTS models – it was only what might best be

↓ **The forged-steel flat-plane crankshaft. The gear at the front of the crankshaft drives the oil pump.**

↓↓ **An inverted side view of one of the cylinder heads, showing the four exhaust ports.**

described as mediocre. As an example, Ferrari claimed a top speed for the Dino 308 GT4 of 156mph (250kmh), whereas their claimed top speed for the 208 GT4 was only 133.5mph (215kmh). This was not really surprising when one considers that the smaller engine was only two-thirds the size, and was propelling a car of the same weight. The same comparison could be drawn between the 208 GTB and the 308 GTB.

Putting trust in the turbocharger solution provided performance worthy of the *Cavallino Rampante* badge on the nose was the right choice at the right time for Maranello. So, the turbo project derived directly from the naturally aspirated 2.0-litre V8 engine fitted to the previous 208 GTB, with the aim of improving performance without succumbing to the fiscal taxation applicable to larger-capacity cars. The F106 D engine, together with the single KKK Turbocharger, succeeded in this aim. The acceleration of the turbo berlinetta was astonishing for its day, with a 0-62mph (0–100kmh) time of only 6.5secs – quicker than the first 308 GTB, which took 7secs! The turbocharger significantly boosted the engine's power without significantly increasing its weight. Compressing the air – to a maximum pressure of 0.6 bar in the case of the F106 D engine – forces more oxygen into the cylinders, allowing more fuel to be added, providing more power. A turbocharger has an exhaust-driven turbine, which drives a compressor that raises the pressure of the intake air flowing into the engine, which provides dense, oxygen-rich air to the engine.

The naturally aspirated engine of the 208 GTB was designed by Angelo Bellei and Franco Rocchi, but the turbo version was reworked by turbocharging specialist Nicola Materazzi, who was working at the time for GES (Reparto Corse Ferrari = Racing Department) at the time of the turbocharged 126 CK F1 car. He became the designer for the Ferrari turbo road-cars, and besides the development of the 208 Turbo, he was also responsible for the projects relating to the GTO (288), and later the F40, both with mid-mounted longitudinal engines and twin turbochargers.

The mechanical components of the F106 D engine were similar to the 2.0-litre naturally aspired F106 CB. With a power output of 220bhp (164kW), compared to the 255bhp (190kW) of the 308, and a maximum torque of 240Nm (177lb ft) at 4,800rpm, the 208 Turbo was capable of reaching a maximum speed of 150mph (241kmh). The most impressive characteristic of this engine was its specific power of 109bhp/litre (81kW/litre)! As this was in the early days of turbocharging,

⬇ **The cylinder block was a smaller-bore derivative of the unit used in the 308 GTB and GTS.**

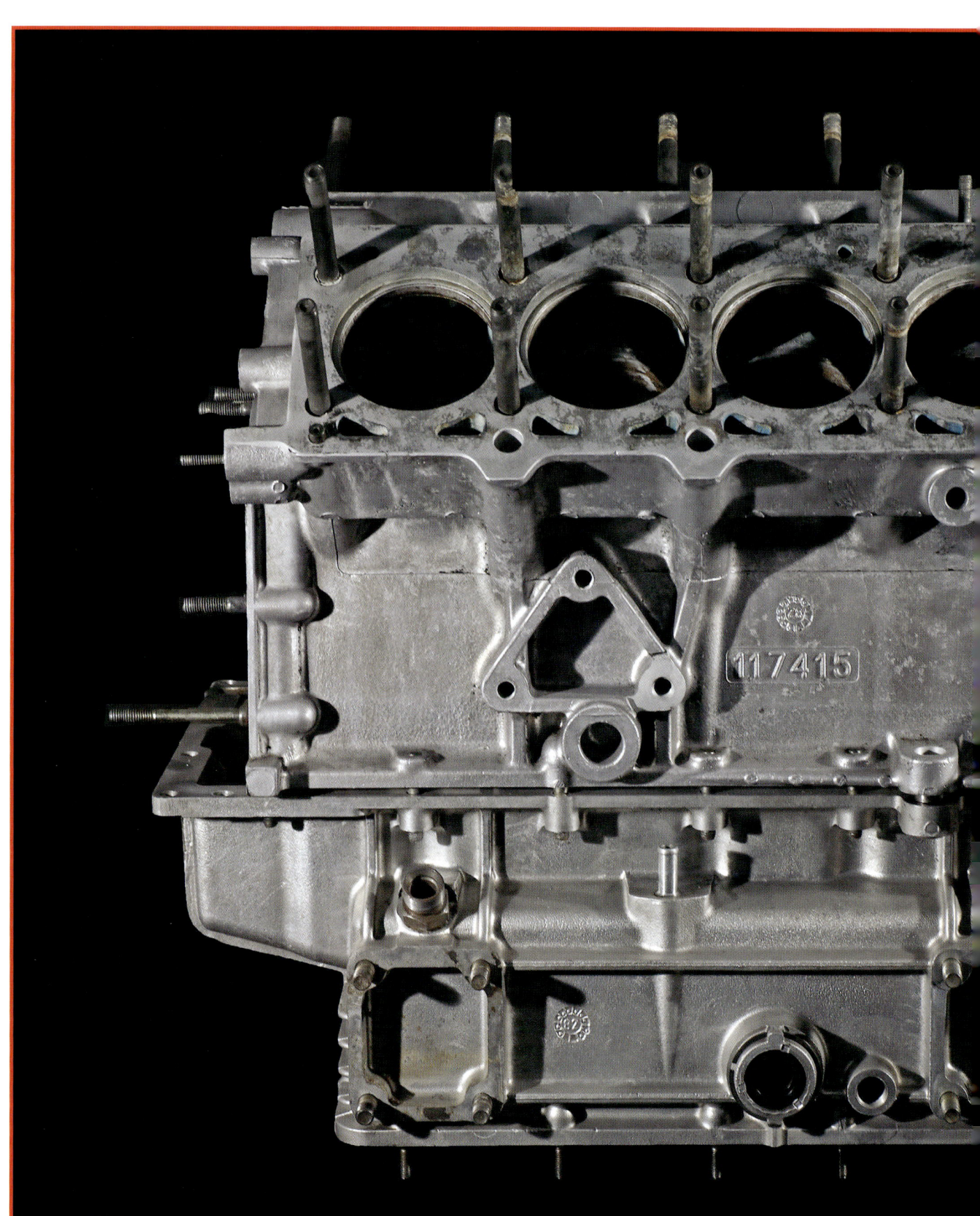

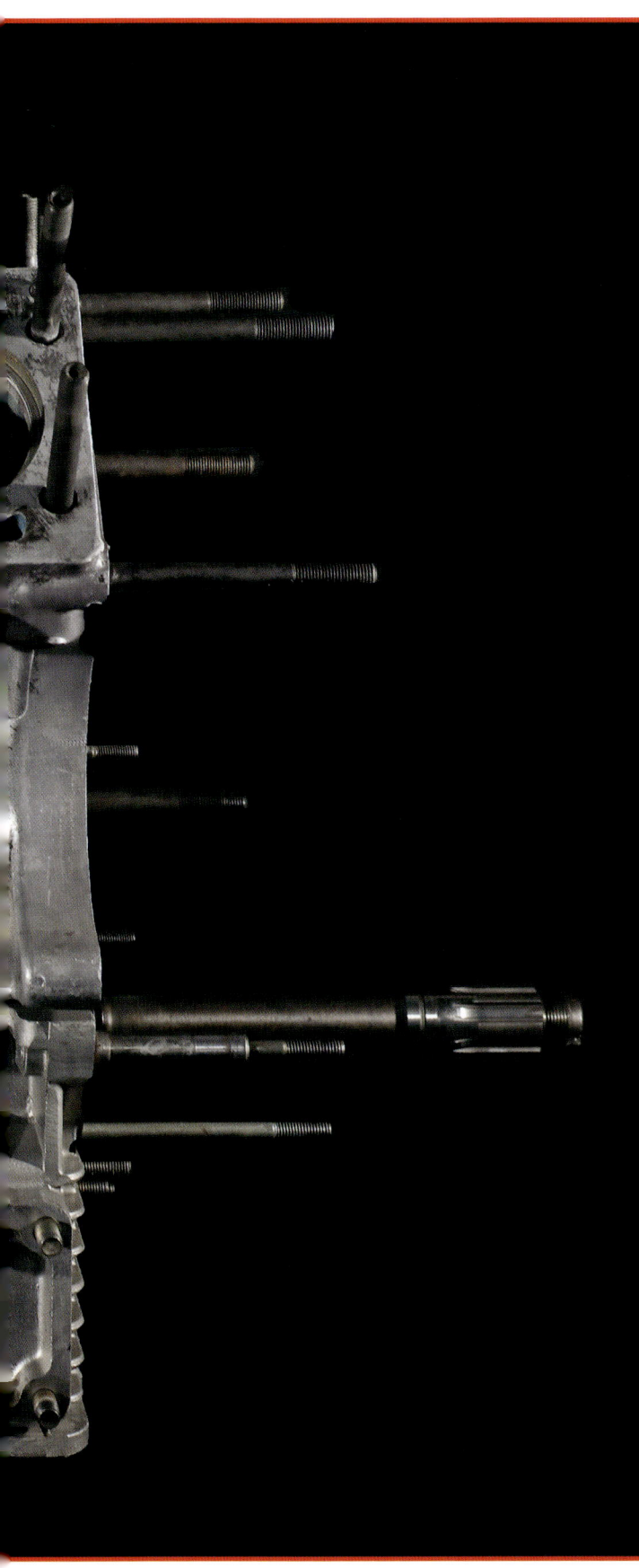

the turbo lag was rather marked, and the presence of boost was only really felt above 3,200rpm. The engine was mounted transversely, in similar fashion to the 308 GTB, with the turbocharger mounted to the rear of the engine.

The 2.0-litre 90° V8 turbo engine featured a cylinder block, heads, timing covers and transmission housing cast in aluminium (as for the 308). The cylinder heads featured two valves per cylinder, and the twin overhead camshafts per bank were gear-driven off the crankshaft with a tensioner assembly by toothed belts. The camshafts operated the valves directly, via bucket tappets. The aluminium pistons were manufactured by Borgo, with steel connecting rods and Nikasil-coated aluminium cylinder liners (as also adopted on the 308 models in 1982, replacing the original cast-iron items), with a bore of 66.8mm, and a stroke of 71mm. The compression ratio was 7:1, and the rev limit for the engine was 7,000rpm. The firing order of the cylinders was 1–5–3–7–4–8–2–6. The steel crankshaft was of the flat-plane type, as with the 308 described on pages 138 to 153. Lubrication was via a wet sump, with a pressure pump driven directly from the crankshaft, and an oil cooler was incorporated in the system. The five-speed transmission was located low and behind the sump, basically the same layout as in the 308 GTB, albeit with different ratios to suit the turbo engine characteristics. The clutch was a single dry-plate unit, connected to the transmission via drop gears.

Fuel delivery was via a Bosch K-Jetronic mechanical fuel injection system, operating in conjunction with a Marelli MED 804A electronic ignition system. The K-Jetronic system was an early injection system in which the fuel was injected continuously upstream of the inlet valves, with the amount of fuel to be injected determined by the volume of air entering the engine.

The temperatures produced by this turbo engine were higher than those of the naturally aspirated version, and thus modifications were made to the bodywork of the 208 Turbo model to aid cooling and heat dissipation. To provide increased airflow through the engine bay, NACA ducts were incorporated into the sill panels just forward of the rear wheels. The spoiler on the trailing edge of the roof was more than simply a device for increasing rear downforce, but also had the task of optimising airflow over the engine cover to extract more air through its louvres. Inside the cabin of the 208 Turbo, a gauge located on the tunnel, close to the gear lever, indicated the instantaneous level of boost pressure. The reliability and performance of this turbo engine was ensured if the instructions in the owner's manual were respected. The most important rule, as for all turbo engines

← **The cylinder block with sump/transmission attached. Note the gearbox input shaft protruding to the right of the transmission.**

↑ A view inside the five-speed gearbox showing the gear clusters and selector mechanism.

← The engine sump casting, with cooling fins on the bottom, along with the oil drain plug.

↙ A view of the underside of the engine/transmission, showing the separate engine (bottom) and gearbox (above) sumps.

↓ The complete transmission assembly, with clutch bellhousing and transfer gears on left, differential in the foreground and gearbox behind.

➔ A forged-steel connecting rod with big-end bearing cap (secured by nuts) fitted.

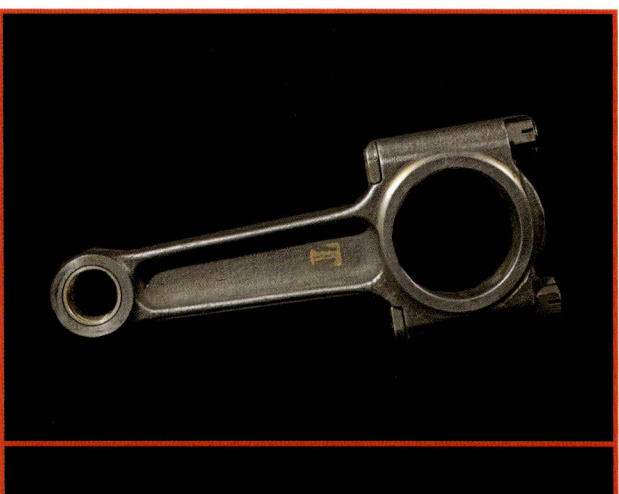

at that time, was to allow the turbo rotor to cool down after use. Thus, before switching off the engine, it was very important to wait for one or two minutes at idle, to allow the temperature to drop to avoid seizing the rotor.

Production of the 208 Turbo lasted for four years, from 1982 to 1985, with 437 examples of coupés and 250 examples of spiders built.

In 1986, in parallel with the introduction of the naturally aspirated transverse 3.2-litre V8 engine of the 328 GTB/GTS, some changes on the 208 Turbo were introduced, as apart from adopting the changes to the bodywork and interior of the 328 GTB/GTS, a new IHI turbocharger (with a maximum operating pressure of 1.05 bar) was fitted, the engine code changing to F106 N. Thanks to the new IHI

➔ One of the flat-top forged alloy pistons with oil control ring and two compression rings fitted.

⬇ A complete set of valves from one cylinder head – exhaust valves on the left and inlet valves on the right.

↑ The single turbocharger, mounted to the rear of the engine. The driveshaft flanges are visible below.

turbocharger system, which increased power to 254bhp (189kW) at 6,500rpm, this new GTB Turbo could reach a maximum speed of 157mph (253kmh) and the turbo power was introduced more gradually from around 3,000rpm. GTB and GTS Turbos were built until 1989 – some 308 examples for the coupé version and 828 for the spider, and these would be the last of Ferrari's 2.0-litre 'tax break specials'.

After production of the F40 ceased in 1992, it would be over 20 years before Ferrari produced another turbocharged road car, which was the front-engined California T, which made its debut in 2014. This was the first model with the new turbo-family V8 engine, which in this model had the code F154 BB, and had a capacity of 3,855cc, producing 560bhp (418kW).

After the successful naturally aspirated mid-engine V8s of the early 2000s (360, 430, 458), Ferrari took the turbo route with the replacement for the 458 model. This was the 488 GTB, the 488 part of the model name harking back to the 'old days' when Ferrari used the approximate swept volume of a single cylinder in the model title, hence 8 x 488 = 3,904cc, the actual capacity being very close at 3,902cc. This engine had type number F154 CB, and featured twin turbos as on the front-engined California T, and that model's replacement, the Portofino. Proud of its

FERRARI 208 TURBO – TECHNICAL DATA

Engine code	F106 D
Engine type	Mid, transverse, V8, 90°
Bore and stroke	66.8 x 71mm (2.63 x 2.79in)
Total capacity	1,990.64cc (121.47cu in)
Unitary capacity	248.83cc (15.18cu in)
Compression ratio	7:1
Maximum power	217bhp (162kW) at 7,000rpm
Power per litre	109bhp/litre (81kW/litre)
Valve operation	Double overhead camshaft per bank, two valves per cylinder
Fuel feed	Bosch K-Jetronic injection, single KKK turbo, external wastegate valve
Ignition	Marelli MED 840A, single spark plug per cylinder
Lubrication	Wet sump
Clutch	Dry, single plate
Maximum torque	240Nm (177lb ft) at 4,800rpm
Firing order	1–5–3–7–4–8–2–6

→ The eight cylinder liners, which fit into the cylinder block to form the bores.

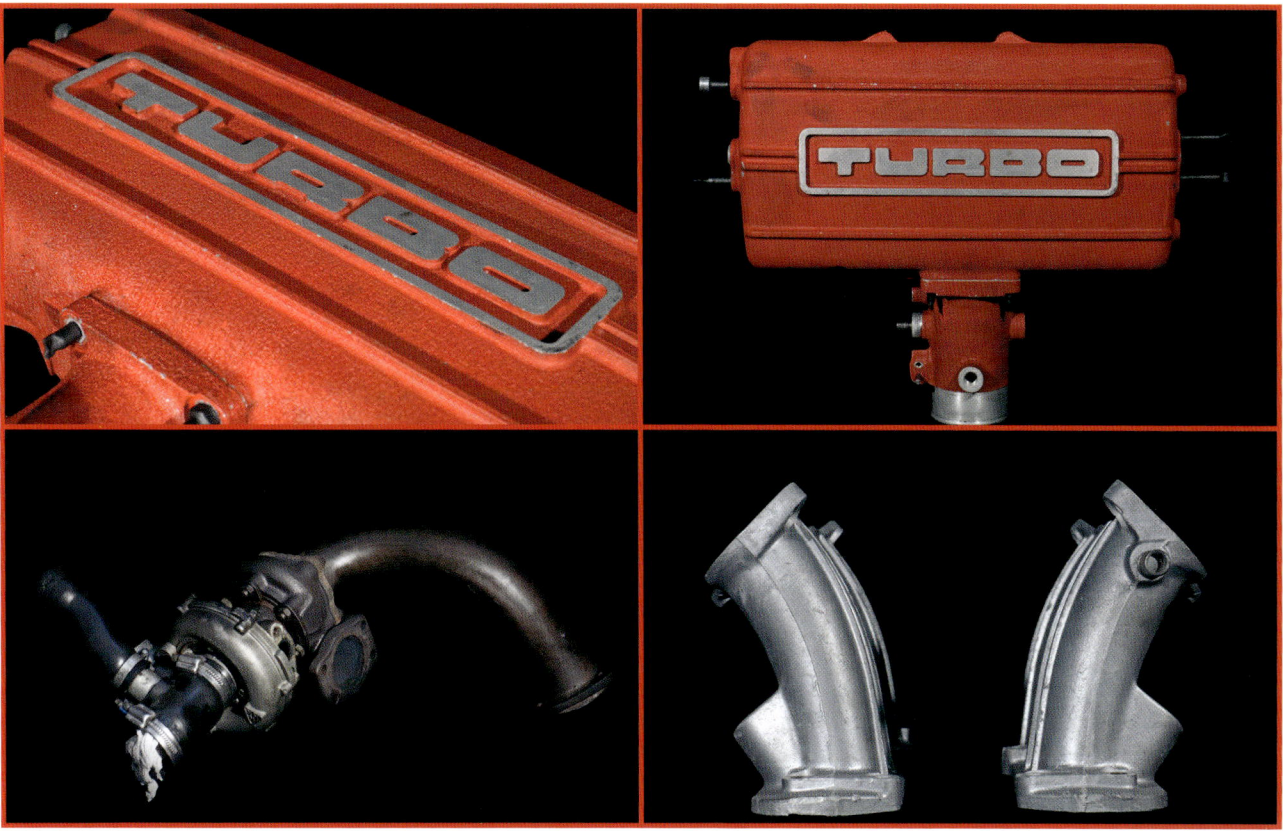

↑↑ A turbo logo is cast into the red-painted plenum chamber which sits on top of the inlet manifolds.

↑ The turbocharger unit removed from the engine, with exhaust outlet pipe attached.

↑↑ A view of the complete plenum chamber casting, with the inlet from the turbo at the bottom of the photograph.

↑ The two cast-alloy inlet manifolds positioned as fitted to the engine. The plenum chamber fits on top of these manifolds.

engineering masterpiece, Ferrari displayed the engine beneath a tempered glass showcase – the extended rear screen, as with the 360 Modena (see pages 218 to 233). The past 25 years had not passed in vain, considering that following the 208 Turbo, which produced 'only' 220bhp (164kW), Ferrari had developed the turbo concept to arrive at the mighty engine used in the 488, producing an impressive 661bhp (493kW) at 8,000rpm. Continuing the story, in March 2018, at the Geneva Motor Show, Ferrari unveiled the most powerful V8 twin-turbo road car engine in Maranello's history – this engine, fitted to the 488 Pista, produced a mighty 720bhp (537kW), exactly 500bhp (373kW) more than the 'little' 208 Turbo!

163

208 Turbo: The first Ferrari turbo road car (1982)

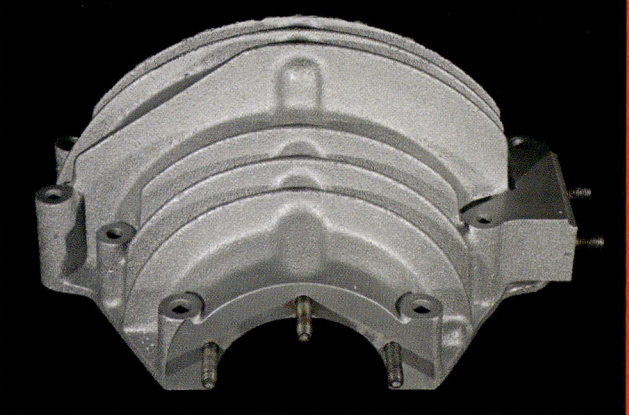

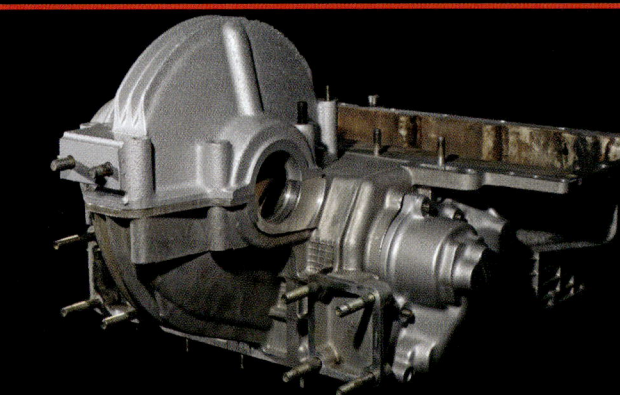

↖ One of the cylinder heads with valves fitted in the hemispherical combustion chambers.

↑ The casting for the upper differential casing.

← The differential and gearbox casings.

↓ The cast-alloy clutch bellhousing and transfer-gear cover.

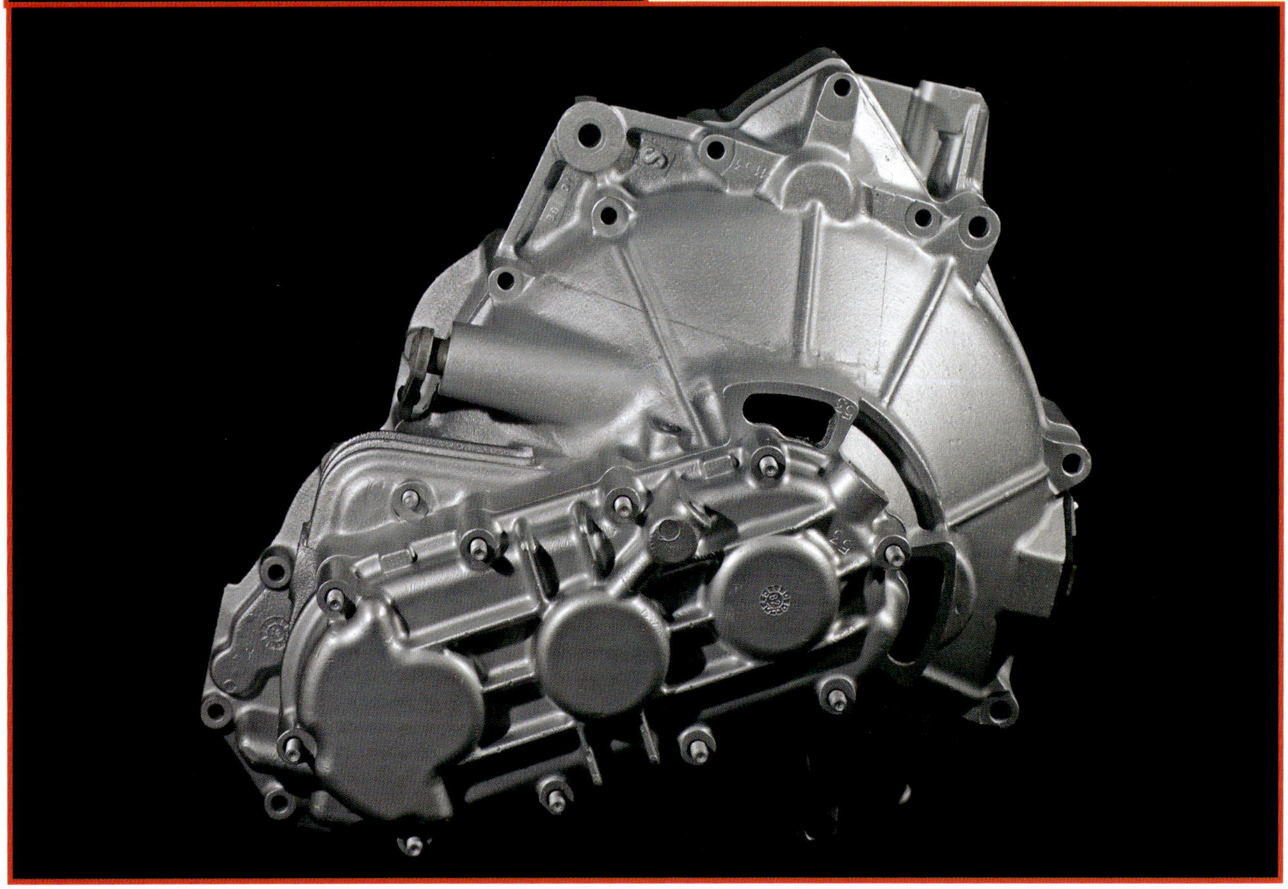

↑ A side view of the gearbox casing, with input shaft on right.

→ A close-up view of one of the cylinder liners.

↓ The cylinder block, sump and gearbox assembled, without crankshaft or cylinder liners fitted. The gearbox input shaft is visible to the right of the gearbox casing.

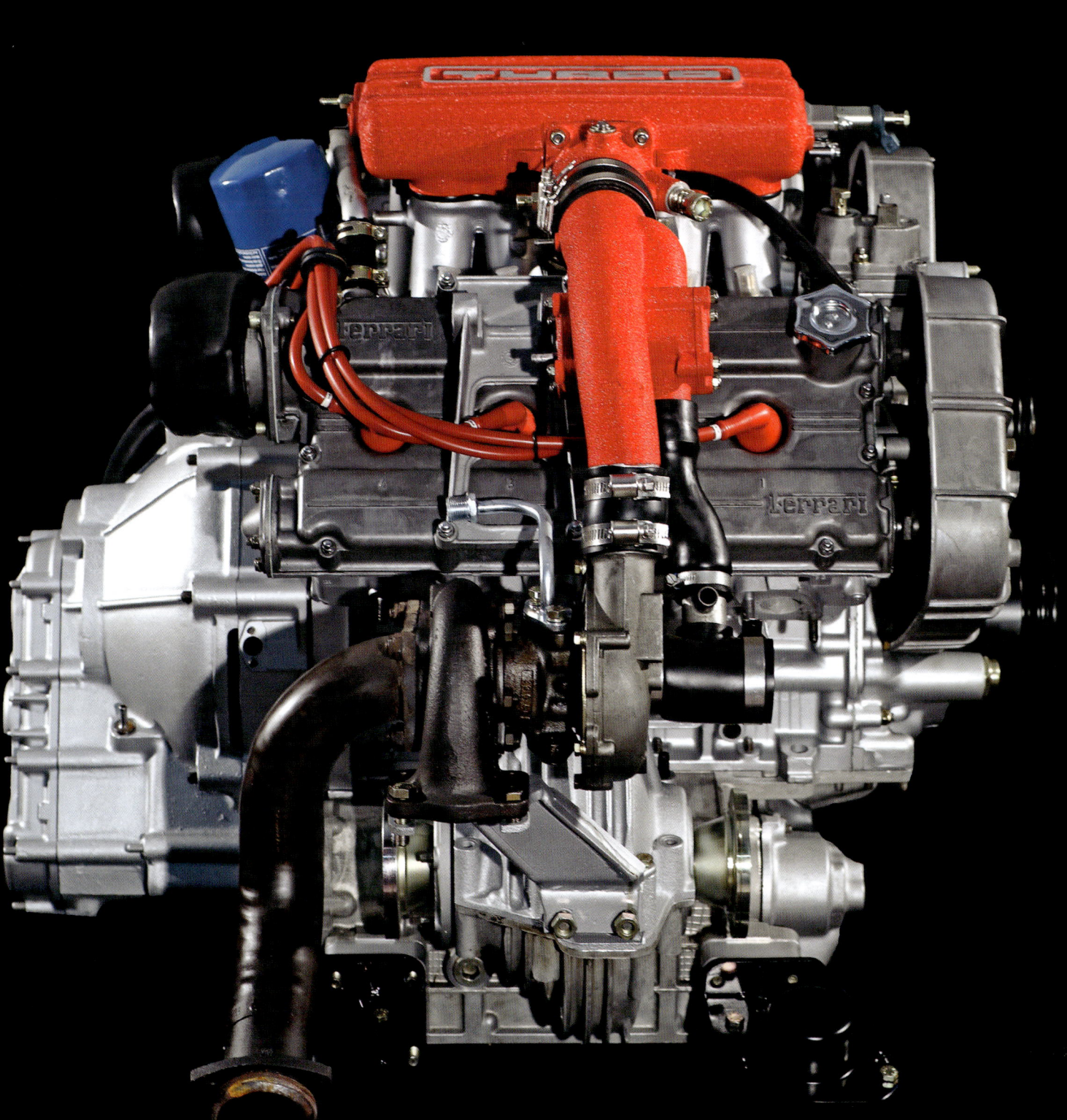

↑ The impressive front view of the 208 Turbo is very similar to its 308 GTB cousin.

↑ The rear of the car is again similar to that of the 308 GTB. The exhaust expansion box is visible below the tail.

➔ The 'pop-up' headlights help to improve the aerodynamics and were de rigeur on Ferraris in the 1970s and 1980s.

↘ The badging carried on the rear clearly identifies this Italian-market car.

↘↘ This aspect of the car's Pininfarina styling, with sail panel and twin round tail-lights shouts 'Ferrari'.

↘↘↘ The black-painted louvres on the nose aid cooling and provide a distinctive styling feature.

↓ The body styling incorporates a NACA duct low down, ahead of the rear wheels, to aid cooling of the engine compartment. The turbo engine generates a significant amount of heat.

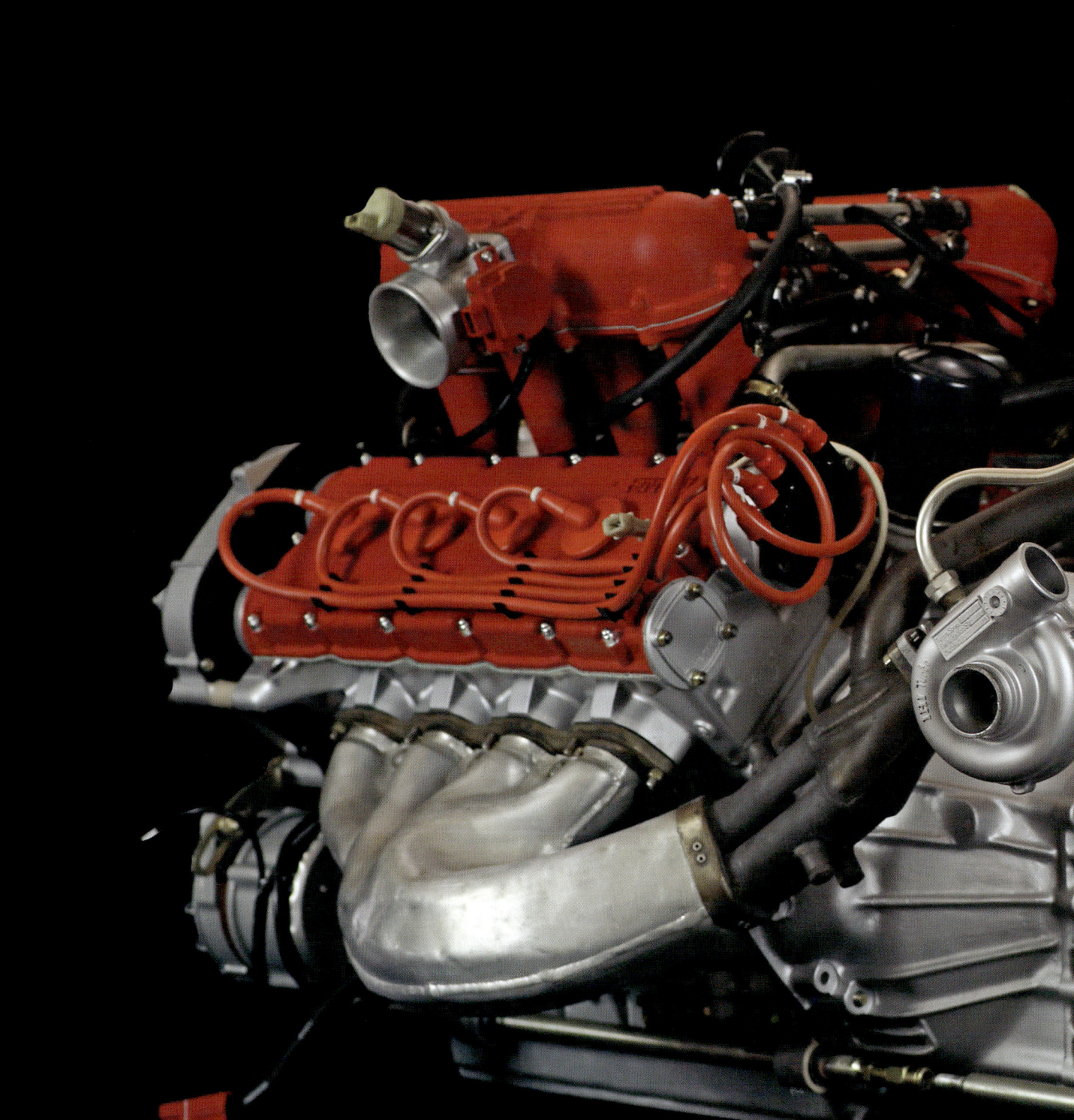

GTO (288)
Twin-turbo supercar (1984)

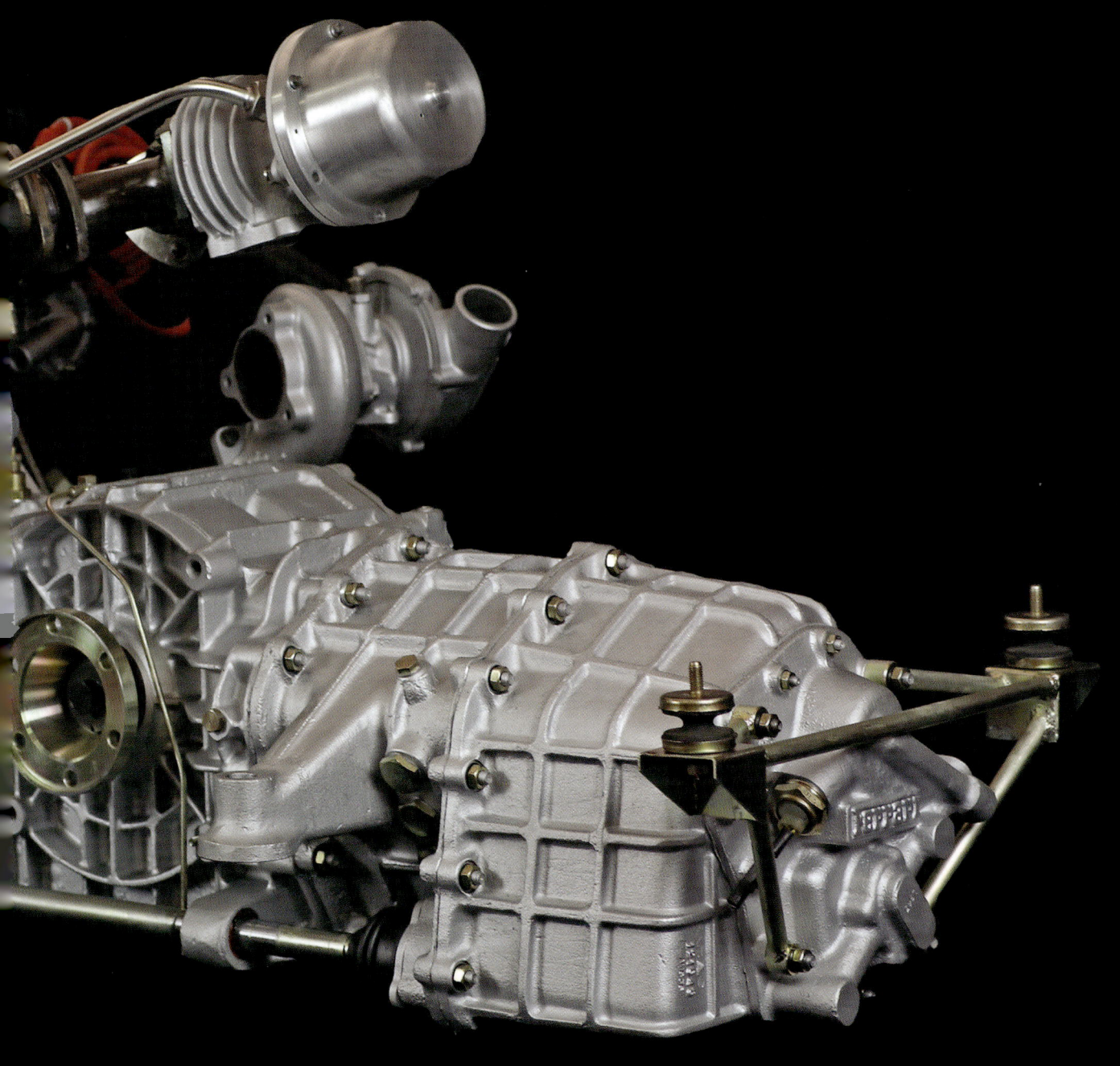

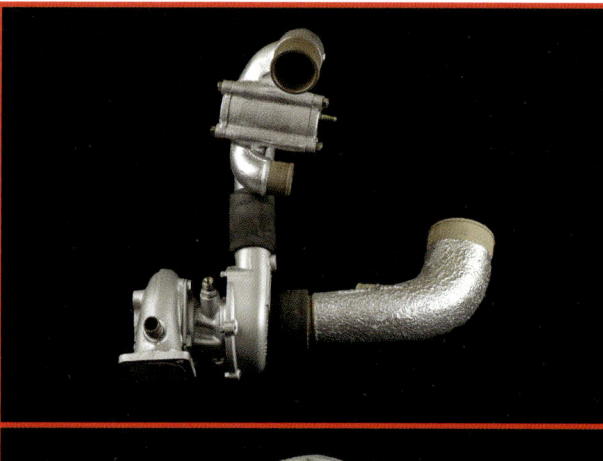

← One of the IHI turbochargers, with the manifold (at top) that supplies pressurised air to the intercooler.

↙ One of the two throttle-body assemblies showing the throttle butterfly valve and operating linkage.

The most illustrious three letters, on which a legend was built, reappeared on a Ferrari 22 years after it was first used on possibly the most iconic Ferrari of all time – the 250 GTO. Any revival of the Grand Turismo Omologato acronym could only be permitted for a very special car, and the GTO, commonly referred to as the 288 GTO, was that car. Conceived to compete in proposed new Group B circuit/rally regulations, the 272 examples built never turned a wheel in anger on the track, because the series was abandoned due to the lack of entries as a result of the regulations.

The birth of the GTO's 2,855.08cc, V8 twin-turbo engine, was due, as often happened in Ferrari history, to the need for speed arising from competition. Racing was the original *raison d'etre* for this engine, which was based on the design of the Ferrari engine that powered the Lancia LC2 sports prototype during the 1983 season. The decision on the capacity was dictated by the FIA's requirement in the Group B regulations for turbocharged engine capacity to be multiplied by 1.4. This provided the GTO with a theoretical engine capacity of 3,997cc, just under the Group B limit of 4.0 litres. Group B required a minimum of 200 homologated examples of the car. The engine type F114 B was born, as noted, as a result of studies to produce a very potent competiton engine, with the emphasis on producing maximum power.

Although originally envisaged as a competition car, the GTO never raced and the 272 cars built remained purely road cars, giving birth to the first instantly collectible special Ferrari, one might even also say the birth of the supercar, to which the F40, F50, Enzo, LaFerrari and LaFerrari Aperta owe a debt of gratitude. The remarkable GTO that was unveiled at the 1984 Geneva Motor Show astonished Ferrari clients and enthusiasts, and all 200 cars which had been planned to be built were sold almost instantaneously. At that time, the GTO was the fastest road car ever built, breaking the 300kmh (186mph) barrier (achieving

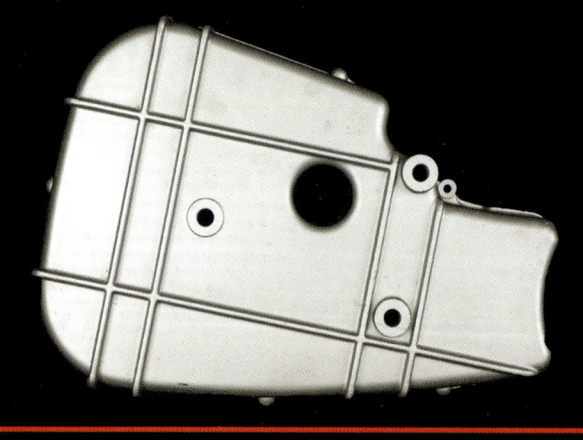

↖ One of the cast-aluminium timing covers that provides protection for the timing belts.

← The single wastegate valve, which regulates the pressure at which the exhaust gases pass to the turbine.

→ The compact, cast-alloy dry-sump pan, which features a single scavenge pump.

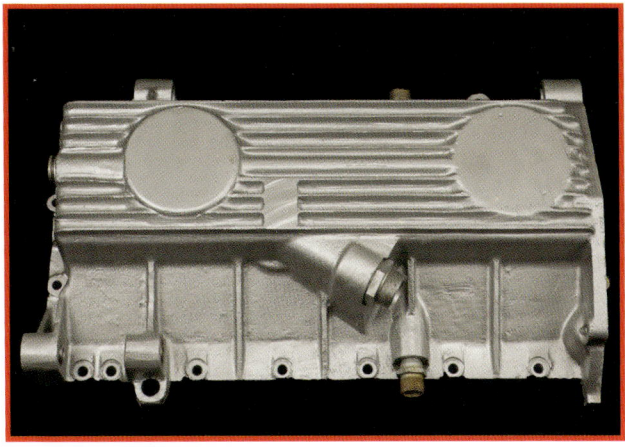

304kmh/189mph to be precise) and scorching from 0–62mph (0–100kmh) in 4.9sec.

At the beginning of the eighties, Enzo Ferrari felt that Maranello's cars has become somewhat less desirable in terms of performance, due to the fact that rival manufacturers such as BMW were building very fast cars, such as the M3, with performance equivalent to the 308 GTB, but at a significantly lower price. It should be noted that at this time Ferrari were in the early days of fuel injection on their cars, to meet more and more stringent emission standards, which had led to a reduction in power output while they came to terms with it. This is one of the reasons why, in 1983, engineer Nicola Materazzi had been appointed to design a turbo engine which would produce significantly more power than the Ferrari engines in production at the time. Maranello was in the process of designing a turbo engine of around 330bhp (246kW) at the time, and when Materazzi discussed this project with Enzo Ferrari, he told him that this engine could be capable of producing at least 400bhp (298kW). Enzo Ferrari said instantly to Materazzi: 'OK, make this engine!' Normally, Ferrari's projects would be handled by one of two design offices, one for production cars and one for competition cars, but for the GTO, the project was born in a third small office, where Materazzi designed the 2.8-litre twin-turbo

↓ The cylinder block with cylinder heads fitted. Note the 16 valve lifters (eight inlet and eight exhaust), visible in the bores in the head.

engine, which was then turned into reality by the Ferrari technical staff. Subsequently, Ferrari promoted Materazzi to head the Technical Production Centre, and so having designed the engine, Materazzi would take care of the overall technical development of the GTO too.

The major difference between the GTO engine installation and that of the 308 GTB was the GTO's longitudinal orientation, rather than the transverse positioning in the 308 GTB. Enzo Ferrari appreciated very much the aesthetics of the engine details visible under the engine cover of the GTO, and complimented Materazzi personally, telling him: 'It's clear that you know what you are doing, and you do it in an orderly and precise way.' Prior to the GTO, only the 250 LM 'road car' (sic) had featured a mid-longitudinal engine layout with a gearbox mounted behind the rear-axle line, and a mid-transverse engine layout lacked the symmetry and equilibrium found in longitudinal layouts. The F114 B was fitted with two large Behr intercoolers, and the engine produced 400bhp (298kW) at 7,000rpm, with a torque of 496Nm (366lb ft) at 3,800rpm. After the originally planned production run of 200 cars sold immediately after Ferrari enthusiasts saw the car at Geneva, Maranello decided to produce a further 72 cars to satisfy the requests of the most

important Ferrari clients. In addition to the production cars, four prototypes were built, three of which were used for crash tests, and one which was owned for a long time by Ferrari, which was recently sold to a collector. The GTO (288) was built from 1984 to early 1986, with chassis numbers in the odd sequence road car range of the period, between chassis numbers 52465–58345. Despite the fact that Group B circuit racing was ultimately cancelled, it was clear from the outset that the GTO was certainly not going to disappoint the Ferrari's fans or customers, even without a place to race.

In terms of its styling, this came from the pen of Leonardo Fioravanti at Pininfarina, and echoed a 308 GTB on steroids (a model also designed by him), but it was radically different beneath the skin. Although clearly following design cues from the 308, the GTO was much more aggressive-looking, and a fitting tribute to the legendary 250 GTO. Like its predecessor, it featured a rear spoiler blended into the tail, and the triple air-outlet slots in the rear wings were a deliberate design link to the pair of slots in the front wings of the 250 GTO. It had a longer wheelbase than the 308 – 2,451mm, instead of the 2,340mm of the 308, in order to accommodate the longitudinal 2.8-litre engine. Aerodynamically, the GTO was refined in the wind tunnel. The chassis structure was built from Ferrari's traditional tubular steel, as was the frame carrying the engine and transmission. Most of the bodywork panels were manufactured from composite materials, or honeycomb and moulded glassfibre, Kevlar was used for the bonnet, and the roof was made from a Kevlar and carbon fibre mix. These materials were derived directly from use in Ferrari's F1 cars. The front lid of a GTO, in Kevlar honeycomb, weighs only 3kg (6.6lb)! These materials contributed significantly to reducing weight while maintaining strength. To accommodate wider wheels, it was necessary to stretch the wheel arches, providing a very aggressive look to this supercar. To supply sufficient airflow to the bi-turbo engine, the bodywork featured a number of air intake and outlet vents, including louvres in the front lid to exhaust air from the radiator, ducts ahead of the rear wheels and in the sail panels to feed air to the engine bay and rear brakes, plus a heavily louvred engine cover to exhaust heat from the engine bay. Another distinctive feature was the pair of 'periscope' door mirrors to allow a clear view rearwards, which were mounted on tall stalks to clear the large rounded wheel arches, together with the pronounced rear spoiler. Enamel *Cavallino Rampante* (Prancing Horse) shields on the upper rear of the front wings provided a link to Ferrari's competition cars. Perhaps surprisingly, the interior of the road-going GTO was not spartan, as it featured either full-black leather-upholstered, or black leather with orange cloth centre, Kevlar-framed bucket seats (styled along similar lines to those of the 365 GTB4 'Daytona'), optional air conditioning, electric windows, an AM/FM radio-cassette player, and a dashboard containing the speedometer, a 10,000rpm tachometer, a turbo boost gauge, oil temperature and pressure gauges, and a water temperature gauge.

← Ferrari's first twin-turbo eventually led to the Engine Of The Year award in 2018 for the 3.9 bi-turbo V8 of the 488 Pista.

The F114 B had two IHI turbochargers, capable of spinning at 180,000rpm, and providing a boost pressure of 11.6psi (0.8 bar) via the two large Behr intercoolers. As with many early turbocharged cars of the period, the turbo-lag effect was considerable, and it was a challenge to control the 400bhp (298kW) of this 'beast', which provided specific power of 140bhp/litre (104kW/litre)! To underline the sporting soul of this V8, the intake manifolds and camshaft covers featured a red crackle finish. The bore and stroke of the type F114 B engine was 80mm x 71mm.

The longitudinal engine layout necessitated a new gearbox configuration that was derived from competitions.

↑ A close-up view of the top of one cylinder head shows the 16 bucket-type valve lifters, operated directly by the cam lobes. The camshaft bearings are machined directly into the cylinder-head casting.

→ The red intake manifolds and plenum chambers resemble two lungs, and supply the fuel/air mixture to the cylinders. The fuel injectors fit into the housings below the plenum chambers.

↓ The 288 GTO is fitted with two large intercoolers to cool the pressurised air from the turbochargers before it enters the engine's inlet tracts.

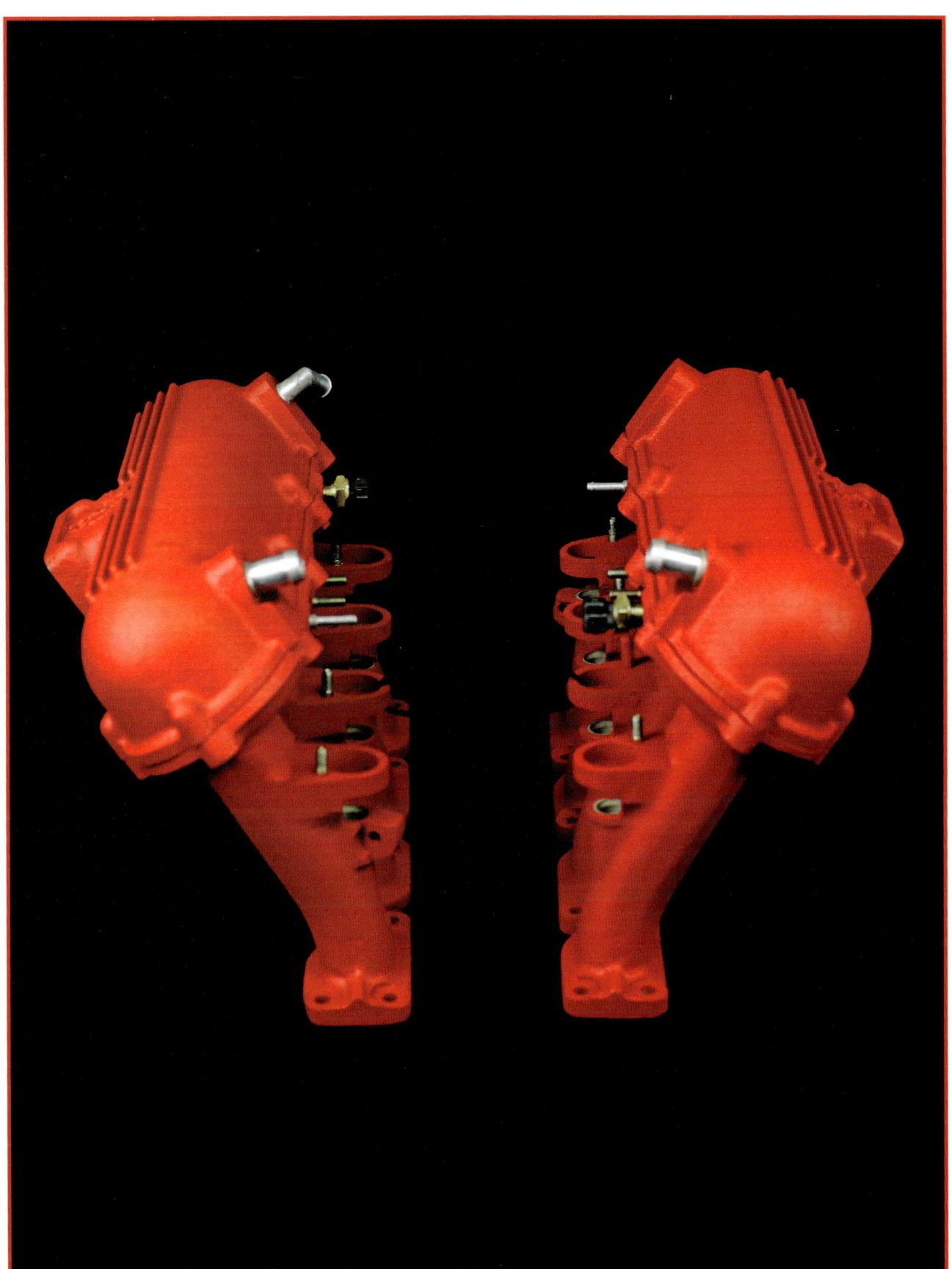

GTO (288): Twin-turbo supercar (1984)

177

↑ A view of the rear of the engine, showing the oil line (foreground) running from the filter mounting to the sump.

FERRARI 288 GTO – TECHNICAL DATA

Engine code	F114 B
Engine type	Rear, longitudinal, V8, 90°
Bore and stroke	80 x 71mm (3.15 x 2.8in)
Total capacity	2,855.08cc (174.22cu in)
Unitary capacity	356.88cc (21.77cu in)
Compression ratio	7.6:1
Maximum power	394bhp (294kW) at 7,000rpm
Power per litre	138bhp/litre (103kW/litre)
Valve operation	Twin overhead camshafts per bank, four valves per cylinder
Fuel feed	Weber-Marelli electronic injection, twin IHI turbos
Ignition	Weber-Marelli JAW electronic, single spark plug per cylinder
Lubrication	Dry sump
Clutch	Dry, double-plate Borg & Beck
Maximum torque	496Nm (365.8lb ft) at 3,800rpm
Firing order	1–5–3–7–4–8–2–6

The gearbox casing hung from the back of the car, mounted longitudinally to the rear of the differential, and a finishing touch was the Ferrari script logo on the rear cover plate of the casing. Bearing in mind the competition use expected when the car was originally designed, the gears were located to enable them to be easily worked on, as gear ratios would have been changed regularly for competition use. To cope with the high power levels, a dry twin-plate hydraulically operated clutch was fitted, supplied by Borg & Beck.

The cylinder block, heads, pistons, timing covers, camshaft covers, sump, gearbox casings, etc, were manufactured from light alloy. The cylinder heads featured four valves per cylinder, and lubrication was via a dry sump, with a remote oil tank located on the right-hand side of the engine compartment, opposite the filler for the 120-litre fuel tank on the left-hand side. The forged-steel DOHC camshafts operated the valves directly via bucket tappets, and the camshaft drive was via twin toothed belts via gears and a tensioner assembly from the crankshaft. The flat plane crankshaft has four crankpins, with two steel connecting rods paired on each crankpin. The same crankshaft was used three years later for the F40 engine. For the first time on a road-going Ferrari, fuel supply and ignition was controlled by a Weber-Marelli

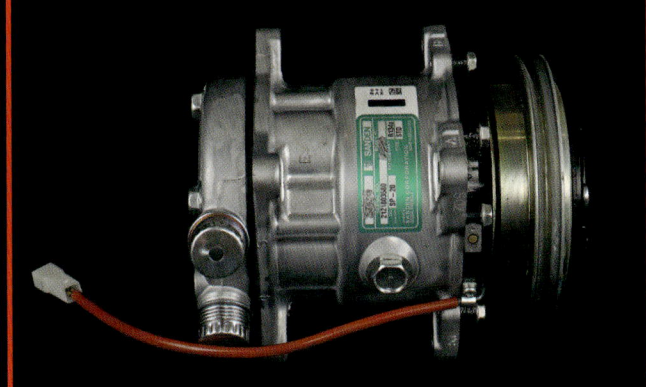

↑ The alloy housing for the water pump and thermostat, which fits at the front of the engine, between the cylinder heads.

↗ The Sanden air conditioning compressor. Air conditioning was an option for the 288 GTO.

→ One of the two distributor caps, with HT leads attached. The distributors are driven from the rear of the inlet camshafts.

↘ A brand-new inlet manifold gasket fitted over the securing studs on one of the cylinder heads.

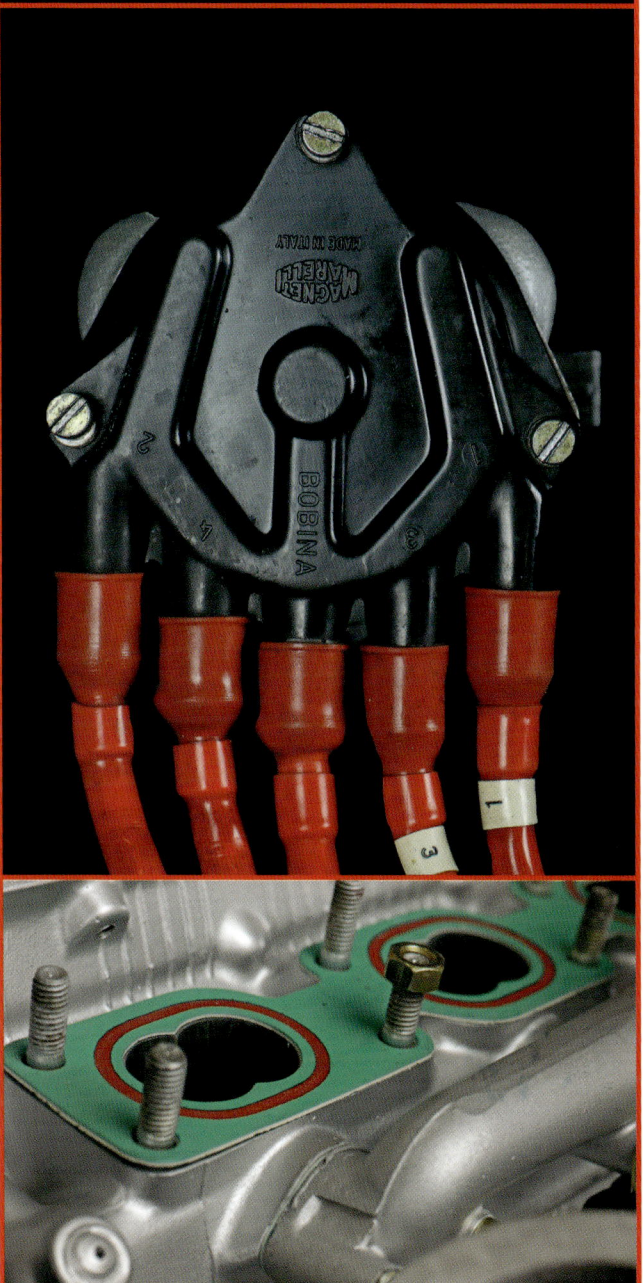

IAW electronic injection system derived from F1. This system provided commands to fire the injectors as the corresponding inlet valve opened. Sensors provided the control unit with information such as engine temperature, throttle position and engine speed in order to compute the optimum fuel/air mixture required by the engine under various operating conditions. The fuel-injection system was indirect, spraying fuel into the inlet tracts, upstream of the valves.

Materazzi later focused on the GTO's F114 B power plant to develop an Evoluzione version, with increased power. Group B regulations had already limited the V8's capacity to 2,885cc, so Materazzi increased the compression ratio from 7.6:1 to 7.8:1, fitted larger turbos, and increased boost pressure substantially from 0.8 bar (11.6psi) to 1.4 bar (24.65psi). This new engine was known as the F114 CR, the 'R' referring to Racing, and produced 530bhp (395kW). After developing the 'CR' engine, the Maranello engineers worked on an even more extreme evolution of the F114 engine. Thanks to larger diameter IHI turbochargers and new inlet manifolds, an upgraded injection/ignition system, and more aggressive cams, power soared to 650bhp (485kW) at 7,800rpm. This engine appeared in 1985 and was the F114 CK. Materazzi

↑ The camshaft covers have red crackle finish. The holes for the centrally mounted spark plugs are clearly visible.

↗ IHI is the abbreviation for Ishikawajima-Harima Heavy Industries, a Japanese heavy engineering company which also produces turbochargers for cars.

↓ The nitrided flatplane crankshaft used in the 2.8-litre V8 of the 288 GTO is the same component used in the later 2.9-litre Ferrari F40 engine.

also involved the famous Michelotto workshop in Padova, which manufactured special parts for the engines and bodywork of the customer competition cars from Maranello. Only five of these F114 CK engines were built, and one was used in a prototype car which featured lightweight Kevlar and composite bodywork, reducing its weight to only 940kg.

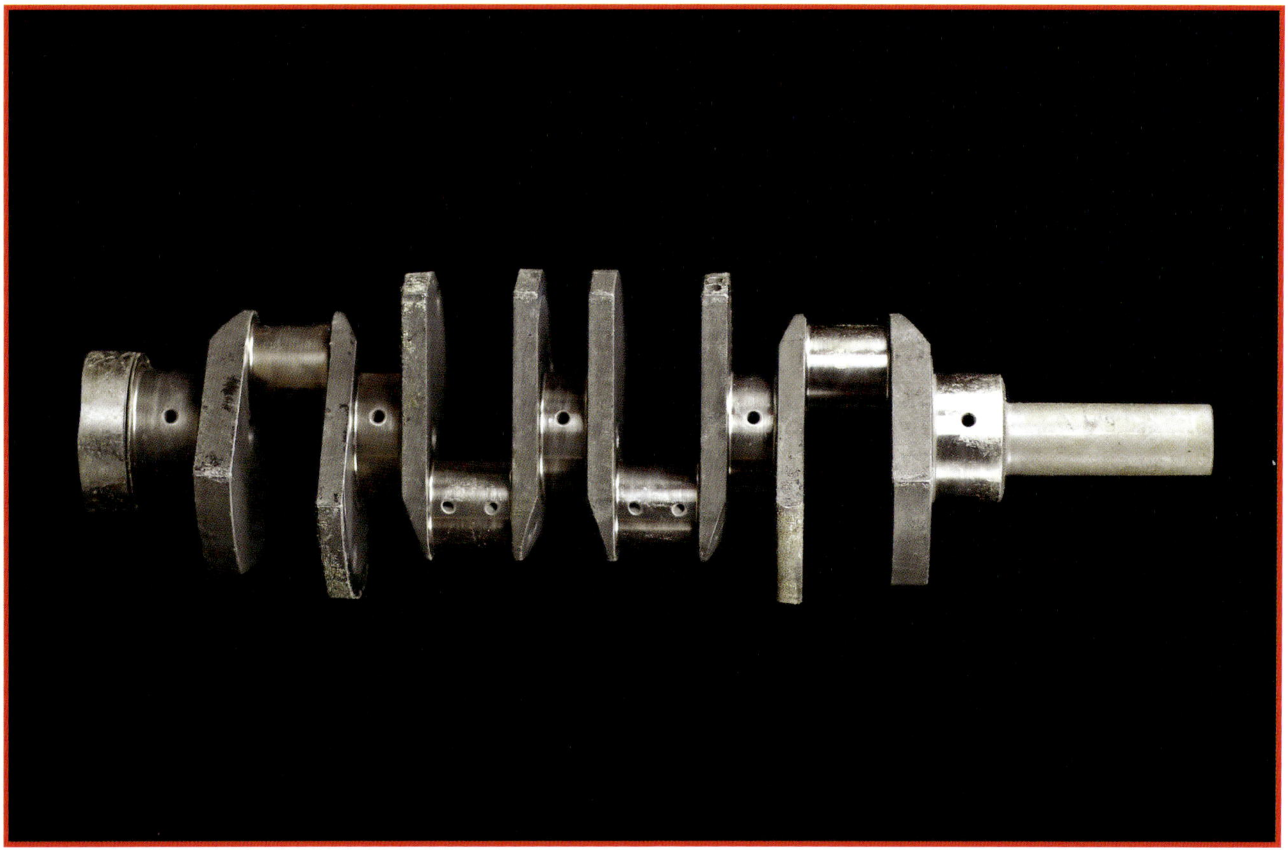

Even though the extreme GTO Evoluzione was never used as Enzo Ferrari would have wanted, this evolution was not built in vain, as it led to the production of Ferrari's 'back to the roots racer for the road' – the spectacular F40. This was unveiled in Enzo Ferrari's presence in 1987,

the last model that he would see launched before his passing the following year, and was called the F40 as a celebration of the company's 40th anniversary. It was equipped with a twin turbocharged 2,936cc V8 based on that of the GTO, producing 478bhp (356kW). As with the GTO, it had a mid-longitudinal engine, with the gearbox located behind the engine. Only 400 examples were scheduled to be built, but, due to overwhelming demand, 1,311 were eventually made. The Ferrari philosophy of producing extreme limited-production-run cars had just begun, and these subsequent cars all owe something to some degree to the GTO (288).

↖ A close-up view of the front end of the engine with the timing cover removed, showing the the end of the crankshaft (with key at the top) and the timing belt idler sprockets above (painted black).

↑ The twin-plate clutch assembly with the inboard friction disc removed showing the outboard friction disc and pressure plate.

↓ The Ferrari logo is cast into the end of the gearbox casing, and is visible with the engine/transmission mounted in the car.

181

GTO (288): Twin-turbo supercar (1984)

↑ To meet customer demand, 272 cars were built instead of the planned 200 – all were sold before production began.

↑ The longitudinal gearbox is located at the rear of the engine for optimum weight distribution. It is visible in this rear view.

➔ The bulging wheel arches front and rear accommodate wider split rim wheels and tyres than fitted to the 308 GTB" – note, the mirrors are door mounted.

↘ Paired driving lights are fitted in each extremity of the radiator grille, just above the brake cooling ducts in the deep front spoiler.

↘↘ Gran Turismo Omologato (GTO) is the legendary name inherited from the 1962 and 1964 Ferrari GTO.

↘↘↘ Three 'gills' in each rear wing allow hot air to escape from the engine compartment and add to the aggressive styling.

↓ Pininfarina was able to create an aggressive interpretation of the well-known shape of the previous 308 GTB.

GTO (288): Twin-turbo supercar (1984)

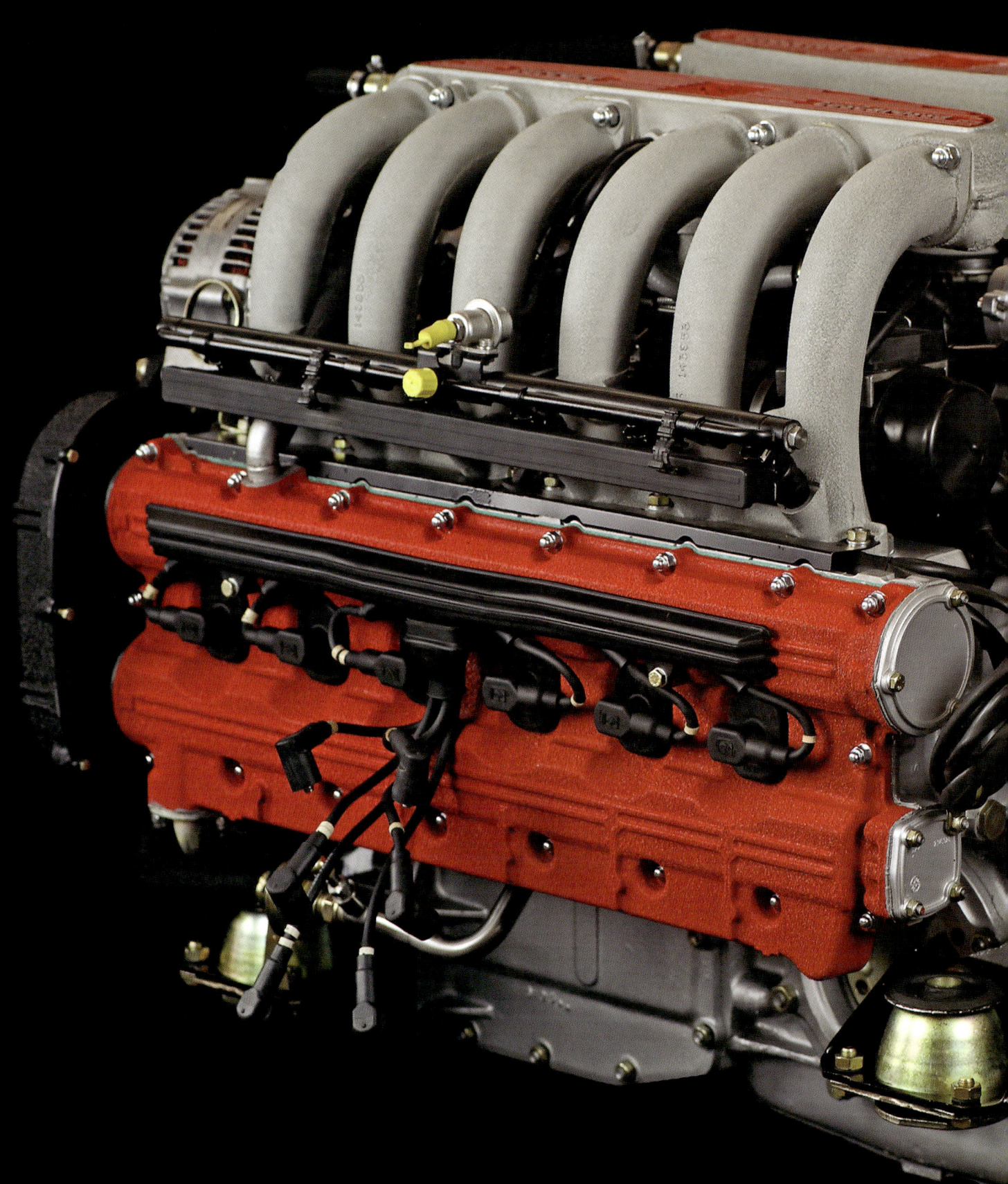

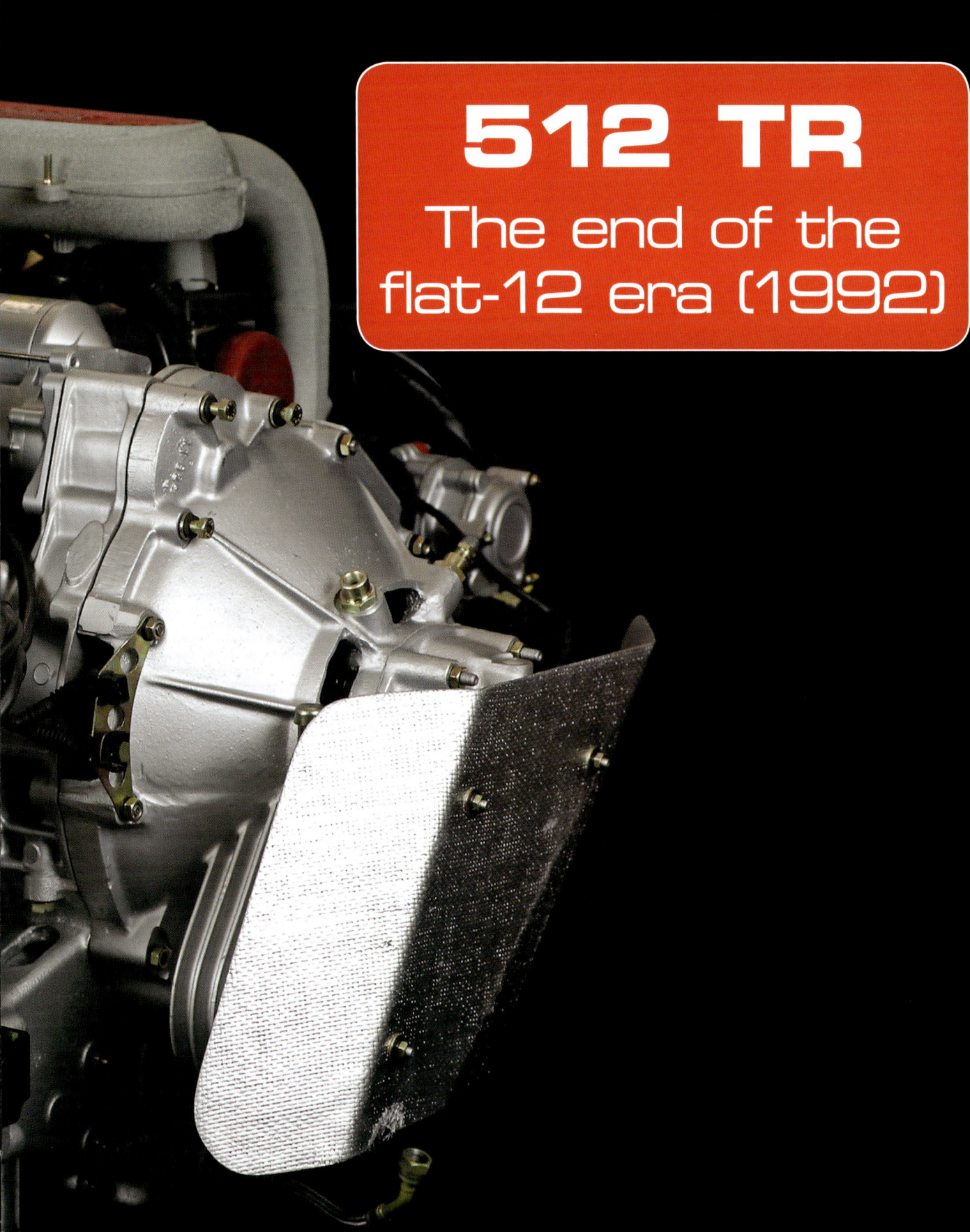

512 TR
The end of the flat-12 era (1992)

← One of the 12 shallow-skirt, lightweight forged-alloy pistons, shown with piston rings removed.

↙ The Ferrari logo (along with 'testarossa') is cast into the plenum chambers rather than into the camshaft covers.

The flat-12 180° vee configuration that Maranello employed for its F1 cars for a decade (from 1970 to 1980) had a longer life on road-going Ferraris. Following the introduction of the first 'Boxer' road car – the 1971 365 GT4 BB – Ferrari continued to develop the flat-12 engine for road use for a further 25 years, the engine evolving to incorporate technological improvements which brought improvements in performance. One of the final evolutions of the engine was unveiled in 1992 at the Los Angeles Motor Show, and was derived from the impressive 1984 Testarossa – a Ferrari with enormous presence due to its vast width and low stance. The car making its debut in Los Angeles was the 512 TR (Testa Rossa), which featured a mid-mounted longitudinal 5.0-litre V12 180° engine – code F113 D – which produced 422bhp (315kW) at 6,750rpm.

Testarossa was an almost mythical name in the Ferrari world, having originated from the 1956 500 TR (Testa Rossa) sports racing car, and its successor the 500 TRC, which was followed by the 250 TR in 1957. The 500 TR was a beautiful spider with bodywork by Scaglietti, intended as a customer car to compete with the Jaguar D-type and Maserati A6GCS, and the 500 TRC was a development of the theme to comply with new Group C regulations in 1957, hence the C suffix. The 250 TR went on to dominate sports-car racing at the end of the 1950s and early 1960s. The name Testa Rossa for both these cars originated from their red-painted cam covers. While the 500 TR was powered by a Lampredi-designed inline four-cylinder engine, the 250 TR featured a V12 engine based on the original Colombo 'short block' design.

At the 1984 Paris Motor Show, Ferrari unveiled an astonishing new top-of-the-range GT car designed by Pininfarina. Its shape was innovative, almost provocative, with aggressive, sharp styling, as if to say to other sport-car manufacturers (in particular Lamborghini): 'Here we are! This is our weapon.' It should be noted that the Testarossa had been designed as a 'world car' from the outset, that is to say that it met emission and crash test standards worldwide,

↖ The forged-steel connecting rods have horizontally split big-ends, with the bearing caps secured by key bolts and nuts.

← A close-up view of one of the inlet manifolds, showing the inlet tracts, with the fuel-injector housings above them.

➔ The central pair of exhaust ports bound the secondary-air injection-ports (part of the exhaust-emissions-control system) on each cylinder head.

particularly important for the large and lucrative US market, where the previous 'Boxer' models had not been sold for these reasons. The Testarossa was powered by a mid-mounted V12 180° engine, code number F113 A, located longitudinally, with a capacity of 4,943cc, the same as that of the other V12 'Boxer' engines in the 113 family, which were derived from Ferrari's first flat-12 road-car engine used in the 365 GT4 BB (see pages 122 to 137).

Enzo Ferrari's decision to use the name Testarossa for the berlinetta revealed in 1984, and the subsequent decision by the Ferrari marketing department to continue using the name for the 512 TR – an evolution of the 1984 Testarossa – could be considered as controversial, as neither of these road cars had any connection to the revered Testa Rossa sports-racing cars. Arguably, the Testarossa road cars and the sports-racing cars from which the name was taken were at opposite ends of the mechanical and aesthetic spectrum. At this time Ferrari seemed to be using names of their revered sports racing models to give kudos to their current production cars, as in 1980 they had used the Mondial name for their new V8 2+2 model, which replaced the Dino 308 GT4.

Stepping forward 36 years from the original 500 TR, we arrive at the 512 TR unveiled in 1992, which continued the large berlinetta philosophy of the 1984 Testarossa, albeit with a more

⬇ A view inside the cylinder-head combustion chambers, showing the valves in place and the threaded spark-plug holes in the centres of the combustion chambers.

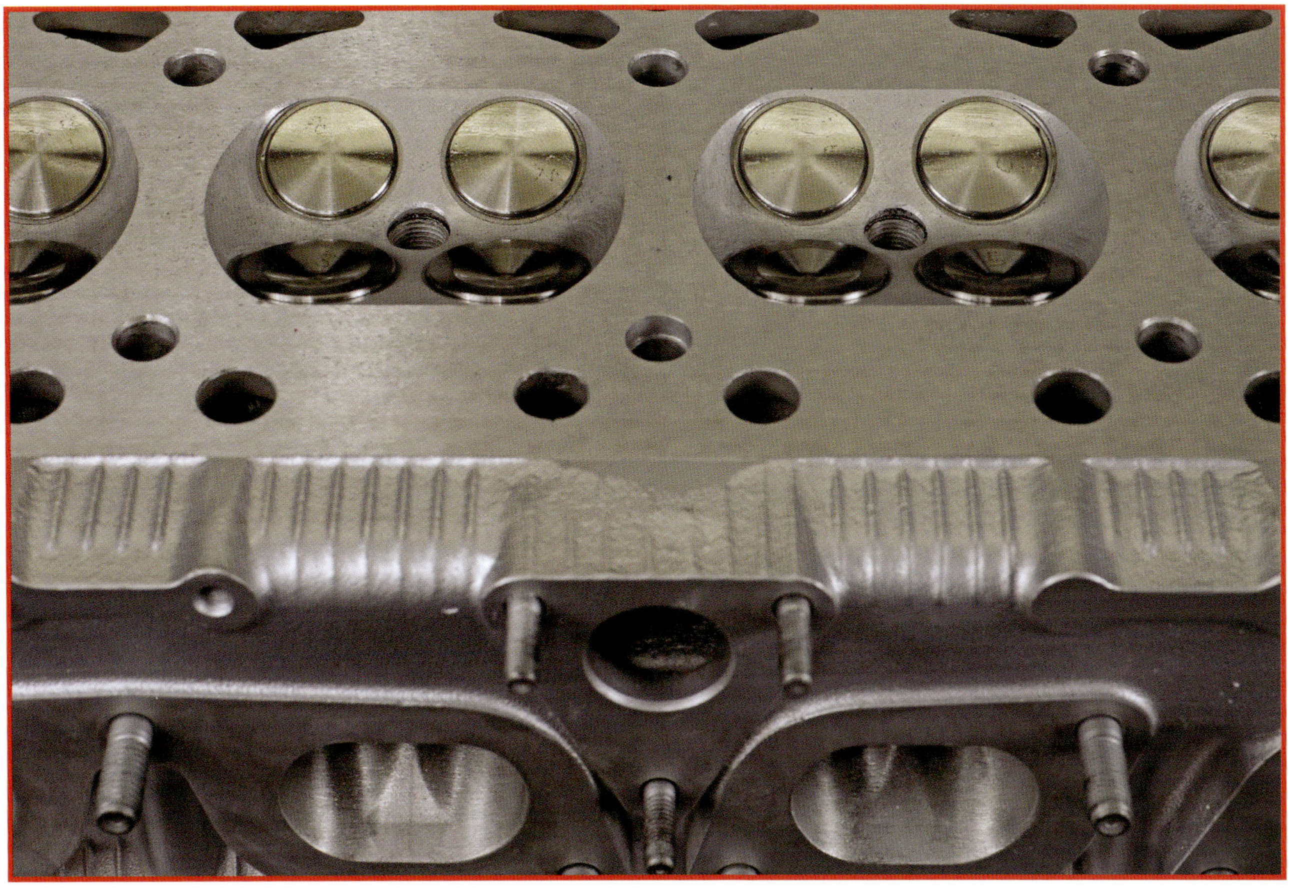

powerful 113-series V12 180° engine. This car was conceived to compete with Lamborghini's new 5.7-litre Diablo, which had captured the imagination of the press and public alike.

The 512 TR's engine, code number F113 D, was built almost entirely from light alloy, with significant modifications from its ancestor used in the Testarossa, including new, shallow-skirt pistons, and a modified crankshaft. The total displacement of this 113 D engine was 4,943.04cc (identical to the 1984 Testarossa), and the unitary capacity was 411.92cc. The bore and stroke was 82mm x 78mm. Nikasil-coated cylinder liners were used, and the DOHC camshaft drive was via toothed belts driven via sprockets from the crankshaft. As with the F113 A engine, the 113 D featured four valves per cylinder, operated directly by steel camshafts (with modified cam profiles) via bucket tappets. The inlet tracts were modified to improve flow and efficiency. As with the 1984 Testarossa, the 512 TR featured twin rear side-mounted cooling radiators, rather than the more usual front-mounted radiator. This led to the prominent strakes on the flanks of the car – a key feature of the styling – which fed cooling air to these radiators. Fuel supply and ignition were via a Bosch Motronic ME 2.7 electronic injection system per bank (the same system as used on the early 116-family engines appearing in the 456 GT). The firing order was

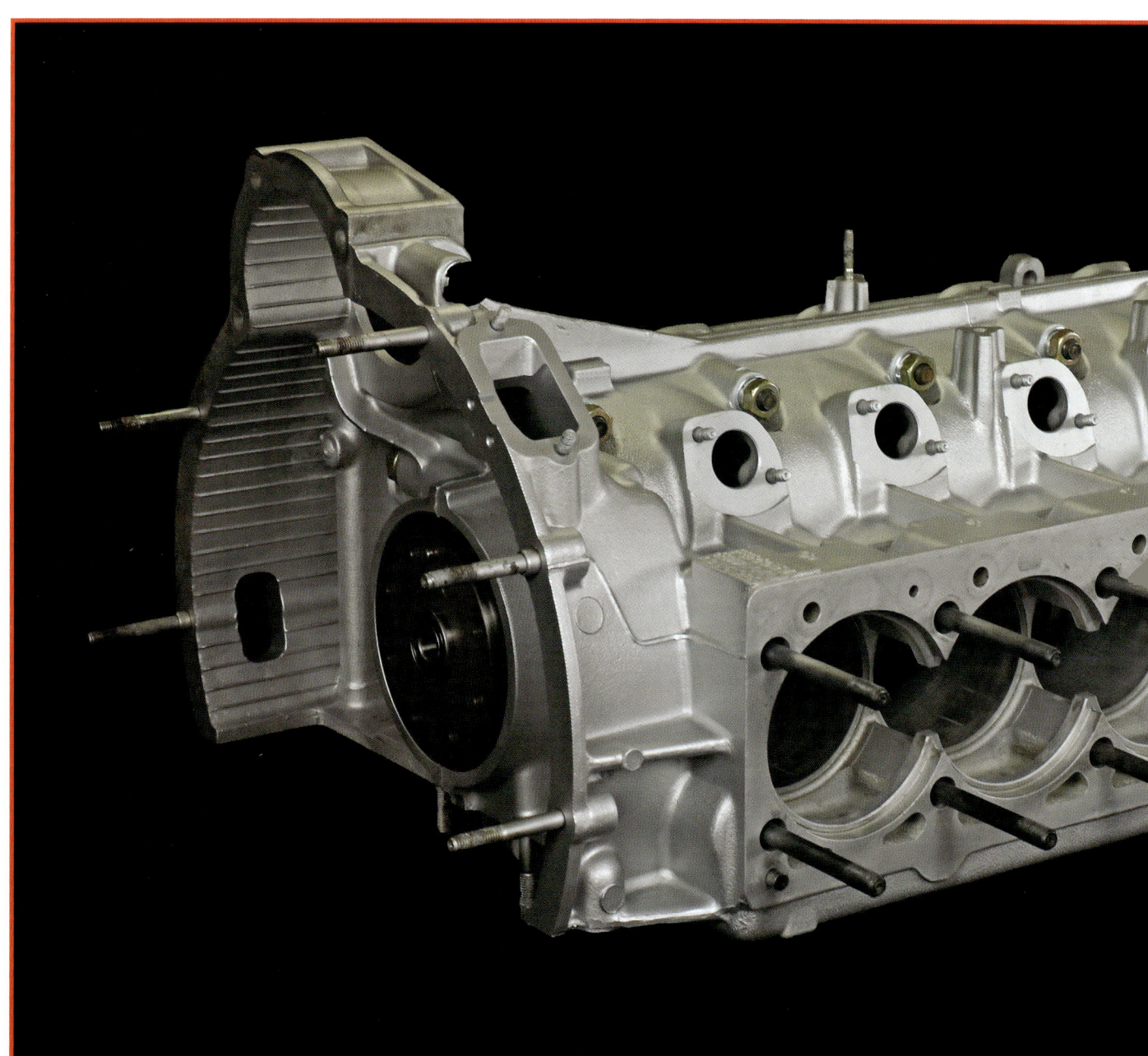

1–9–5–12–3–8–6–10–2–7–4–11. Lubrication was via a dry sump. The compression ratio of the F113 D was increased to 10:1 (instead of 9.3:1 for the Testarossa). The clutch was a single, dry-plate unit, and the 512 TR featured a modified gearbox which provided a smoother gearchange and improved reliability. Specific power for the 5.0-litre flat-12 was 86bhp/litre (64kW/litre) – up from the 78bhp/litre (58kW/litre) of the Testarossa. The results of these improvements were immediately evident in the overall performance of the engine, with a 37bhp (28kW) improvement in maximum power, to 422bhp (315kW) at 6,750rpm, with a slight improvement in torque to 491Nm (362lb ft) at 5,500rpm. All this took the maximum speed to a remarkable 195mph (314kmh), with a 0–62mph (0–100kmh) time of 4.8 seconds!

The mid-engine layout, with the engine located between the axles, provided excellent weight distribution, providing optimum stability and handling, with a weight distribution of 41% front and 59% rear.

The suspension was modified, with the adoption of twin gas-filled dampers at each corner, and larger cross-drilled brake discs were fitted – 315mm diameter at the front, and 310mm at the rear.

Modifications and improvements were also made to the bodywork compared with the Testarossa, with revised styling for the nose and engine cover. Compared with the Testarossa, the 512 TR bodywork was 5mm shorter and 5mm higher. There were changes to the front and rear tracks, the front increasing by 14mm, and the rear being reduced by 16mm, with a change in wheel size from 16-inch to 18-inch diameter, and tyre profile (235/40 ZR 18 at the front axle and 295/35 ZR 18 at the rear), which accounted for the difference in the overall height of the car. Thanks to the use of lighter materials for the bonnet and engine cover, the weight of the 512 TR decreased to 1,473kg, from the 1,506kg of the Testarossa.

One of the most prominent styling features of both the Testarossa and 512 TR was the side strakes, sometimes referred to as 'cheese graters' or 'egg slicers', that ran through the door panels into the rear wings. Another unusual feature of both models was a rear light arrangement that differed from Ferrari's 'standard' circular layout, as the rectangular combination light units were hidden behind a full width satin-black-finished slatted grille. The interior of the 512 TR was redesigned, with a new upgraded, updated and more functional cockpit, a brand-new steering wheel (with air bag) and new leather seats.

The Testarossa/512 TR/F512 M series ran from 1984 to 1996, in four different versions, and around 10,000 cars were built: 7,177 examples of the Testarossa (first and second series – essentially series 1 cars had single nut wheel fixing and a single exterior mirror and series 2 cars had five-bolt wheel fixing and paired mirrors), 2,261 examples of the 512 TR, and just 501 examples of the F512 M, the final version, built from 1994 to 1996. Among the large number of cars produced was a one-off spider for Fiat President Gianni Agnelli, who ordered his car to mark the 20th anniversary of becoming President of the multinational company FIAT S.p.A. Agnelli's car was painted in silver, with a blue stripe around the cabin and base of the bodywork, a vestigial soft top, and a blue leather interior. This car was sold in 2016 at auction

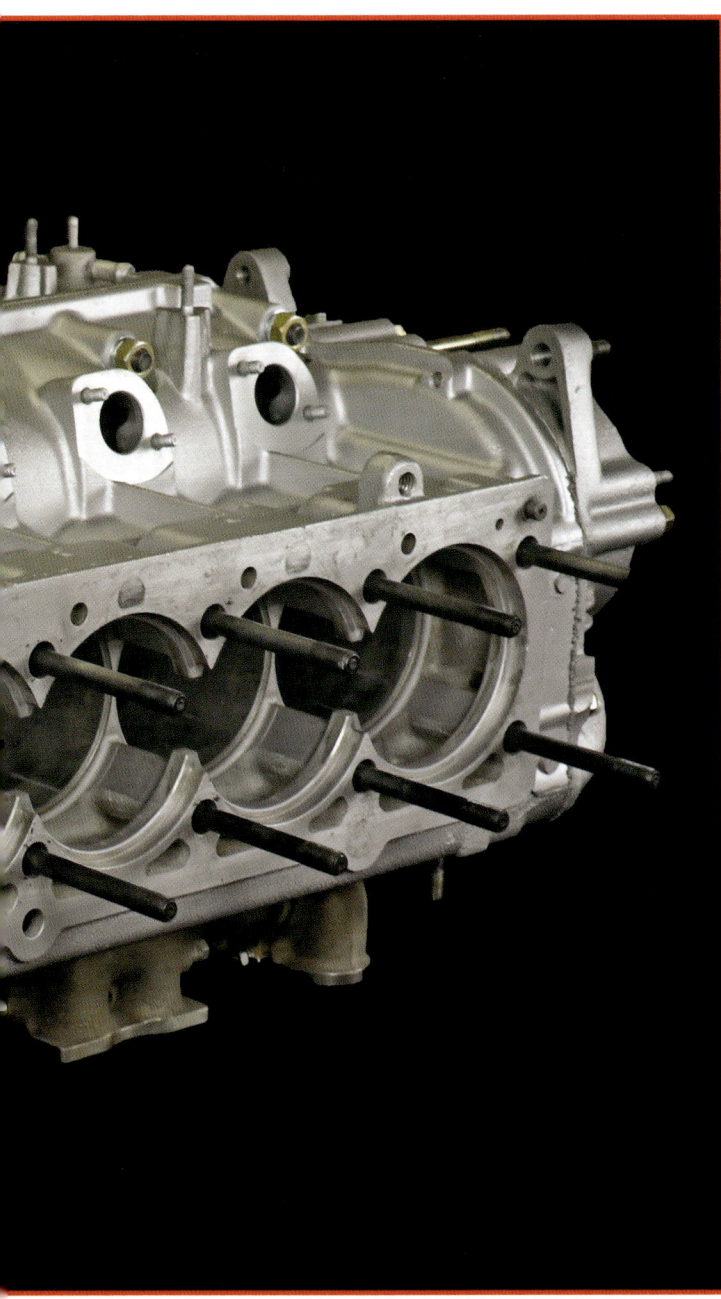

← **The complete cylinder block (two halves bolted together) with the crankshaft, but no cylinder liners fitted.**

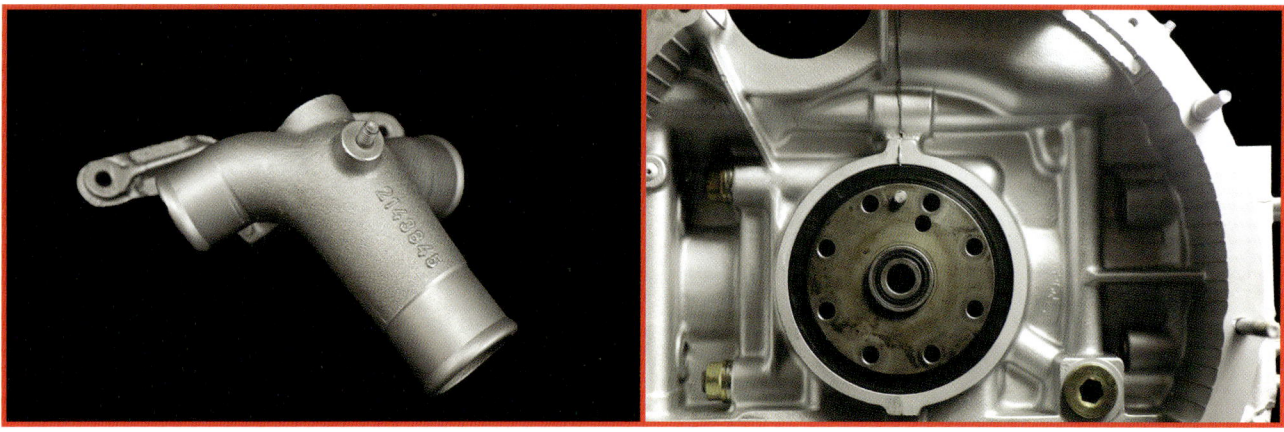

↑ Most of the engine covers and housings, including this coolant elbow, are cast from light alloy.

↑ A view of the rear of the cylinder block showing the flywheel-mounting flange on the crankshaft.

for 1,210,080 Euros! It also won the Best of Show Street Car prize at the 70th Anniversary Ferrari celebration at Maranello/Fiorano in September 2017. Subsequently, the car was exhibited from November 2017 to April 2018 at the Design Museum in London, at the 'Ferrari Under the Skin' exhibition. Pininfarina are understood to have built a spider example – said to have been commissioned by Olivier Gendebien, who won at Le Mans in 1958 driving a 'true' Testa Rossa, a 250

→ A view inside the top of one of the cylinder heads showing the valves in place, but camshafts removed.

↘ One of the Nikasil-coated cylinder liners.

↓ One of the inlet manifold/plenum chamber assemblies. Note the 'Ferrari' and 'testarossa' script cast into the plenum chamber.

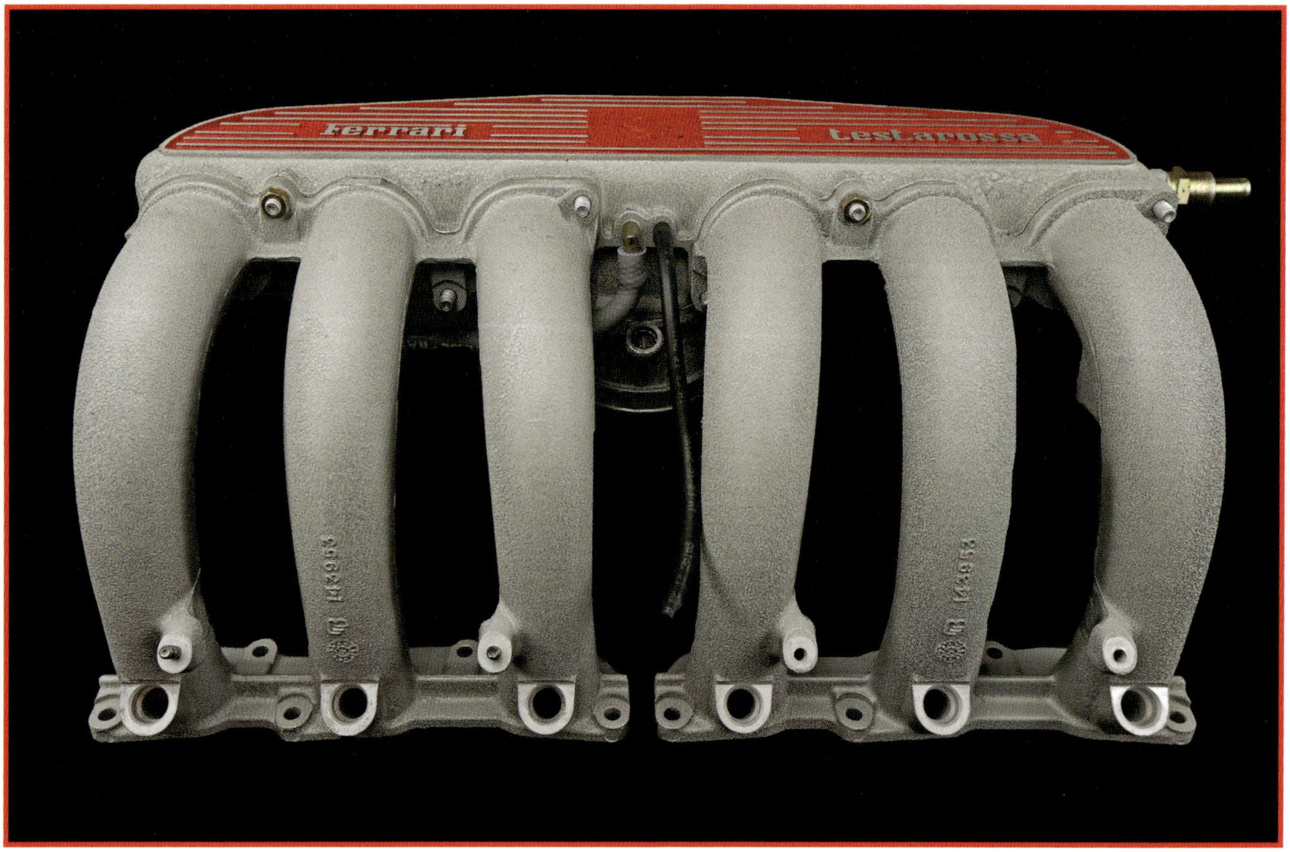

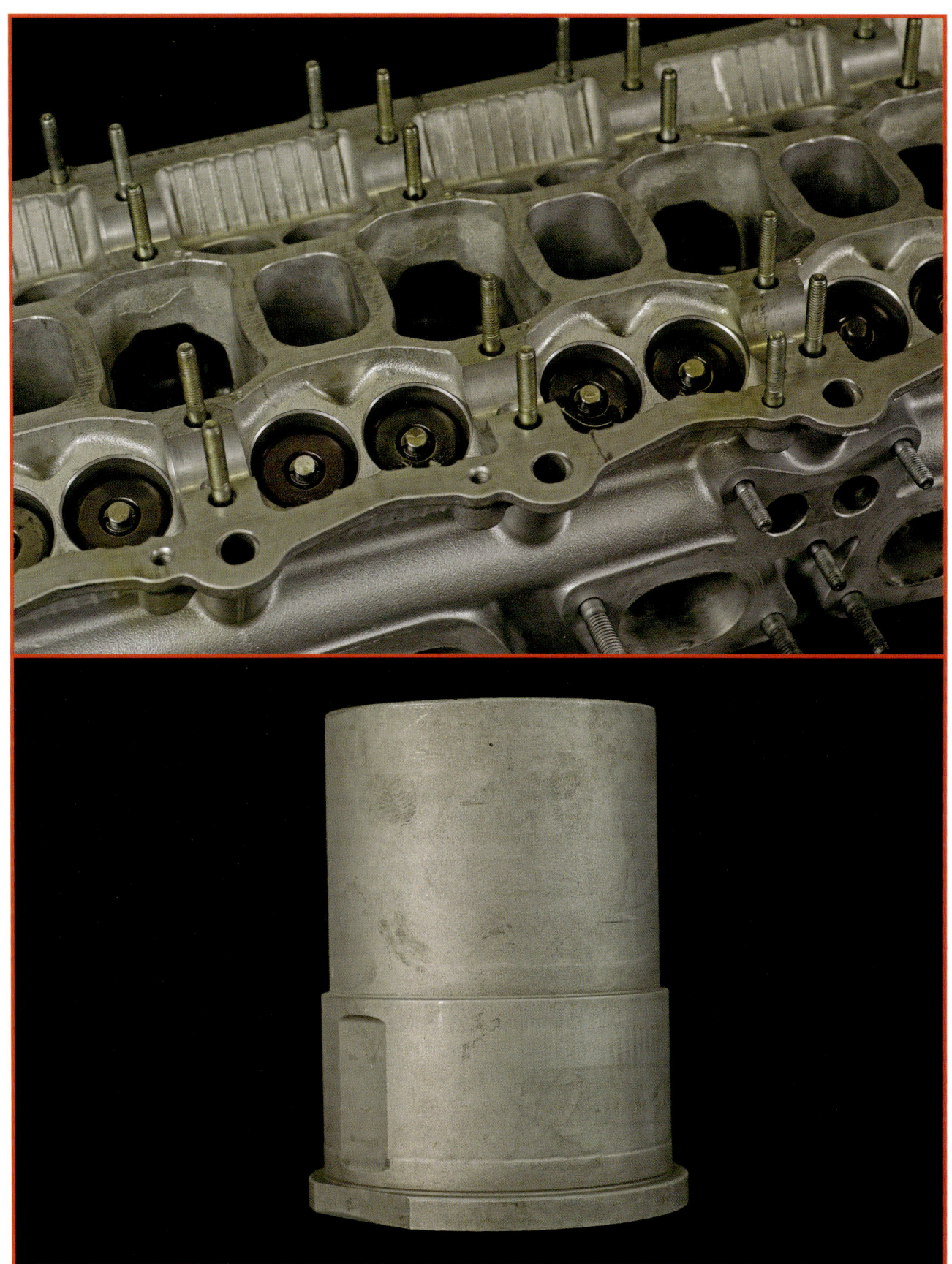

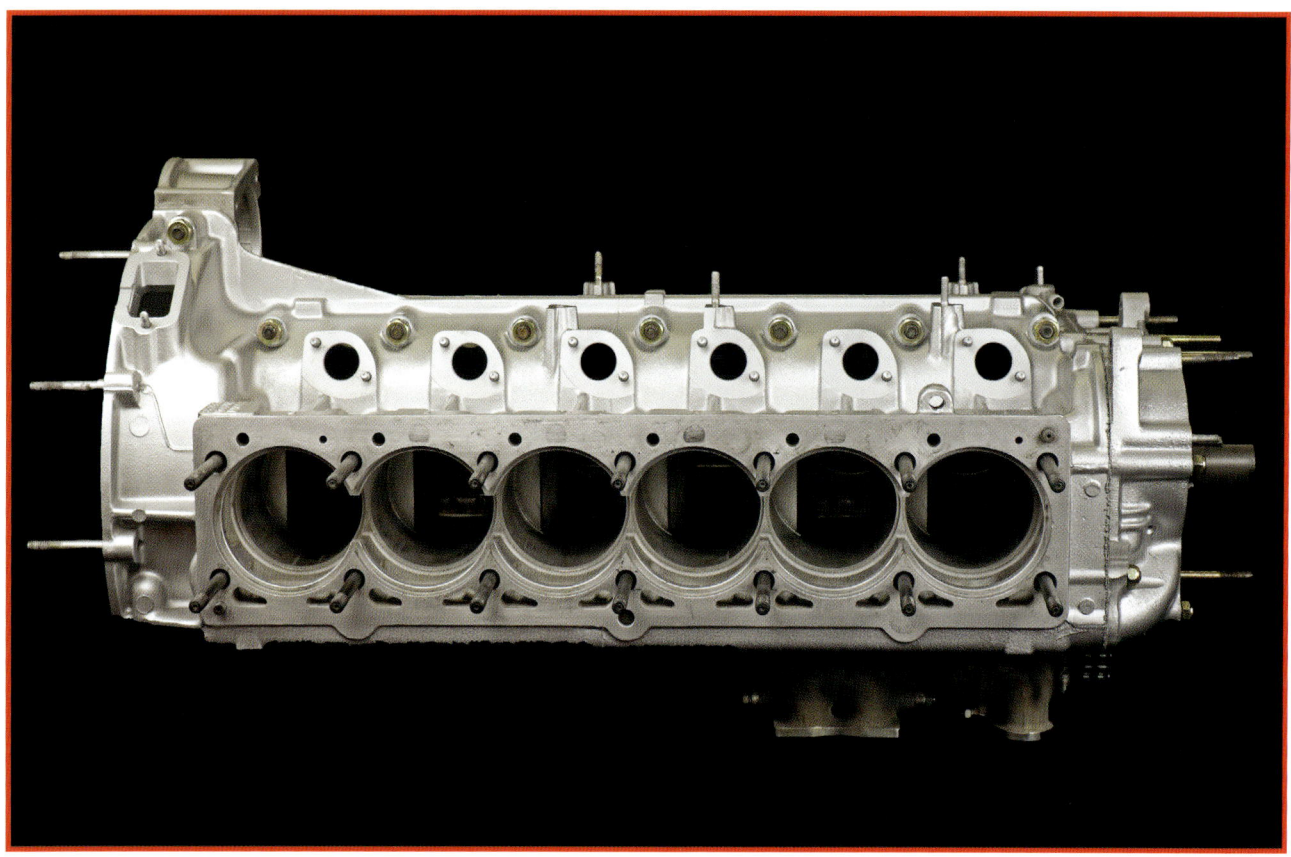

↑ A side view of the cylinder block, showing the bores for the cylinder liners.

FERRARI 512 TR – TECHNICAL DATA

Engine code	F113 D
Engine type	Mid-rear, longitudinal, V12, 180°
Bore and stroke	82 x 78mm (3.22 x 3.07in)
Total capacity	4,943.04cc (301.64cu in)
Unitary capacity	411.92cc (25.13cu in)
Compression ratio	10:1
Maximum power	423bhp (315kW) at 6,750rpm
Power per litre	86bhp/litre (64kW/litre)
Valve operation	Double overhead camshafts per bank, four valves per cylinder
Fuel feed	Bosch Motronic M2.7 electronic injection
Ignition	Bosch Motronic M2.7 electronic, single spark plug per cylinder
Lubrication	Dry sump
Clutch	Dry, single plate
Maximum torque	491Nm (362.1lb ft) at 5,500rpm
Firing order	1–9–5–12–3–8–6–10–2–7–4–11

TR – which was built in 1989. This car was painted in metallic black, with black retractable roof and a red interior. It featured in the Italian motoring magazine *Auto Capital* in period. Pininfarina also built a series of ten Testarossa spiders for the Brunei Royal Family, in a variety of colours.

Two other famous Testarossas that contributed to the success of, and promoted, the car in the US market, were the pair gifted by the Maranello factory to Hollywood for the well-known TV series *Miami Vice*. Universal Studios initially used a fake 365 GTS4, built on a Corvette C3 chassis, in the first series, but the Ferrari lawyers did not appreciate this, and in order to resolve the problem, Ferrari agreed with the studio that the fake 'Daytona Spider' would meet a 'catastrophic' end, to be replaced by the Testarossas. Initially the cars supplied were black, but in order to make them more suitable for night shooting, they were repainted white.

As mentioned previously, the final evolution of the Testarossa, and the final Ferrari road car to use the mid-mounted longitudinal flat-12 engine, was the F512 M, which was introduced at the 1994 Paris Auto Show. Ferrari dropped the TR suffix and added the M that stood for Modificata (Modified). The F signified 'Ferrari', and was used during that period in the nomenclature for several berlinettas (such as the F355). With the engine code number 113 G, the F512 M featured improved weight distribution – 42% front

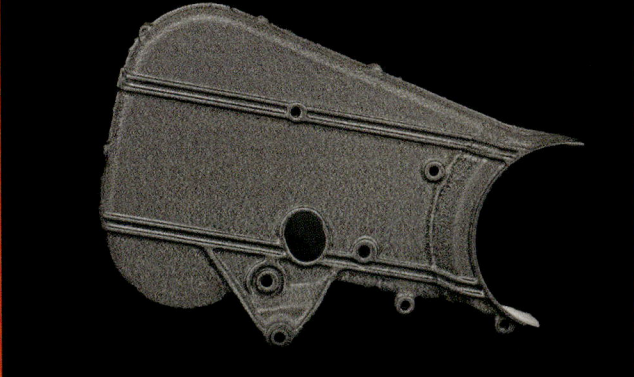

↑ A view of one of the red-painted camshaft covers, with holes for the spark plugs in the centre.

↗ One of the cast-alloy timing covers, with elongated hole to accommodate the timing-belt tensioner.

→ The cast-alloy inlet manifolds fit between the cylinder heads and the plenum chambers.

↓ The Nippondenso alternator, mounted on the front of the engine, is belt-driven from the crankshaft.

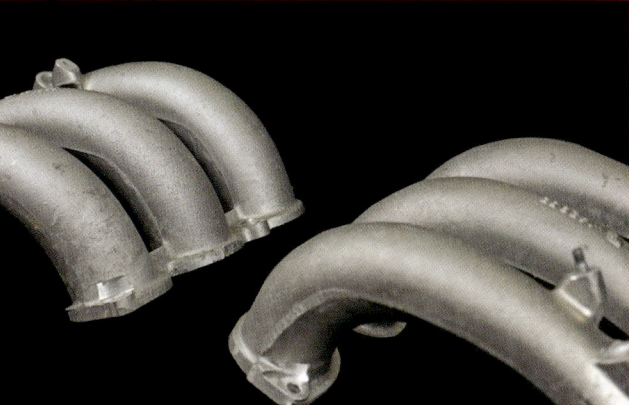

and 58% rear. This berlinetta produced 434bhp (324kW) at 6,750rpm, 12bhp (9kW) more than the previous 512 TR. The compression ratio was increased to 10.4:1, and the engine featured a new lightened crankshaft and titanium connecting rods. This was the final chapter in the Ferrari flat-12 road-car story, after 23 years of commercial success. After this period (in reality from 1992, with the unveiling of the 456 GT 2+2), the Maranello factory relied on a new family of V12 65° engines, initially fitted in a front longitudinal position, then in a mid-mounted location in the F50 and Enzo, and with the addition of hybrid technology, in the LaFerrari and LaFerrari Aperta. With these new mechanical layouts, we arrive at the present, looking towards Ferrari's technological route to the future.

↑ The 12 forged-alloy pistons and steel connecting rods form an impressive line-up.

→ A top view of the assembled engine, with plenum chambers and inlet manifolds dominating the view, the air-conditioning compressor (bottom left), the alternator (bottom right) and the starter motor (top, between the plenum chambers).

↓ A view of one of the cylinder heads, showing the exhaust ports and the studs for the camshaft cover (top).

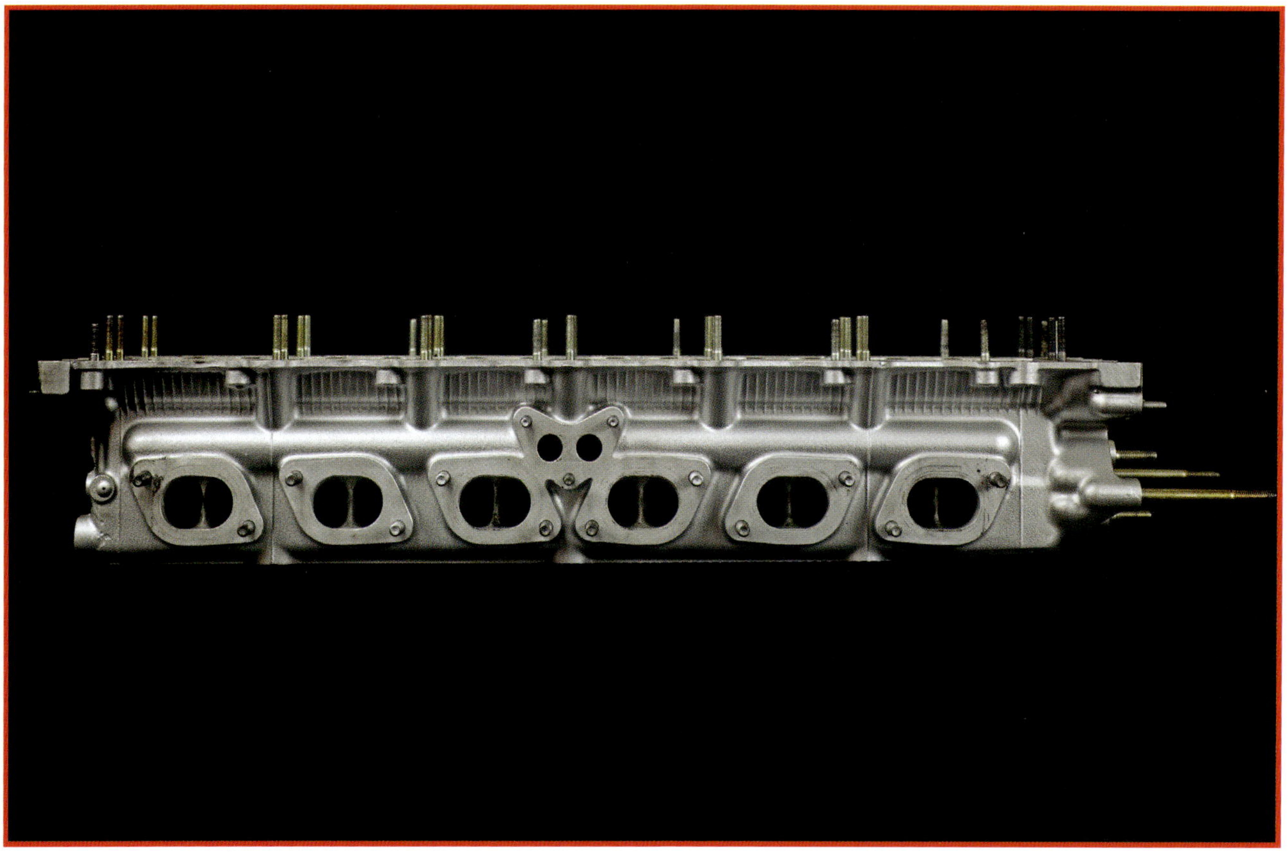

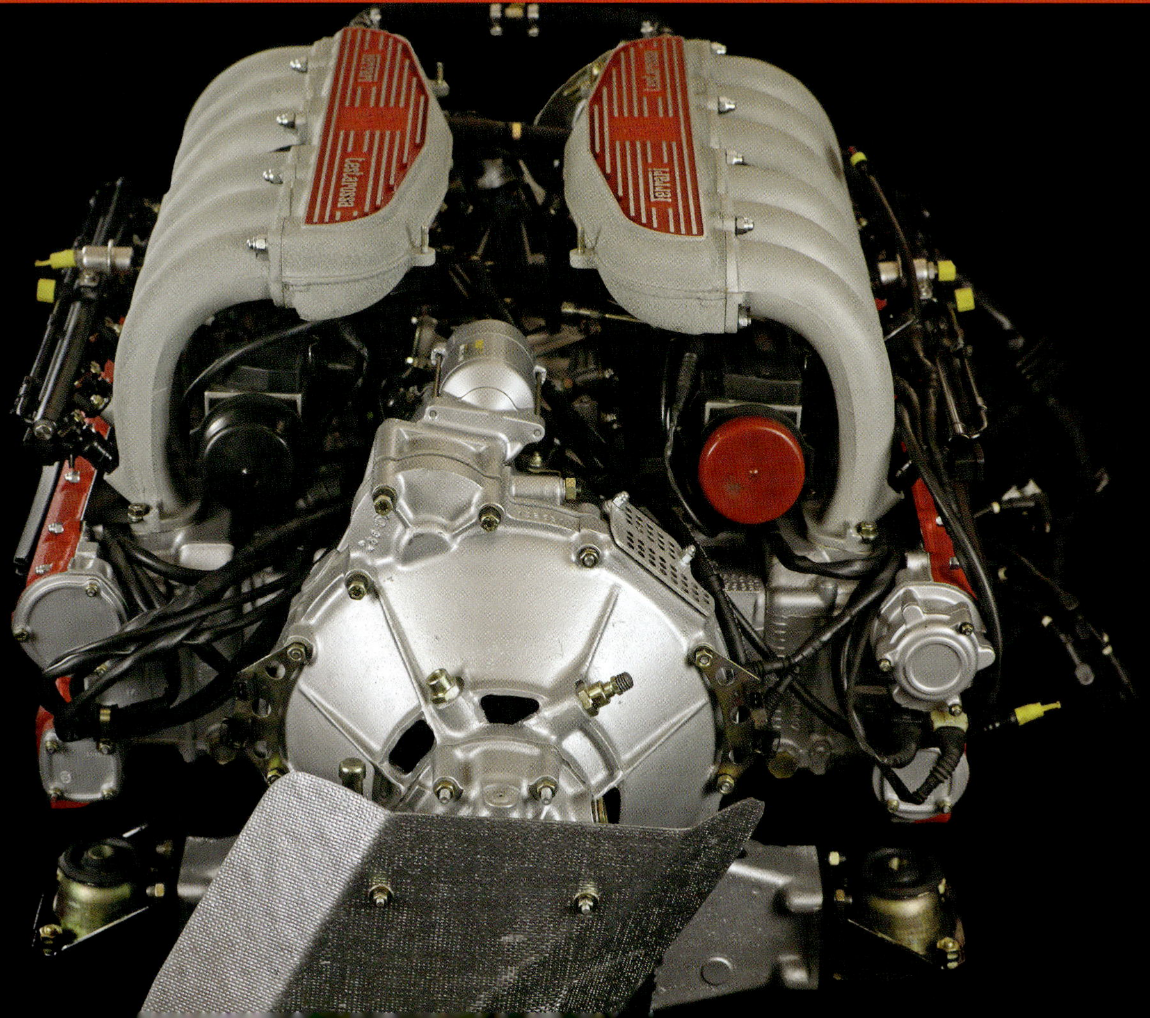

↑ The front view of the 512 TR is similar to that of the Testarossa. The later 512 M featured Plexiglas-covered headlights.

↑ The width of the car is obvious from this imposing rear view, with broad tail and wide rear tyres.

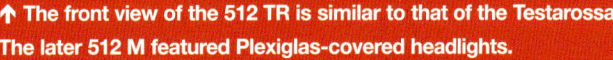

➔ One of the most prominent styling features is the side strakes, sometimes referred to as 'cheese graters' or 'egg slicers'!

↘ The five-spoke alloy wheels, with a Ferrari logo on the centre caps, cover large drilled brake discs.

↘↘ Unusually for a Ferrari, the rear light clusters were hidden behind a satin-black-finished slatted grille.

↘↘↘ The elegant 'twin boom' door mirror that featured on the second series Testarossas and subsequent models.

↓ The side view is dominated by the strakes running from the doors to the rear wings. The apertures in the wings, behind the strakes, feed air to the side-mounted radiators.

512 TR: The end of the flat-12 era (1992)

456 GT M
V12 back to the front (1998)

← The F116 cylinder block was the first road-going 12-cylinder Ferrari with a vee angle of 65° instead of the previous 60°.

↙ The engine code and 'internal identification number' are stamped into the cylinder block.

A true revolution in the Maranello factory's V12 DOHC configuration took place with the creation of a new engine family – the F116/F133 – the first Ferrari road-going 12-cylinder engine with a vee angle of 65°, instead of the previous 60° – an important turning point in the story of the Ferrari V12 engine, and a configuration which has been maintained since then for all Ferrari V12 engines to the present day. The first engine of this series was the 116 B, unveiled in 1992, and fitted longitudinally under the front bonnet of the 456 GT 2+2, designed by Pininfarina. This brand-new 5.5-litre engine saw Ferrari return to its historic model nomenclature, designating the new coupé by the engine swept volume of each cylinder – 456cc. The 116 B engine was a very powerful unit, capable of punching out 436bhp (325kW) at 6,250rpm, and pushing the considerable weight (1,790kg) of the 456 GT to a speed of around 186mph (300kmh) – absolutely worthy of the high standards of the Maranello factory.

The 456 GT launch celebrated the anniversary of the partnership between Enzo Ferrari and Jacques Swaters – the Belgian racing driver and then Ferrari dealer, who founded the famous Ecurie Francorchamps racing team, a racing stable mainly associated with Ferrari, in 1952. So, in September 1992, the Ferrari factory revealed its new 456 GT 2+2 to the guests at Ecurie/Garage Francorchamps 40th anniversary celebrations at a gala dinner at the Cinquantenaire in Brussels . With this superb four-seater, officially unveiled one month later at the Paris Motor Show, Ferrari launched its new big-displacement engine family (the largest engine produced by Ferrari at the time), carrying the code number F116, and then later, for the 550 Maranello, with type number F133. The revolutionary F116 (the engine shown in this chapter is that of the 456 GT M, code number F116 C, almost identical to the 116 B) was a completely new project, and the engine had a capacity of 5,474cc, with 48 valves (four per cylinder). The bore was 88mm and the stroke 75mm, producing the unitary capacity of 456.16cc. The cylinder block, heads, sump, timing covers and cam covers were all manufactured from light alloy.

↖ The light-alloy cylinder head features four valves per cylinder, with the spark plug positioned in the centre of the valves.

← A view of the bottom of the cylinder block, showing the bearing locations and the main-bearing-cap studs.

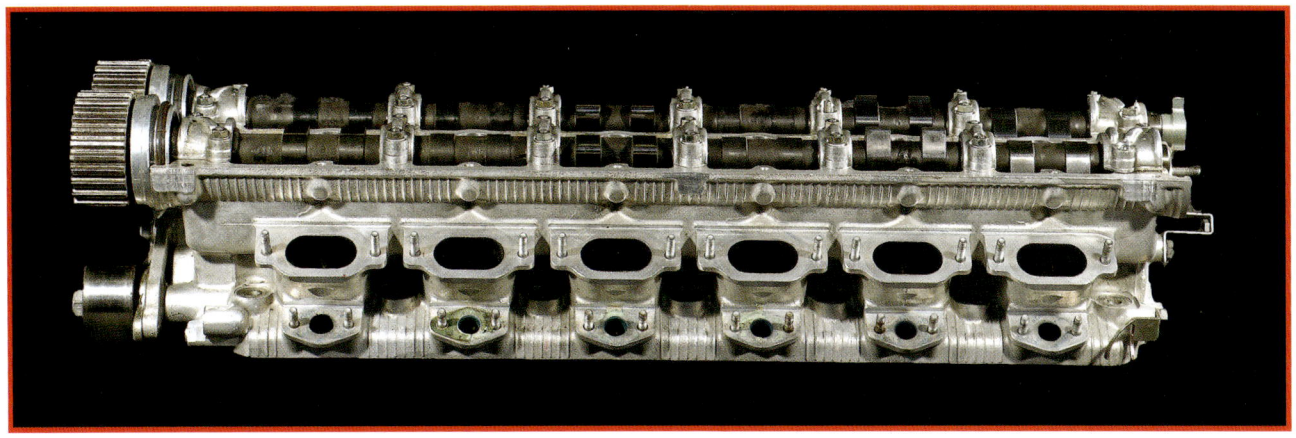

↑ **One of the cylinder heads, with its two camshafts (with drive sprockets fitted) in place.**

The steel, nitrided crankshaft was supported by seven main bearings, and was fitted with a torsional damper at the front end. The alloy cylinder liners were treated with Nikasil. The pistons were light alloy, with shallow skirts to reduce weight, while the connecting rods were titanium – lighter and stronger than the steel ones employed on previous engines. The dry, single-plate clutch was manufactured by the French company Valeo. Lubrication was via a dry sump, providing a more compact engine, enabling it to be fitted lower in the chassis, and helping to avoid oil starvation during sporty driving. The lubrication system featured twin oil pumps, twin filters and an oil cooler integral with the engine-cooling radiator. The gearbox was integral with the rear axle, as was the case on previous cars (275 GTB/GTS, 330 GTC/GTS, 365 GTC/

↓ **A view of the cylinder block showing the crankshaft main-bearing locations and the hole for the starter motor (top left).**

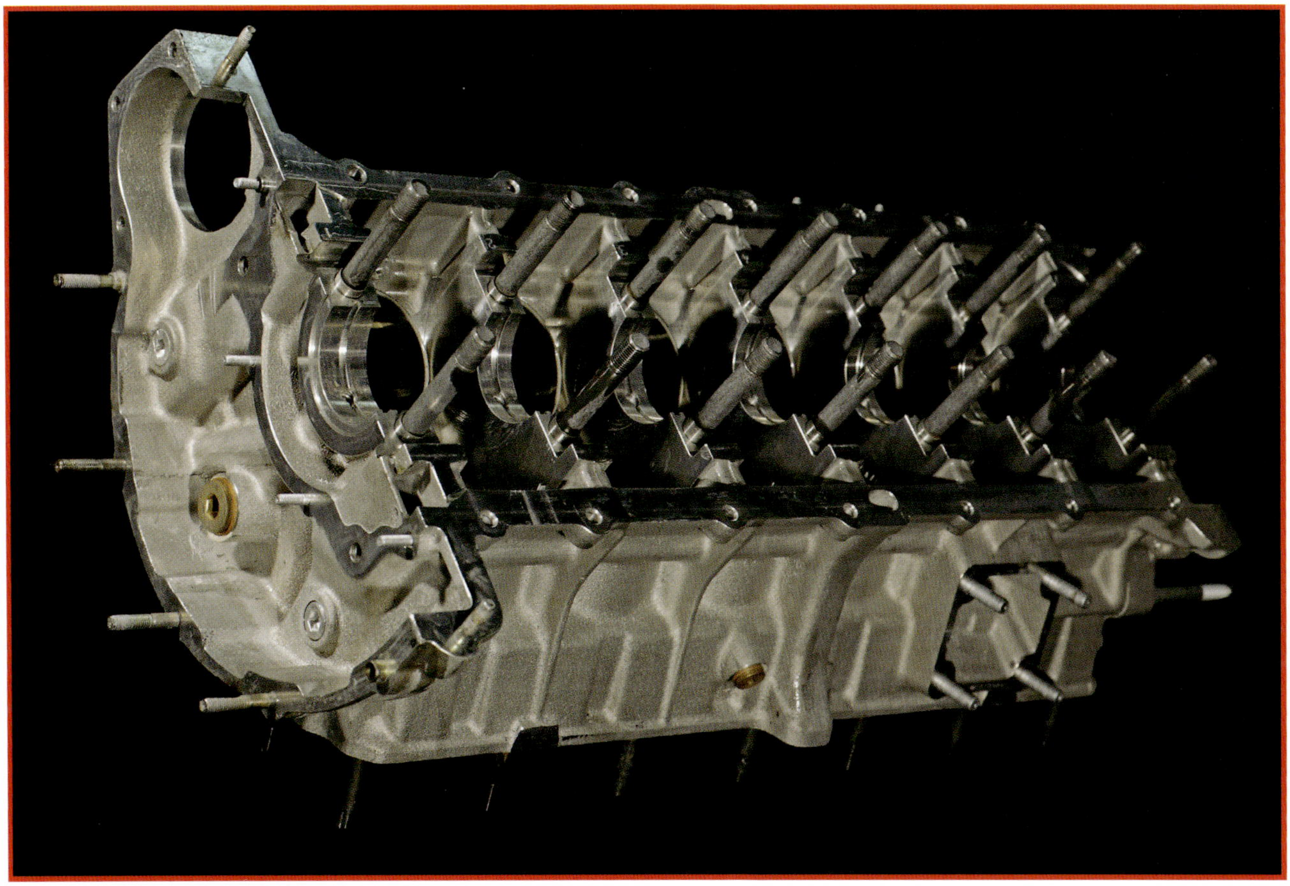

GTS, 365 GTB4 and GTS4 'Daytona', but this was the first six-speed transaxle produced by Ferrari for a road car. The hydraulically actuated single-plate clutch was mounted on the engine flywheel. Drive was transmitted from the engine to the gearbox through a three-bearing propeller shaft housed in a steel tube rigidly connecting the engine to the transaxle. The six-speed gearbox had double-cone synchromesh with a low-friction direct sixth gear. The differential was a limited-slip ZF unit. The transmission was pressure lubricated by a pump and a transmission oil cooler was fitted. The camshaft drive was provided by primary sprockets gear-driven from the crankshaft, via two toothed belts – one per bank, each of which drove the twin camshafts per bank, actuating the twin inlet and exhaust valves for each cylinder. The engine featured straight inlet tracts, and the combustion chambers had a low surface area/volume ratio to provide improved efficiency. The inlet manifolds crossed over within the engine vee. The first engine of the family, code number F116 B, was identical to the 116 C, but employed a digital Bosch Motronic ME 2.7 system to control fuelling and ignition, instead of the Bosch Motronic ME 5.2 system of the updated 116 C. The injection system was a multipoint sequential system, with twin ignition coils. The two engines had a different firing order – with the F116 B firing in the sequence 1–12–5–8–3–10–6–7–2–11–4–9. On

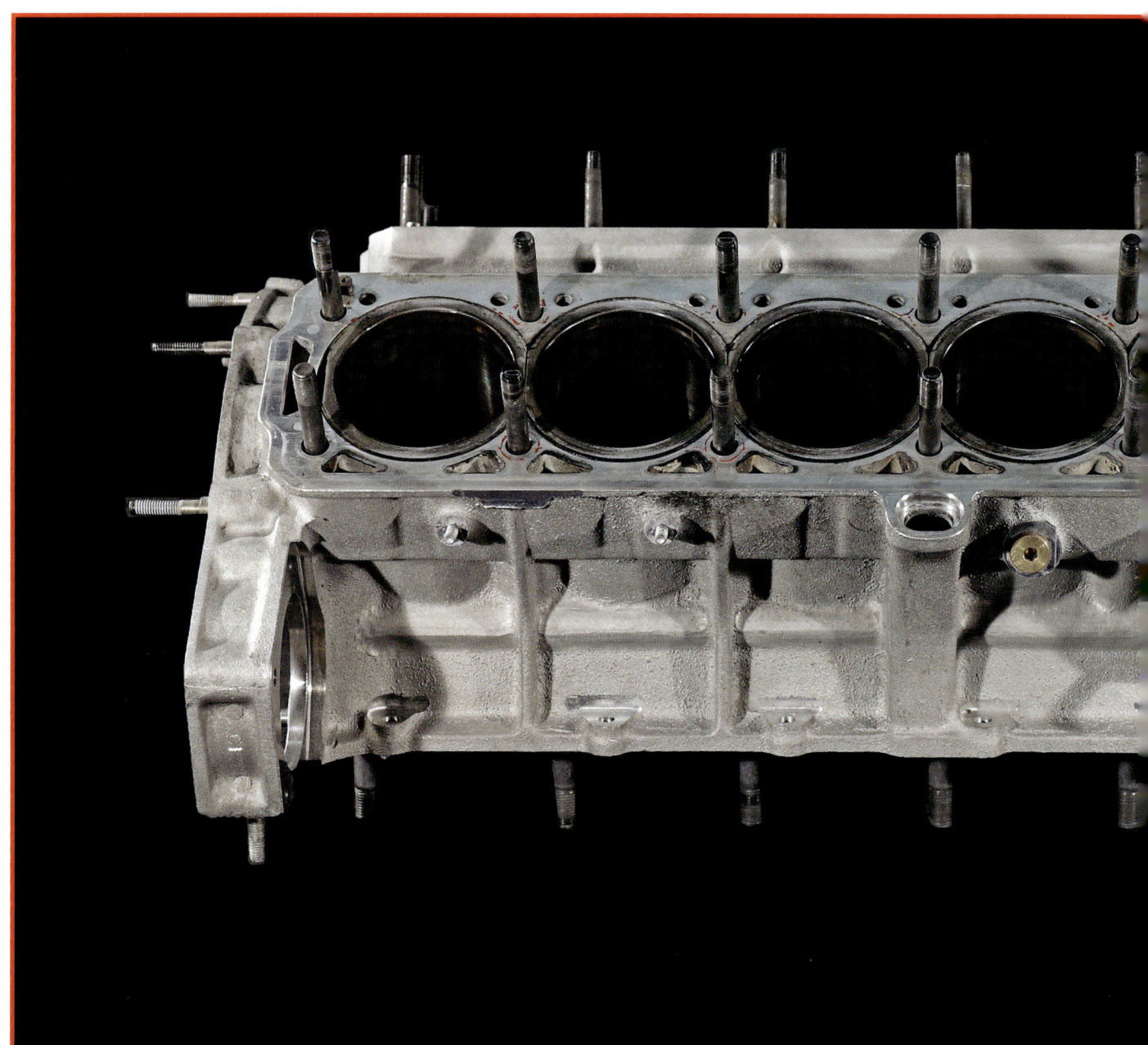

the 116 C unit, the firing order was changed to 1–7–5–11–3–9–6–12–2–8–4–10. The 116 engine family was fitted with two catalytic converters, with evaporation recovery via an activated carbon canister. The exhaust manifolds were tuned to optimise performance and to control the sound of the engine.

In true Ferrari tradition, much of the advanced technology incorporated in the 456 GT 2+2 was derived from F1 experience. The 65° vee angle was similar to the 640 F1 car, the first V12 single-seater from Maranello to adopt this new configuration, after many years of 60° and 180° engines. All the innovative features incorporated on the F116 and F133 engines were recognised in 2000 when the F133 engine (the sister engine as fitted to the 550 Maranello) became the winner of the International Engine of the Year competition in the 'Best Above 4.0-litre' category. The decision to fit this engine to a four-seater coupé followed Enzo Ferrari's philosophy, underlining that 'racing improves the breed', ie, that the precious competition experience gained by the *Cavallino Rampante* was transferable to all types of road-going Ferraris. Another connection with F1 technology on the 456 GT 2+2 was the use of light alloy for the main body shell and doors, and composite material for the large bonnet (substituted on the 456 GT M with carbon fibre). The aluminium body was spot-welded to the tubular steel chassis using a Feran interleaf, which overcame the two materials' normal incompatibility. This solution contributed substantially to minimising the weight of this large but well-balanced four-seater coupé.

The 456 GT replaced the previous 412 model, which had ceased production in 1989. In comparison to the previous four-seater, with its angular lines, the 456 GT was more aesthetically pleasing, with a beautiful aerodynamic shape, designed by Pietro Camardella of Pininfarina, taking cues from the 365 GTB4 'Daytona', from which the new coupé derived the long bonnet, retractable headlights, and the rear end with a twin tail-light arrangement in a modern single housing clearly inspired by the Daytona. This streamlined four-seater, developed under the supervision of Lorenzo Ramaciotti, set a new record for the longest production run of any Ferrari – in its two series, the 456 continued in production for 12 years, from 1992 to 2004!

The first car in the series – the 456 GT – featured a manual six-speed gearbox with the typical Ferrari open selector gate. In 1996, the GTA was introduced, with an automatic four-speed gearbox available as an option with the intention of providing greater appeal to the American market. On the early cars, produced up until 1998, an electrically actuated automatic rear spoiler was fitted to the lower rear of the car, integrated with the bumper: its angle was variable according to the speed of the car, increasing the downforce as the speed rose. This device was abandoned on the second series 456 GT M cars, built from 1998 until 2004, on which improvements were made to mechanical and electronic details, and the interior.

The first series of cars was built with the chassis code number F116 CL, for a total of 1,548 456 GT cars, and chassis code F116 CLA for 402 examples of the 456 GTA. The second series was built with the chassis code number F116 CL for 640 examples of the 456 M GT and chassis code F116 CLA for 631 examples of 456 M GTA. Then Ferrari F1 driver Michael

← A top view of the cylinder block with the Nikasil-coated cylinder liners in place.

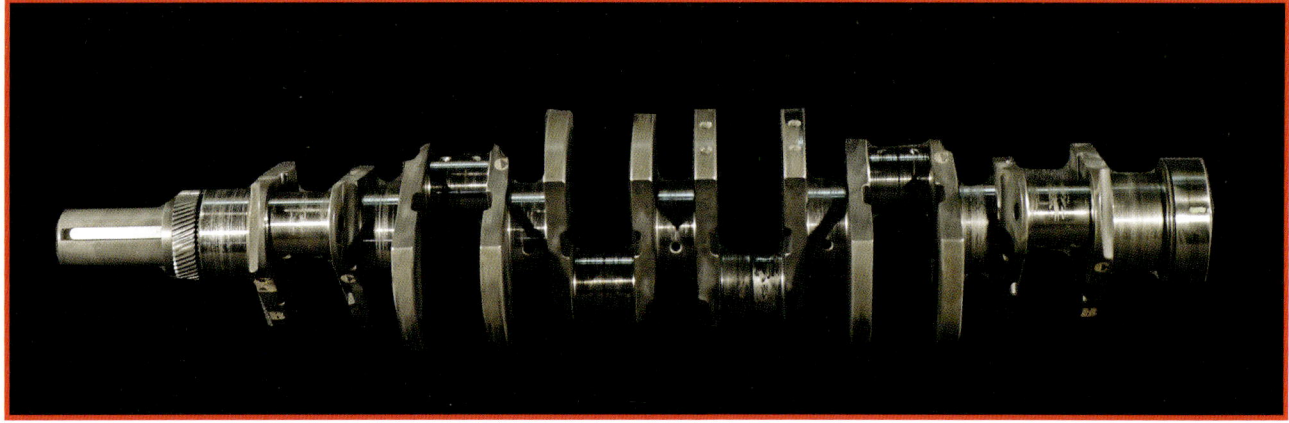

↑ The steel, nitrided, seven-main-bearing crankshaft, with shared big-end-bearing journals.

Schumacher had a special duotone silver and dark grey example of the 456 M GT, and Ferrari produced a limited edition run of this model in their Carrozzeria Scaglietti programme in this colour scheme with a grey leather interior and a Michael Schumacher plaque. The production figures include a number of special examples codenamed Venice, converted by Pininfarina from standard cars into four-door saloons, station wagons and cabriolets specifically for the Brunei Royal Family.

The decision to build a large-capacity and very expensive Ferrari in the early 90s – a difficult period for luxury cars – proved a winning strategy, and the sales figures were unexpected for this type of 'comfortable' Ferrari. Indeed,

→ An interesting arrangement of components for one cylinder, showing (from bottom to top): the titanium connecting rod fitted to a piston; the bucket tappets and shims; valve-spring caps; valves and double valve springs.

↓ A view of the cylinder head, with valves fitted, showing the shallow combustion chambers and four valves per cylinder.

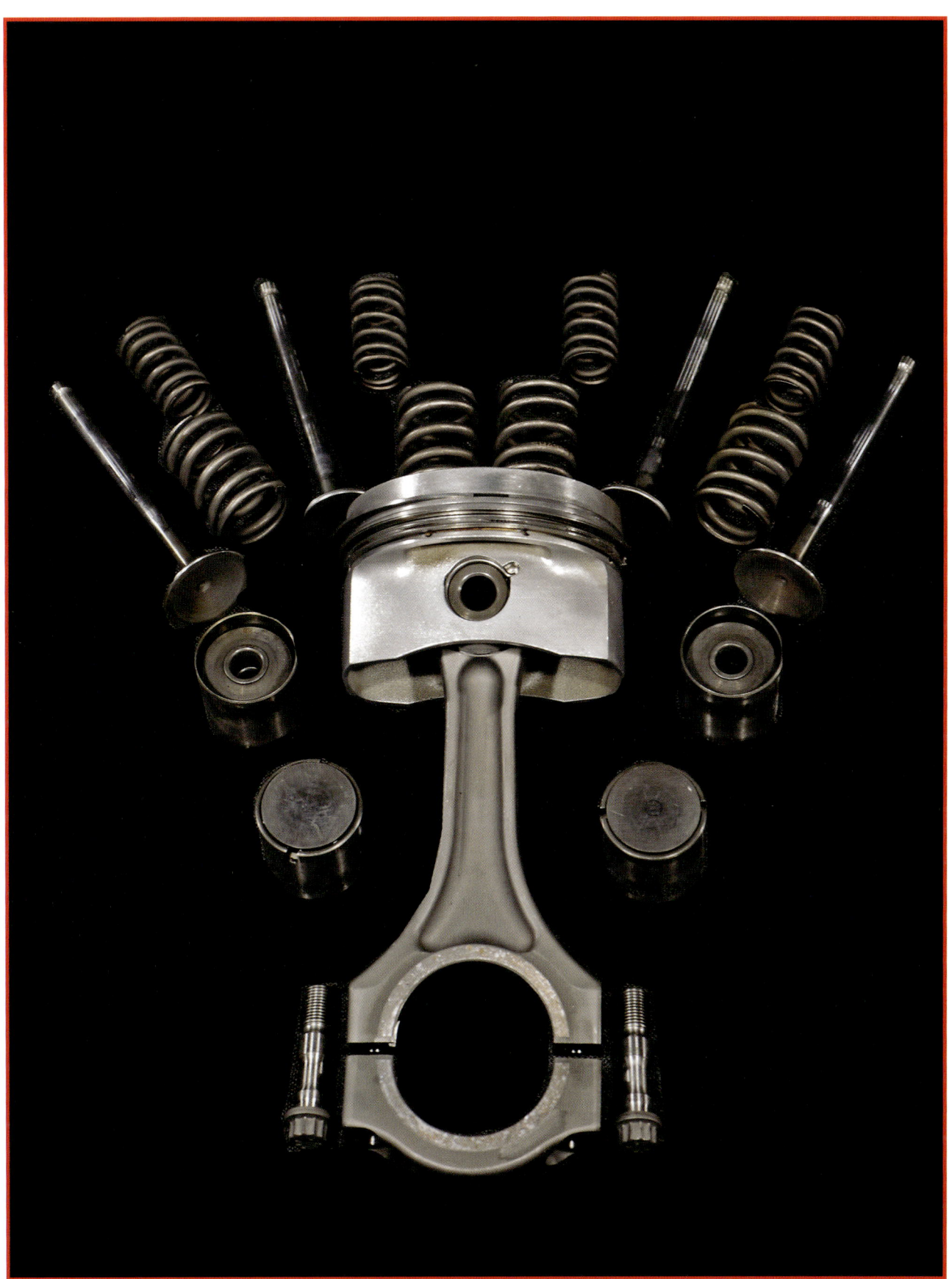

↑ The two cylinder heads, with camshafts in place, and camshaft sprockets and timing belt tensioners in the foreground.

FERRARI 456 GTM – TECHNICAL DATA

Engine code	F116 C
Engine type	Front, longitudinal, V12, 65°
Bore and stroke	88 x 75mm (3.46 x 2.95in)
Total capacity	5,473.92cc (334.04cu in)
Unitary capacity	456.16cc (27.83cu in)
Compression ratio	10.6:1
Maximum power	436bhp (325.09kW) at 6,250rpm
Power per litre	80bhp/litre (59kW/litre)
Valve operation	Double overhead camshaft per bank, four valves per cylinder
Fuel feed	Bosch Motronic 5.2 electronic direct injection
Ignition	Bosch Motronic 5.2 electronic
Lubrication	Dry sump
Clutch	Dry, single plate
Maximum torque	550Nm (406lb ft) at 4,500rpm
Firing order	1–7–5–11–3–9–6–12–2–8–4–10

the total number of 456 variants sold was 3,252! Referring back to the past, to understand the genesis of this GT 2+2, we need to travel back to 1960, when Enzo Ferrari decided to produce his first four-seater coupé (Ferrari had produced models with 'four' seats in the early fifties, but the rear seats were only suitable for small children), with the aim of enlarging his international market. The 250 GTE 2+2 was a big Ferrari (2,600mm wheelbase) with a 3.0-litre engine producing 237bhp (177kW) at 7,000rpm, fitted with four comfortable leather seats. Enzo Ferrari himself owned an example of this car for a long time (with registration MO 54083) to travel from Maranello to his home in Modena. This first Ferrari four-seater was designed to appeal to customers who were more used to driving comfortable cars, and wanted space for the family. Thirty two years later, with a power increase of 202bhp (151kW), the same wheelbase of 2,600mm, and with technological advances made through competition experience and the introduction of advanced new materials, the modern four-seater equivalent of the 250 GTE 2+2 was launched by Maranello.

The 456 GTM (the model featured in this chapter) was updated to incorporate technological features such as new anti-dive front-suspension geometry and retuned shock absorbers for improved low-speed ride. The GT M also featured a dynamic stability control system (ASR), which optimised traction via the

↑ The single Valeo clutch friction disc.

↗ The flywheel, with starter-motor ring gear and crankshaft position sensor teeth around its periphery.

→ The clutch pressure plate assembly, showing the diaphragm-spring assembly.

→ The two compact cylinder heads, with camshaft covers removed, showing the camshafts in place.

↘ One of the throttle valves (shown closed here – one valve for each bank) inside the throttle housing on the plenum chamber.

↓ A close-up view inside one of the cylinder heads, showing the camshaft lobes and camshaft bearing caps.

211

456 GT M: V12 back to the front (1998)

ABS system and engine throttle control, with three settings to chose from – Normal, Sport and Off.

After the 5.5-litre 116 B and 116 C engines, the revised F133 appeared in 1995, featuring the same capacity of 5,474cc, but with power increased to 478bhp (356kW) at 7,000rpm.

The front-engined V12 456 series epitomised Enzo Ferrari's mantra that 'the horse should pull not push the cart'. The new design philosophy introduced by the incoming Ferrari President Luca di Montezemolo was to produce more comfortable and user-friendly sports cars, whilst maintaining peak performance. With power continuously increasing, the Ferrari design team would face challenges ahead, but the future of the front-engined V12 appeared to be secure!

↖ A close-up view of the crossover pattern of the inlet manifolds, with each manifold tract running to the opposite cylinder bank.

↑ The complete twin-inlet-manifold assembly, with throttle housing and plenum chamber on each side.

➔ A view looking forwards from the rear of one of the cylinder heads with camshafts and bearing caps in place.

↓ A view of the underside of one of the cylinder heads, showing the impressive line-up of four valves per cylinder for six of the 12 cylinders.

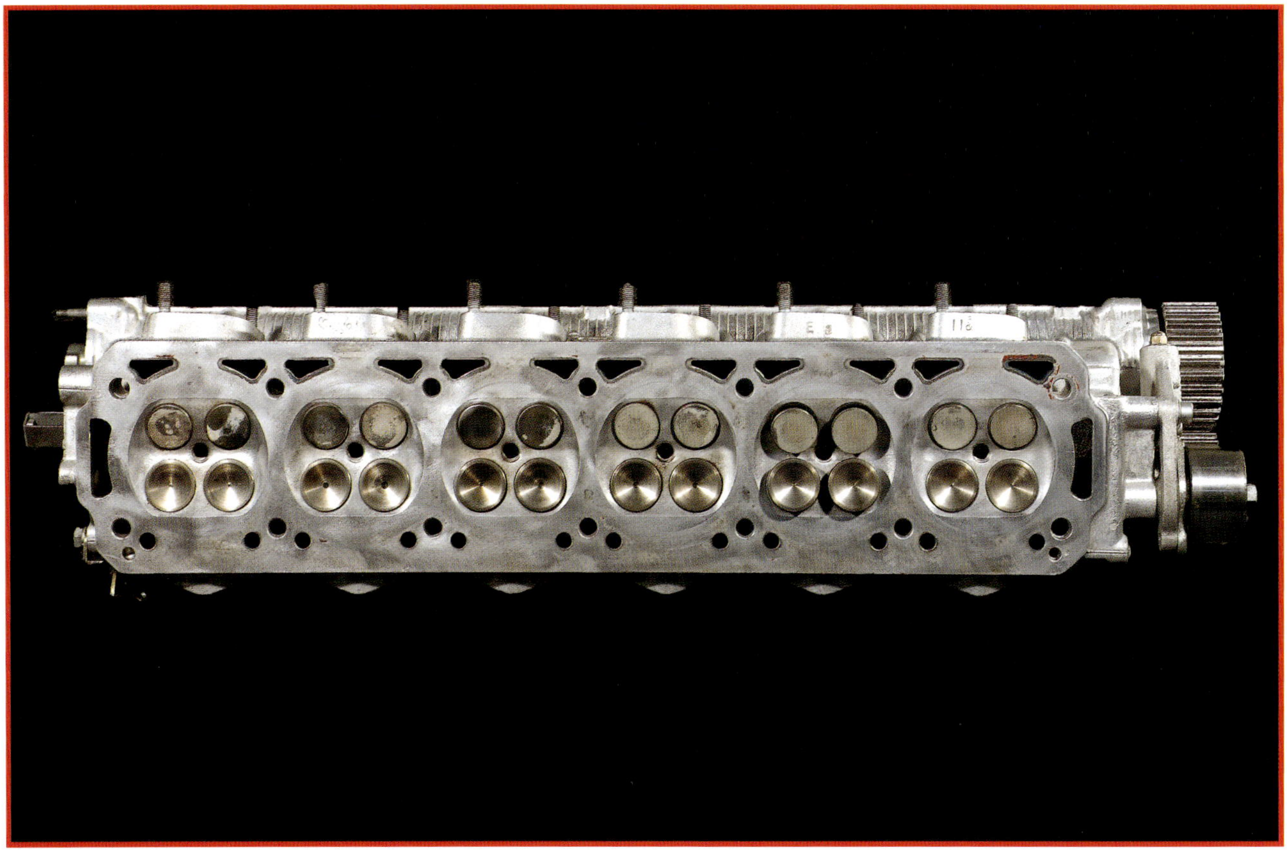

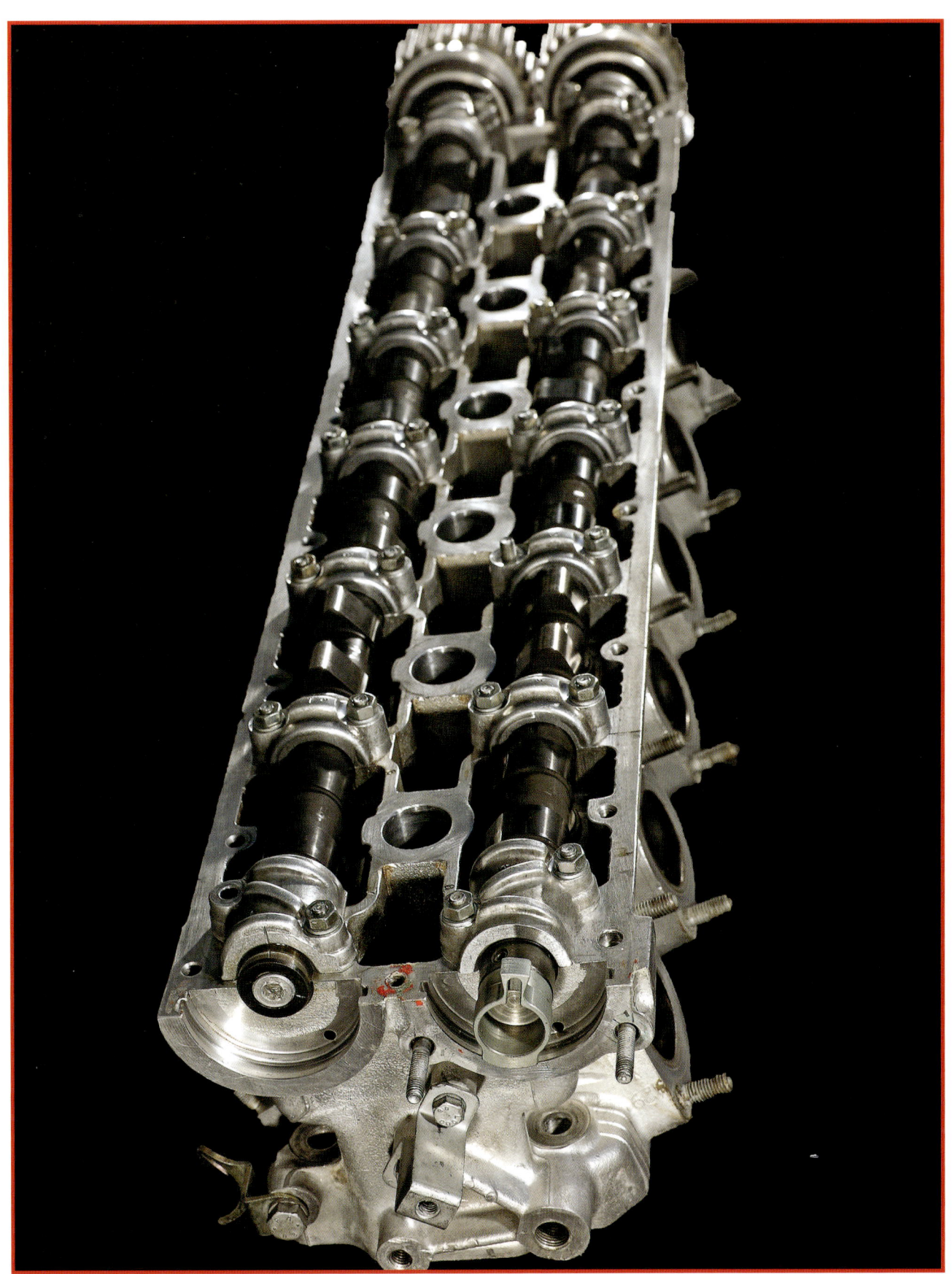

↑ The front of the 456 GT M is a harmony of curves, with retractable headlights enhancing the clean lines.

↑ Round tail-lights, grouped together into a single unit on each side, mirror the four exhaust tailpipes.

➔ The retractable headlight sits subtly above the bumper, with the fog light recessed into the grille panel.

↘ Even when the headlights are extended, the 456 GT M looks sleek and powerful.

↘↘ The paired rear light assemblies in a single housing provided a link to Ferrari's classic twin rear light arrangement.

↘↘↘ The sculpted recesses running along the doors of this 2+2 GT car serve to disguise the large air-outlet vents at the rear of the front wheel arches.

↓ The styling cues provided by the 'Daytona' are obvious in this side view of the sleek, front-engined 456 GT M.

360 Modena
The V8 reborn (1999)

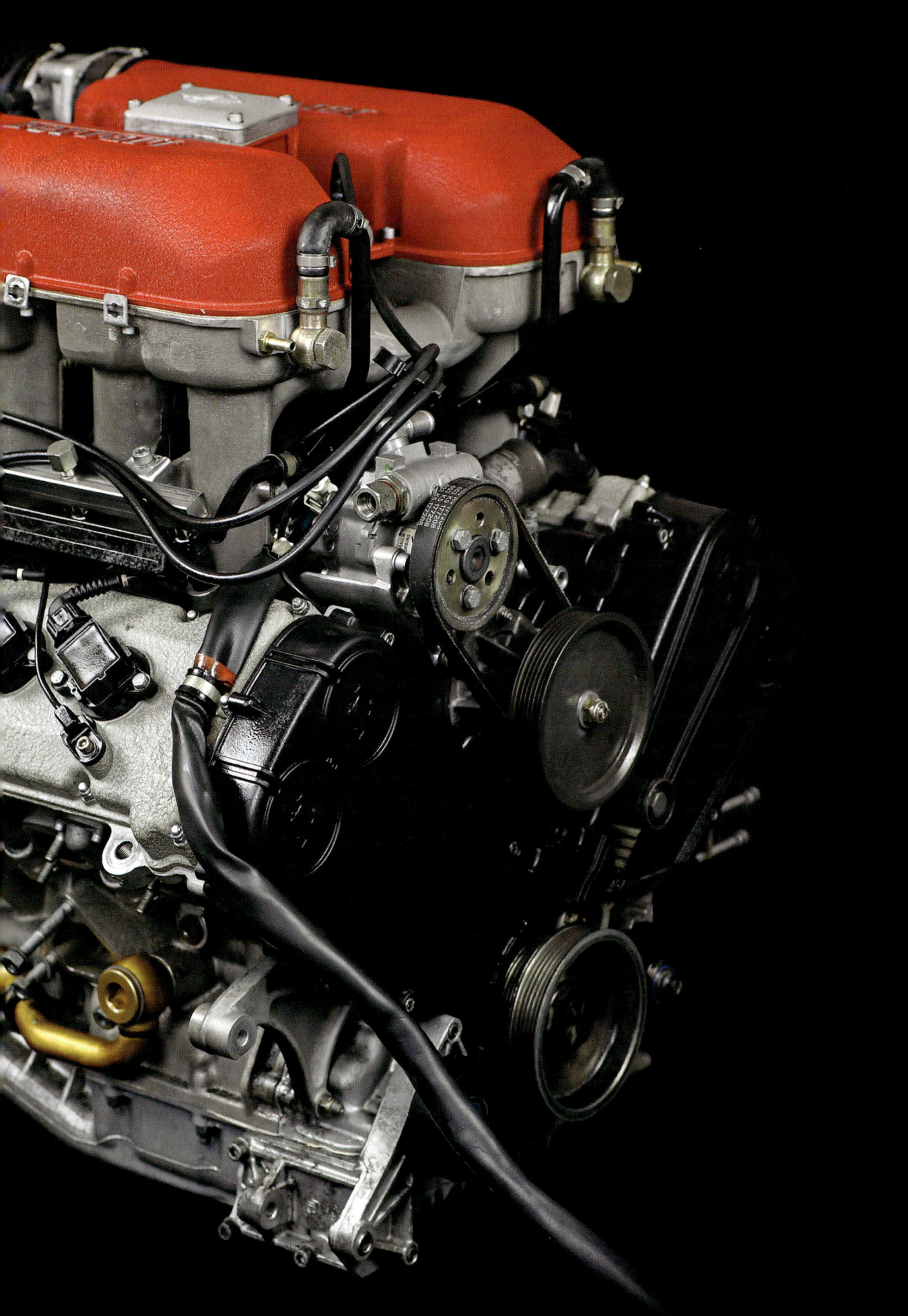

Ferrari's car for the new millennium was a drastic departure from the previous classic Ferrari shapes, taking the company into the 21st century with a series of innovations to maintain its position as a world leader in sports-car engineering. This car was the 360 Modena, powered by a mid-mounted longitudinal 90° V8 engine producing 400bhp (298kW) at 8,500rpm. The 360 Modena was launched in 1999 at the Geneva Motor Show, one of Maranello's favourite venues for unveiling its cars, followed by a spider version in 2000.

The Maranello V8 road-car story began with the Bertone-designed Dino 308 GT4 model with a 3.0-litre engine in 1973, and moved into the new millennium with the 3.6-litre F131 engine fitted in the 360 Modena Berlinetta. The engine formed part of the visual impact of the 360 Modena, as it was visible through the extended rear screen/engine cover. The car featured a number of advanced characteristics, including the six-speed F1 electro-hydraulic gearbox system, operated by two paddles behind the steering wheel – a system which first appeared on the F355 in 1997. Additionally, the type F131 engine featured five valves per cylinder, three intake and two exhaust, and a variable-geometry intake manifold, with valves governed via electronic throttle management, which altered the routing of the inlet air depending on rpm and the prevailing engine-operating conditions. This system provided

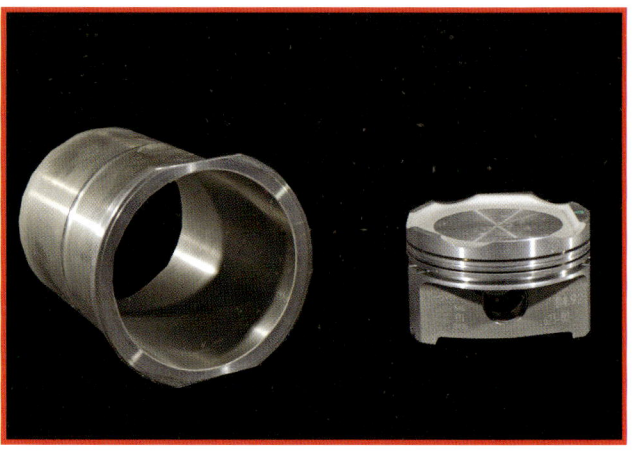

↑ One of the eight Mahle forged-alloy pistons, together with the cylinder liner in which it slides.

→ The forged-steel flat-plane crankshaft, showing the five main bearing journals and shared big-end-bearing journals.

↓ A line-up of the eight forged-alloy pistons, complete with their titanium connecting rods.

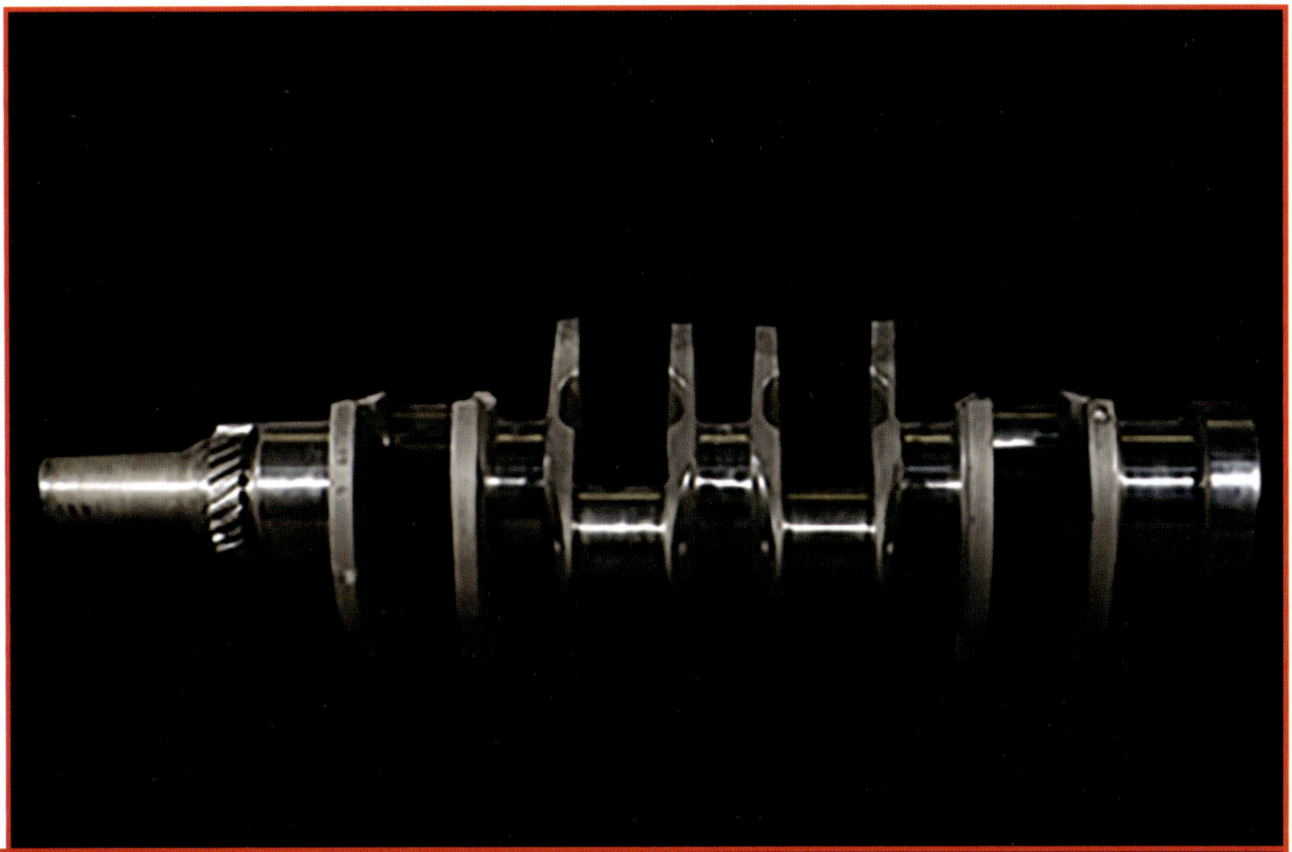

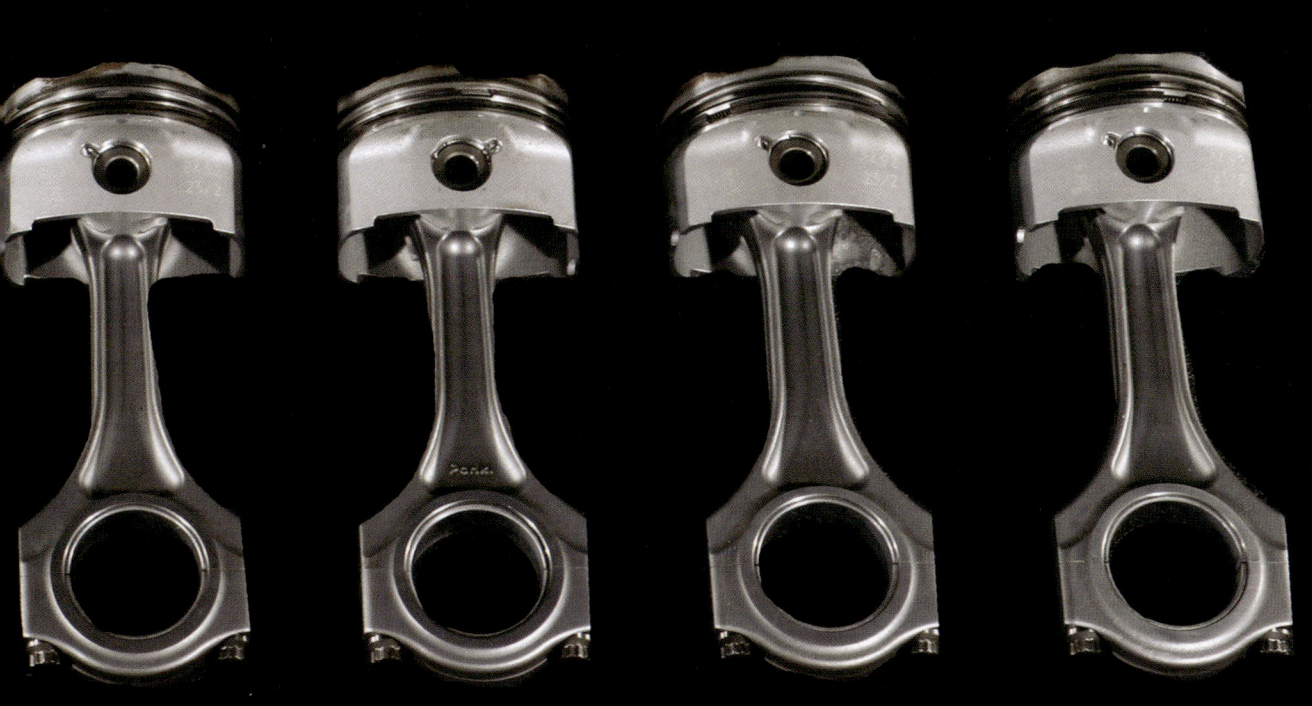

221
360 Modena: The V8 reborn (1999)

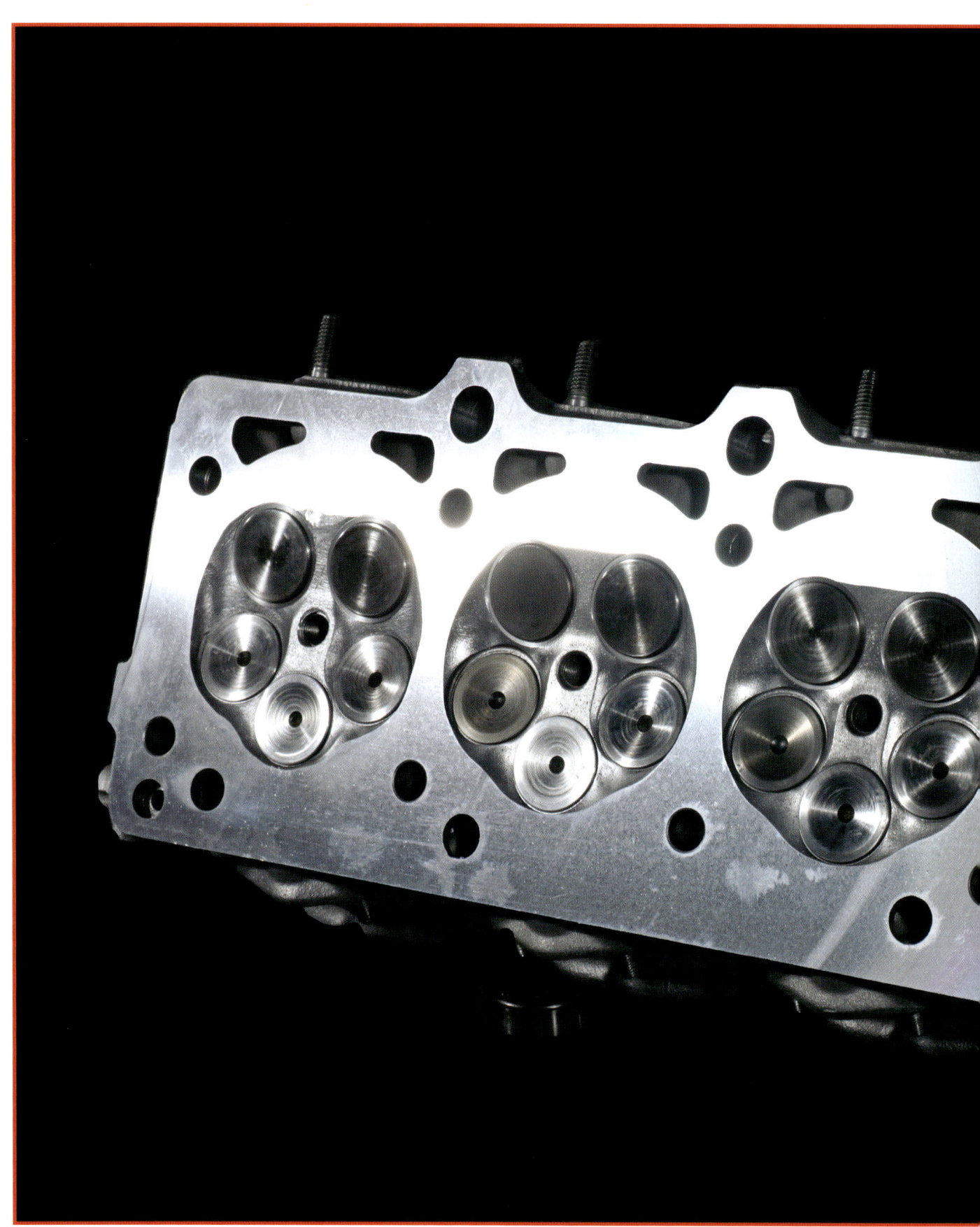

improved torque and optimum power. Both these innovations were derived from the Ferrari 641 F1 car, designed by the English designer John Barnard.

For optimum power, Ferrari continued with the five-valves-per-cylinder configuration used on the preceding F355 model, featuring steel valves with a hydraulically controlled variable-valve-timing system. This system not only controlled the valve timing, but also aided optimum air/fuel mixture flow. The majority of the engine components including the cylinder block, heads, timing covers, inlet manifolds, sump etc were light alloy, with a forged-steel, flat plane crankshaft, and titanium connecting rods which were manufactured by Pankl.

The attention to detail for this engine was truly astonishing, although the titanium connecting rods were abandoned on the subsequent F430 models, probably due to the production cost, as were the five valves per cylinder. The cylinder liners were Nikasil treated, and the light-alloy pistons were manufactured by Mahle, with narrow skirts for lightness. The compression ratio was 11:1. The twin overhead camshafts per bank were belt-driven via sprockets from the crankshaft incorporating a tensioner assembly. A Bosch Motronic ME 7.3 engine management system was used, with separate coils for each spark plug (coil-over-plug), and an electronic drive-by-wire throttle system was used. The firing order of the engine was 1–8–3–6–4–5–2–7. Lubrication was via a dry sump, with the oil tank located above the differential to the rear of the cylinder block. Thanks to all the sophisticated components and systems, the specific power was 112bhp/litre (84kW/litre), and maximum engine speed was 8,500rpm. The technological package of the F131 engine, which employed the best resources available at the time, was state-of-the-art technology.

Another notable feature of the F131 engine was its amazing sound, enhanced thanks to a special exhaust system, designed both to optimise performance and to modulate the sound of the engine (4-into-1 manifolds with a catalytic converter for each bank, which fed the exhaust gases through a variable back-pressure system).

A computer-controlled ABS/ASR braking/traction control and variable damping system was fitted, which offered the choice of three settings, 'Normal', 'Sport' and 'Off'. This incorporated anti-dive and anti-squat to the suspension geometry, and controlled the vertical movement of the wheels relative to the chassis, the degree depending upon which setting was chosen, together with a braking effort proportioning valve (EBD) and a MSR system to prevent wheel lock-up under rapid deceleration.

For the first time on a road Ferrari, the chassis was built completely from aluminium, using a combination of

← **The underside of the cylinder head showing the combustion chambers, each with three inlet and two exhaust valves.**

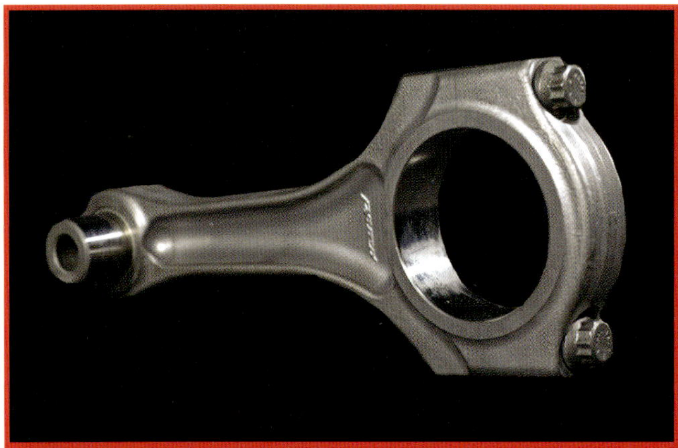

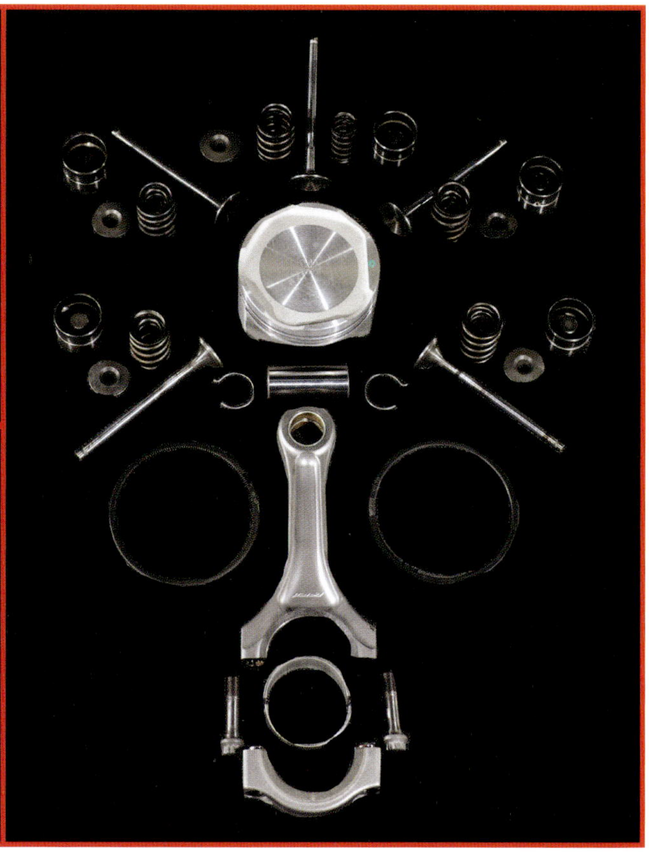

extruded box sections and cast units, with the light-alloy bodywork riveted and bonded to it to form a monocoque structure. Ferrari cooperated on the chassis design with Alcoa – a multinational company working mainly in the aerospace sector, with whom they had previously worked on the 408 RM four-wheel-drive prototype. The alloy body panels and monocoque, together with light-alloy suspension components, helped to reduce the weight of the car to 1,290kg, as opposed to the 1,440kg of the preceding F355 model. The wheelbase was 2,600mm (150mm longer than the F355), and the front and rear tracks were 1,679mm and 1,617mm respectively (again, an increase over the F355).

↖↖ One of the titanium connecting rods with gudgeon pin and bearing cap fitted.

↖ The chain-driven oil pump, which fits inside the sump pan.

↑ An artistic layout of the piston, connecting-rod and valve components for one cylinder.

↙ A view of the camshaft sprockets on one of the cylinder heads.

↓ The Ferrari logo and scipt are displayed prominently on the plenum chambers.

↑ A view of the cylinder block without the cylinder liners fitted. In the foreground is one of the engine-mounting brackets.

The refined aerodynamic features of this car necessitated a pair of radiators, one either side, in the nose, which gave the model a distinctive appearance. This allowed air to be channelled centrally across the flat bottom of the car to a pair of rear diffusers, which provided increased downforce through 'ground effect' without resorting to the use of a rear wing.

The lower weight of the 360 Modena compared to the F355 added to the overall performance provided by the already exuberant F131 V8, of 3,586.20cc capacity, producing 400bhp (298kW) at 8,500rpm, propelling the 360 Modena to a top speed of 183mph (295kmh), with 0–62mph (0–100kmh) in just 4.5sec.

As mentioned previously, Ferrari offered the six-speed electro-hydraulic F1 gearbox as an option for the 360 Modena. It was faster than that version fitted to the earlier F355, and was capable of making a gearchange in around 100 milliseconds. The system allowed automatic downchanges, and the roar produced by the engine during sequential downchanges was an aural delight for the enthusiast, thanks to the mid-mounted engine just behind the ears of the passengers. Even though the F1 gearbox was specified by the majority of customers, standard equipment for the 360 Modena was a manual six-speed gearbox with the classic metal open gate. A dry single-plate clutch was fitted, manufactured by Valeo.

Thanks to its aesthetic qualities and performance, which made the car very attractive for Ferrari's customers, over 18,000 examples of the 360 Modena and F131 engine were built (with chassis Nos. from 104376 to 140647). Towards the end of the production run a more extreme road version was created, the limited-production Challenge Stradale. This, as its name implies, was a street (stradale) version of the Challenge series race car, and was a full 110kg lighter than the standard car, which obviously translated into improved performance. This was further enhanced by fine tuning of the engine to provide a then record for a naturally aspirated engine of 118.5bhp/litre (88.4kW/litre). The F131 engine was also fitted in a spectacular one-off spider built to a commission by Gianni Agnelli as a wedding gift for Luca di Montezemolo – Ferrari's President at the time. Pininfarina designed an exclusive and beautiful barchetta body for this car, finished in silver (Argento Nürburgring), with a very low and steeply raked windscreen dipping in the centre, without any side support. The rear panels behind the headrest were a different shape to the standard spider, and there was no roof, which would have disturbed the aesthetics of this masterpiece. Montezemolo

↑ A view inside the plenum chambers showing the electronically controlled valves (closed in this photograph) that operate the variable-length inlet-tract system.

FERRARI 360 MODENA – TECHNICAL DATA

Engine code	F131
Engine type	Mid, longitudinal, V8, 90°
Bore and stroke	85 x 79mm (3.34 x 3.11in)
Total capacity	3,586.20cc (218.84cu in)
Unitary capacity	448.29cc (27.35cu in)
Compression ratio	11:1
Maximum power	394bhp (294kW) at 8,500rpm
Power per litre	110bhp/litre (82kW/litre)
Valve operation	Double overhead camshafts per bank, five valves per cylinder
Fuel feed	Bosch Motronic ME7.3 electronic injection
Ignition	Bosch Motronic ME7.3 static electronic, single spark plug per cylinder, separate coil-over-plug for each cylinder
Lubrication	Dry sump
Clutch	Dry, single plate
Maximum torque	373Nm (275.1lb ft) at 4,750rpm
Firing order	1–8–3–6–4–5–2–7

was a fan of the 360 Modena project even before this gift, declaring it a success all over the world, due to the balance between performance and driving pleasure, testified by its sales success. Another fan of this car was Dario Benuzzi, at that time Ferrari's chief test driver, who, after the launch of the spider version of the 360 Modena, described it as the best V8 convertible Maranello had ever produced. He said that the driving pleasure was due to the throttle response, and that the handling was extraordinary.

↓ Another view of one of the cylinder heads, with valves fitted and exhaust ports visible on the side of the head.

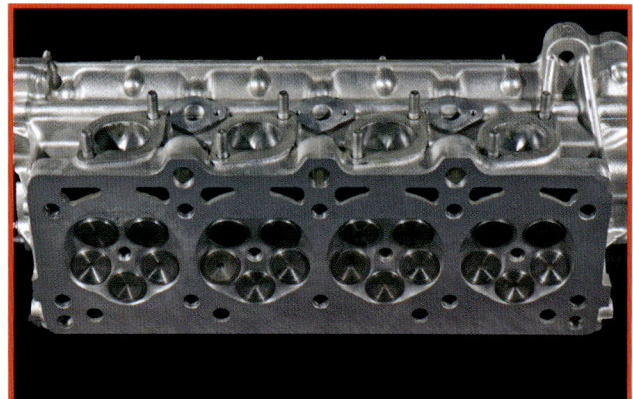

↑ The assembled clutch and flyweel assembly. Note the (shiny) drilled holed where the assembly has been balanced.

↗ The single, dry Valeo clutch friction disc.

→ The light-alloy casting for the dry-sump pan. Note how shallow the sump is compared to a wet sump.

↓ A view of the inlet manifolds with variable-length inlet-tract system (covers removed) – technology which filtered down from Ferrari's F1 cars.

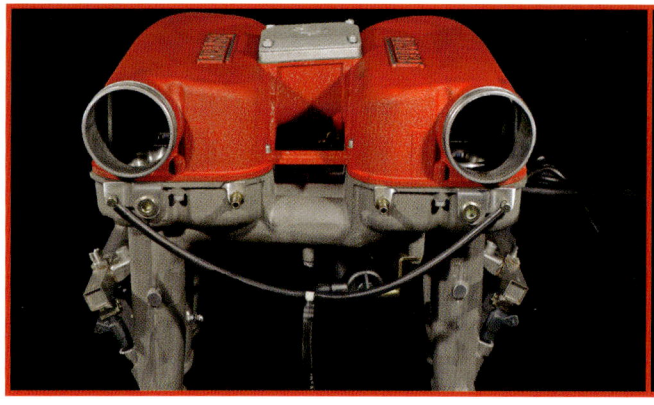

From 2000 to 2006 the 360 Modena was used for racing (as were the previous 348 and F355), both in the Ferrari Challenge Series, and the FIA N-GT Championship. Ferrari worked with its long-time collaborator Michelotto Automobili to develop a more powerful version of the 360 Challenge car, creating the 360 N-GT for international GT racing. The race version of the F131 V8 was developed by the Ferrari Corse Clienti department in Maranello with Michelotto, and featured lighter pistons, high-lift camshafts, reshaped combustion chambers and a re-mapped engine management system, together with body modifications. In 2001, the JMB Competition Team (as the official Ferrari-supported team) won the N-GT Class in the FIA GT Championship with this

↖ Another view of the inlet manifolds with red-painted plenum-chamber covers fitted.

↑ One of the two four-into-one exhaust manifolds, with heat-shielding in place.

↓ A view of the light-alloy cylinder block (inverted), with crankshaft main-bearing locations visible. The long protruding studs locate the main-bearing caps.

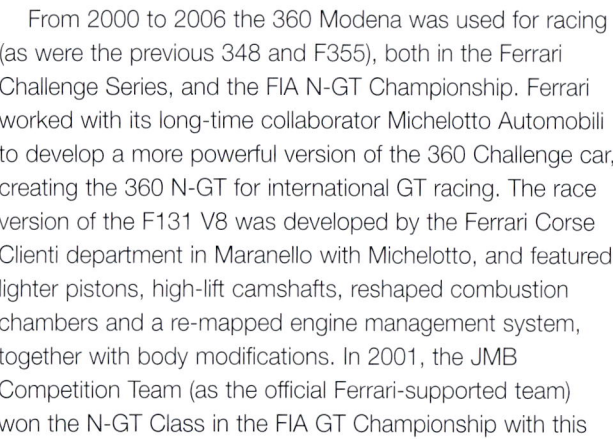

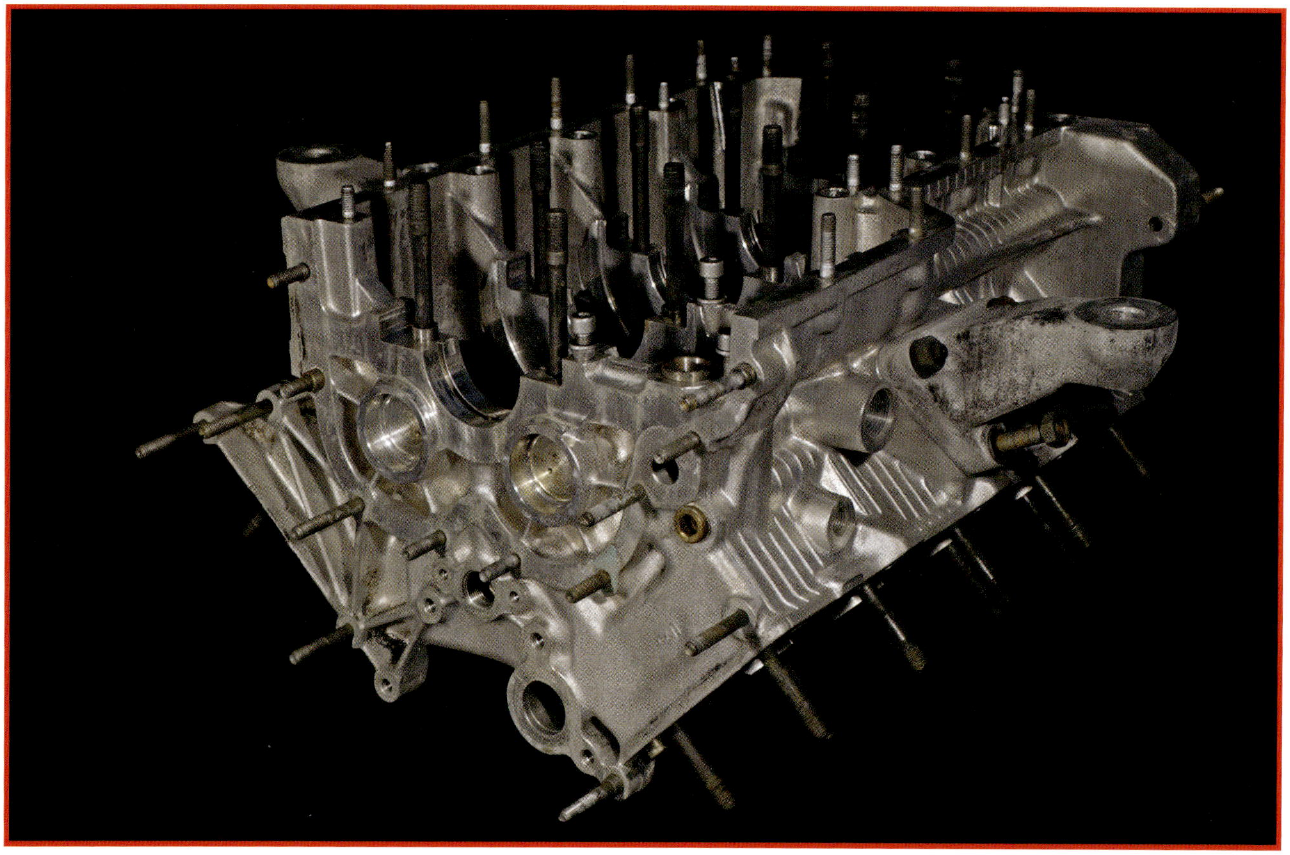

car. In 2003 Ferrari Corse Clienti with Michelotto developed the 360 GTC, which was powered by a 450bhp (336kW) version of the F131 V8, and the weight was reduced to the minimum required by the N-GT class regulation (1,100kg), thanks to the use of composite materials for the bodywork.

The racing evolution of this successful 90° V8 engine was just one of the many steps that prolonged its life. Indeed, after more than 18,000 360 Modenas had been built, the flat plane-crankshaft V8 was fitted to the succeeding Ferrari F430 model, in which the capacity was stretched to 4.3 litres and the power to 440bhp (328kW), the engine evolving into the type F136 E. In 2009 the engine capacity was increased again, resulting in the 4.5-litre type F136 F engine, used in the 458 Italia model. Due to ever tightening emission controls worldwide this was probably the last naturally aspirated Ferrari V8 engine, a derivative of which was used in the front-engined California model. It won the award for the Best Performance Engine Above 4.0 Litres in the 2011, 2012 and 2014 International Engine of the Year awards. Today, the V8 is still in production as a 3.9-litre twin-turbocharged unit – type F154 CB, which in 2016 won the Best New Engine prize and, in 2017, both the International Engine of the Year and the Best Performance Engine awards. This twin-turbo unit is fitted to the 488 GTB Fiorano, which with its 670bhp (500kW) output is able to reach 205mph (330kmh) and accelerate from 0–62mph (0–100kmh) in just 3.0sec. Like its predecessor, a derivative has been used in the California T and Portofino front-engined V8 models. More excitement is no doubt in store from the next evolution of this 45-year-old V8 Ferrari engine!

↑ The forged-steel crankshaft lying in position in the cylinder block, but without main-bearing caps fitted.

↓ The assembled cylinder heads in place on the bare cylinder block, with sump fitted.

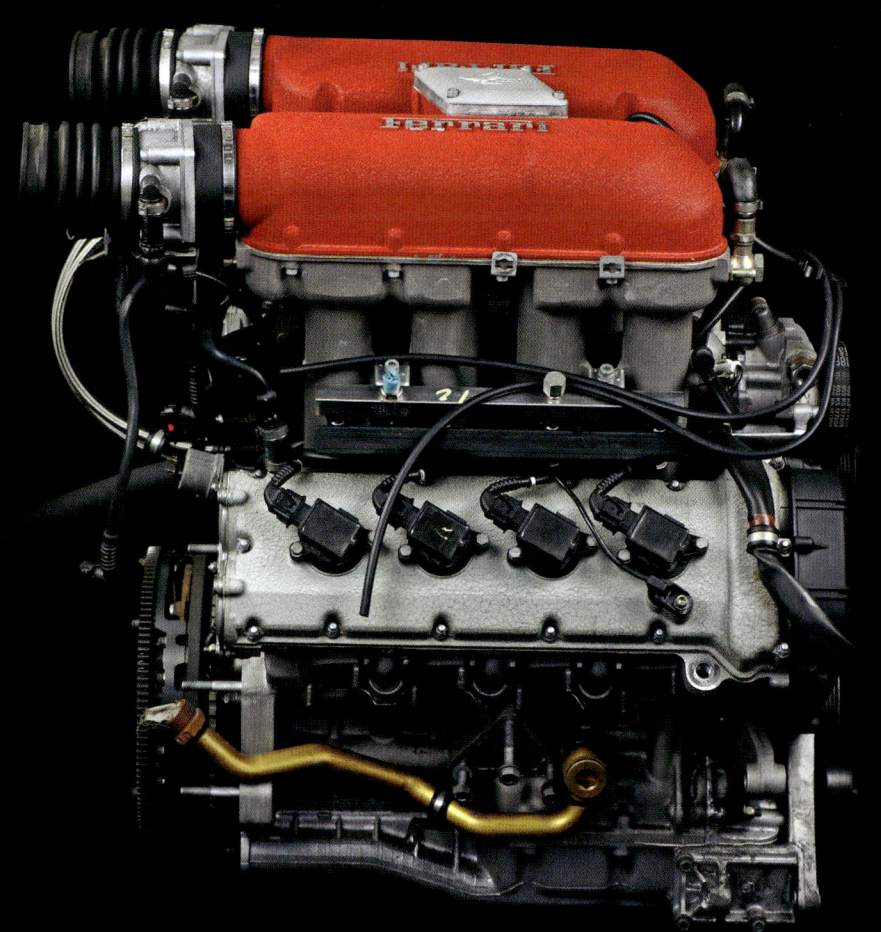

↑ For the first time on a Ferrari road car, the front grille is replaced by two air intakes, styled with a nod to the 156 F1 car.

↑ The classic round tail-lights and Prancing Horse badge leave no doubt as to the identity of this car.

➜ The apertures surrounding the exhaust tailpipes mirror the air intakes at the front of the car.

↘ Air intakes recessed into the curvaceous bodywork behind the doors are reminiscent of the 250 Le Mans.

↘↘ Plexiglas covers over the front lights aid aerodynamics and add another element to the curved design theme.

↘↘↘ The five-spoke light-alloy wheels cover large ventilated brake discs and calipers carrying the Ferrari script.

↓ Pininfarina's styling of the 360 Modena, taking cues from several of the car's predecessors, created another instant Ferrari classic.

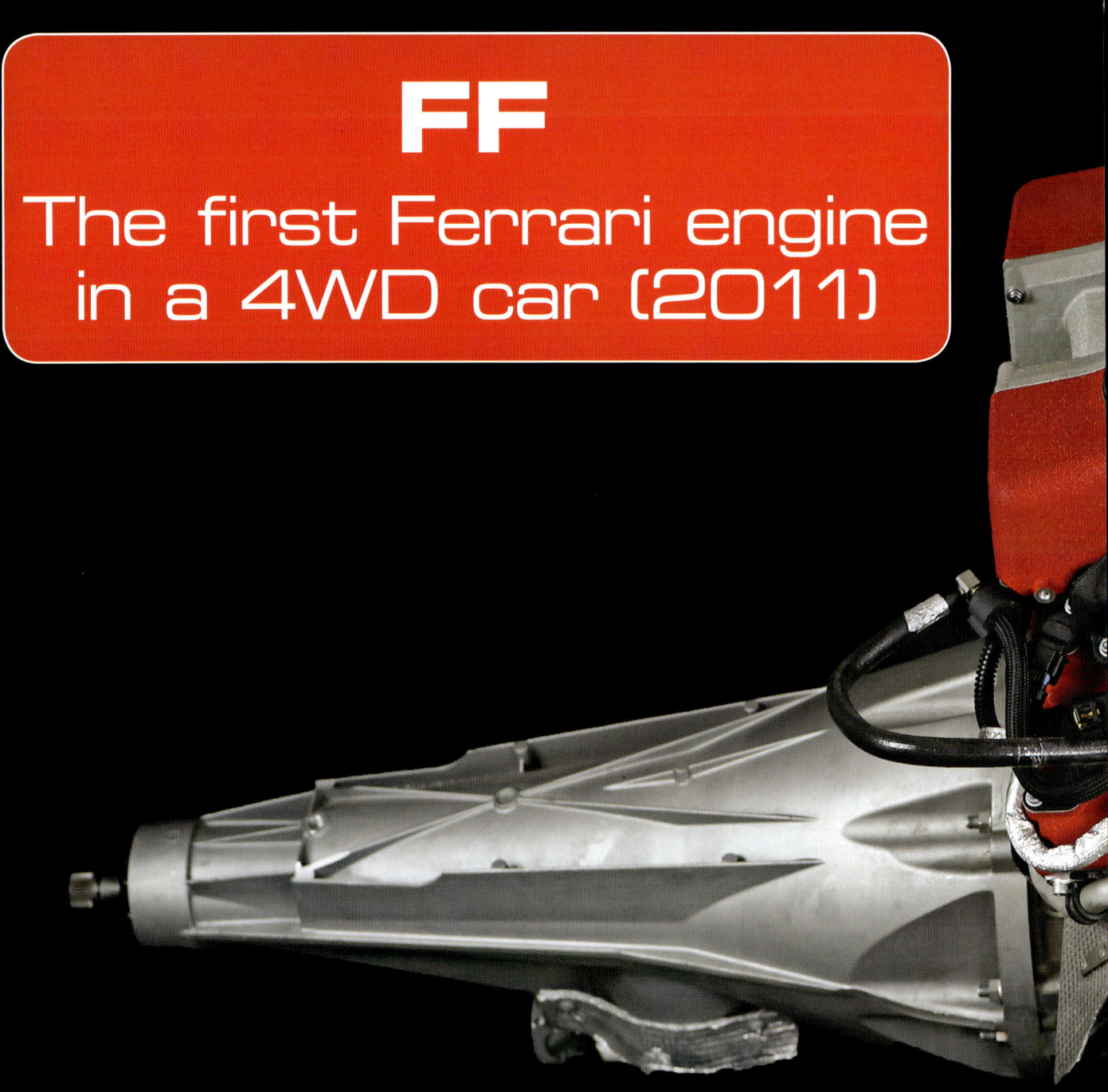

FF
The first Ferrari engine in a 4WD car (2011)

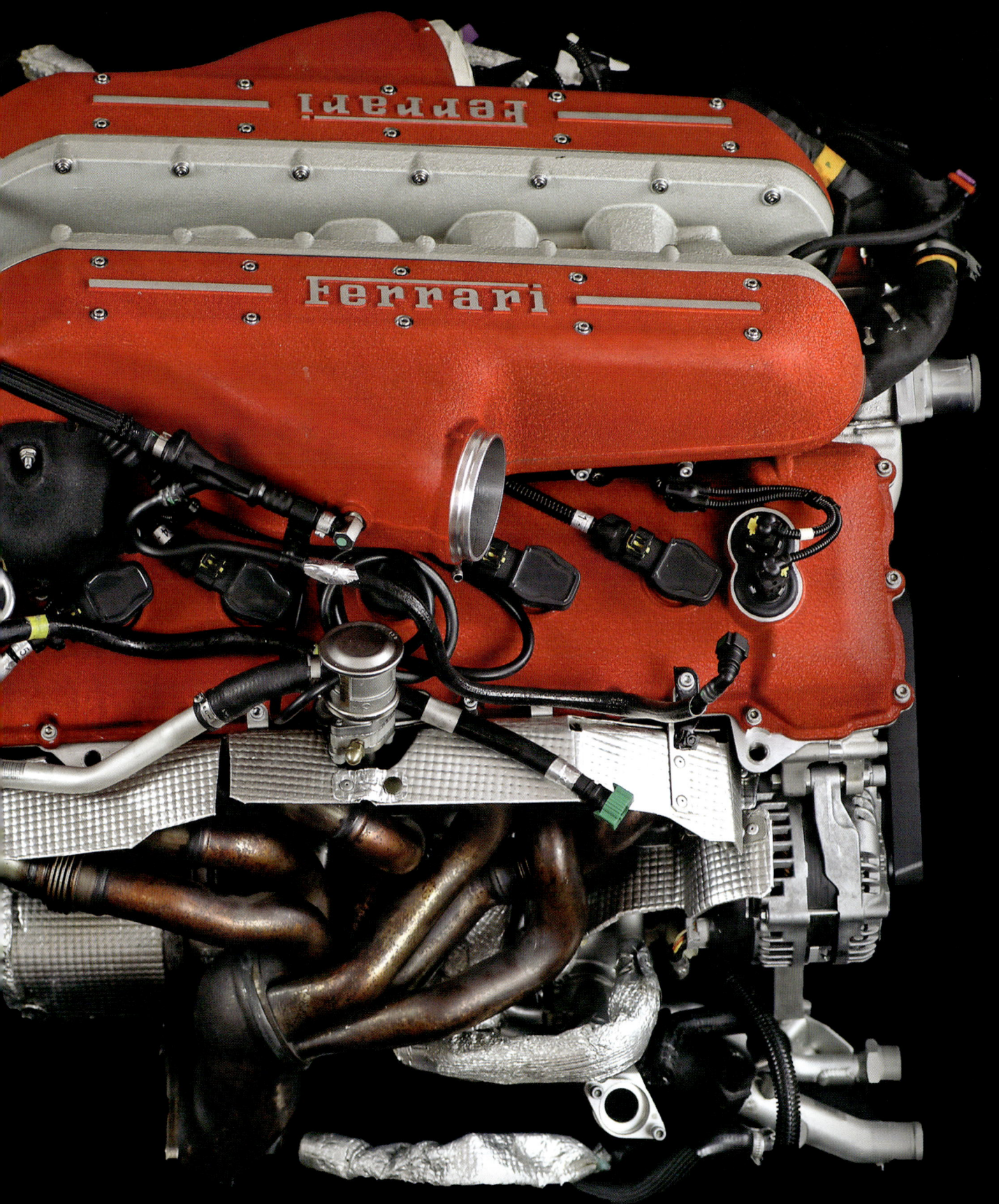

← The engine code and chassis number are stamped into the sump casting.

↙ One of the unusual 'apple-shaped' combustion chambers with four valves in place. The direct-injection fuel injector sprays into the 'stalk' at the top of the combustion chamber.

At the time of its unveiling in 2011, the Ferrari FF (an acronym of Four-wheel-drive, Four-seater), was powered by the largest-capacity road-car engine built by the Maranello factory – the naturally aspirated 6.3-litre (6,262cc), V12, 65° DOHC engine, identified by the code number F140 EB. The FF was intended to be an extreme Gran Turismo car. This large-capacity unit started a new engine family, that was fitted, with minor modifications, in front, longitudinal configuration on the F12 Berlinetta (engine code F140 FC), F12 TdF (engine code F140 FG), and the GTC4 Lusso (engine code F140 ED). Additionally, this powerful engine (with engine code F140 FE) was also fitted to the first-ever hybrid-powered Ferrari – the mid-rear-engined LaFerrari (500 examples built) and LaFerrari Aperta (210 examples built). In hybrid form, the engine was supplemented by a 161bhp (120kW) 'HY-KERS' unit.

As Ferrari tradition dictated, this 'shooting-brake' GT car was developed to incorporate technology derived from competition, and featured an electronically controlled rear differential ('E-diff'), together with the latest evolution of Ferrari's stability-control system ('F1-Trac').

With the FF, a four-wheel-drive Ferrari finally became a reality after a project for such a car had been hiding in a drawer for decades. Indeed, Mauro Forghieri – one of the most important Ferrari engineers in the company's history, who started as a young engineer, eventually becoming technical director, in almost 30 years with the company (from 1960 to 1987) – developed an experimental four-wheel-drive road car. This was 408 4RM (4 RM = 4 Ruote Motrici = 4 Wheel Drive), which was unveiled at the Detroit Motor Show in 1987, four months before the departure of Forghieri from Maranello. Two examples of this first Ferrari four-wheel-drive road car were produced – one in red (chassis No. 70183, shown at Detroit) and one in yellow (chassis No. 78610), built in 1988. This second prototype had a bonded-aluminium

↖ A close-up view of one of the red-painted camshaft covers with holes for the spark plugs.

← The crown of each forged-alloy piston has cut-outs to accommodate the valve heads, and also incorporates an extension of the combustion chamber.

monocque chassis, a feature that would become production reality with the 360 Modena model in 1999. The innovative four-wheel-drive system for the 408 featured two mechanical differentials, which under normal driving conditions could supply a power split of 29.3% to the front axle and 70.7% to the rear axle. There was a hydraulic control system to modify the power split according to the driving conditions. The engine used in the 408 prototypes was a mid-longitudinally mounted V8, 90° DOHC unit, with four valves per cylinder and a capacity of 3,999.66cc, producing 300bhp (224kW) at 6,250rpm, with a compression ratio of 9.8:1. This engine was derived from the V8 road car family, at which time the 328 GTB and GTS were the current models, with increased capacity. The quirk was that this engine was built only for use in these two prototypes. Making a leap forward of nearly 25 years, we arrive at the largest V12 Ferrari engine ever built – the F140 EB – capable of supplying 660bhp (492kW) at 8,000rpm, with enormous torque.

In March 2011, for the international press launch of the FF, Ferrari chose an appropriate location to demonstrate the qualities and characteristics of the car, taking two examples of this brand-new car (together with a Boeing CH-47 Chinook helicopter) to the ice and snow of Plan de Corones, in the Italian Dolomite mountains. The car had innovative

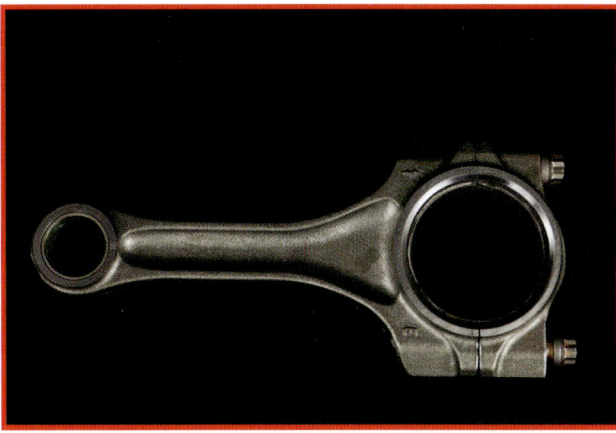

↑ **One of the forged-steel connecting rods, with the big-end bearing cap secured by bolts.**

'shooting brake' styling, designed by Flavio Manzoni (of the Ferrari Styling Centre), collaborating with Lowie Vermeersch, former Design Director at Pininfarina. The engineer

↓ **The light-alloy cylinder-block casting, with Nikasil-treated cylinder liners fitted.**

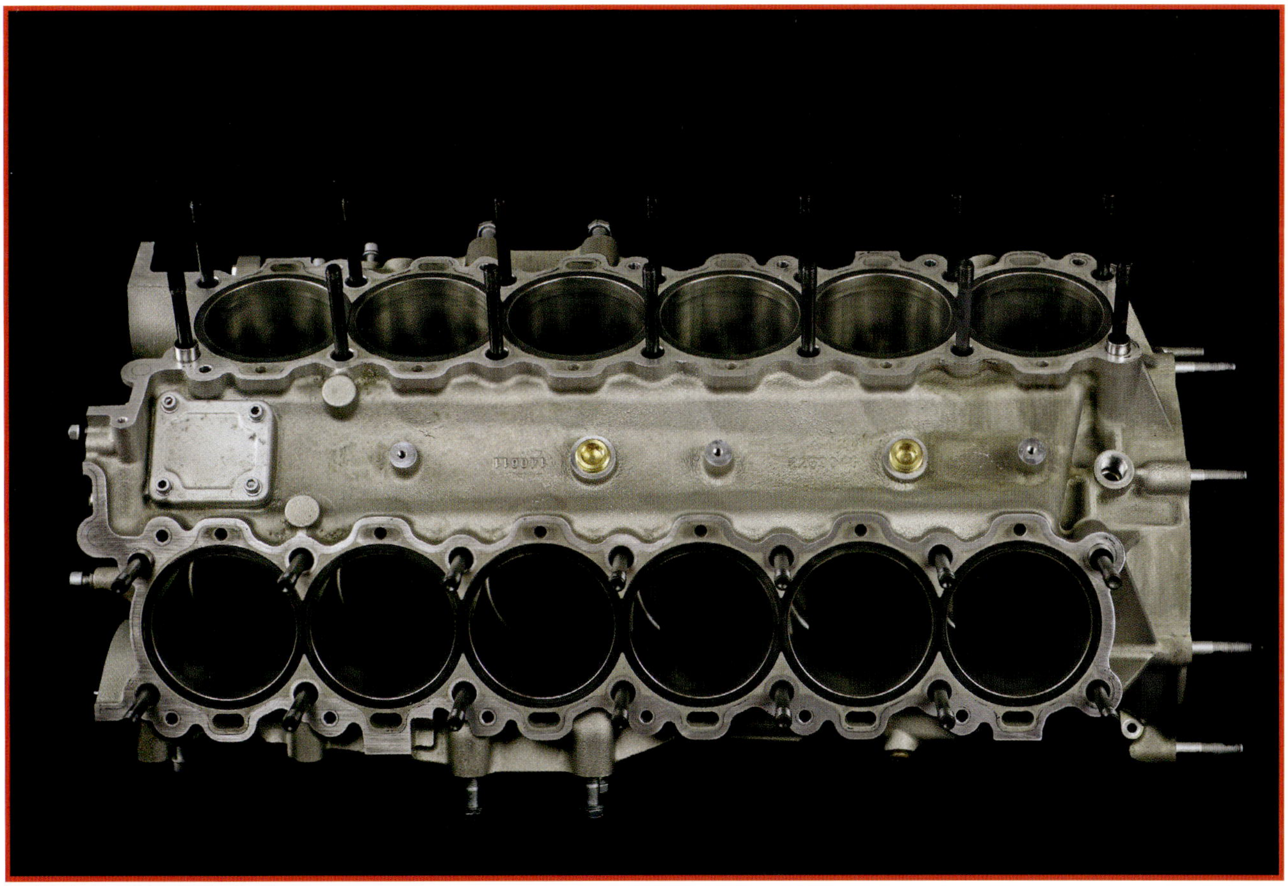

responsible for the layout of the car was Franco Cimatti, who developed the car with inspiration from Forghieri's 408 RM project, studying the innovative power-transfer unit for managing the driven front axle.

The FF appears to take styling cues from the 458 Italia, from which it takes the shape of its headlights, and the twin circular tail-lights. The car also takes inspiration from the 2007 Sintesi concept car, created by Pininfarina. Shooting brake styling takes aims to incorporate the features and practicality of an estate car, with a wide rear provided with a tailgate. The origin of Ferrari's development of this design began in 1996, when Pininfarina was commissioned to build a series of 456 GT-based cars for the Brunei Royal Family, which carried the project name 'Venice', and five of these were shooting brakes. The bodywork of these shooting brakes was 20cm longer than the bodywork of the production coupé. For this unusual request, the Brunei Royal Family allegedly spent US$9 million. After this unofficial series produced by Pininfarina, 15 years later Ferrari produced their own shooting brake for general sale.

The front, longitudinal V12 configuration of the previous four-seater Ferrari – the 612 Scaglietti – remained basically unchanged for the FF, but the engine capacity was increased from the Scaglietti's 5,748cc to 6,262cc. To optimise the

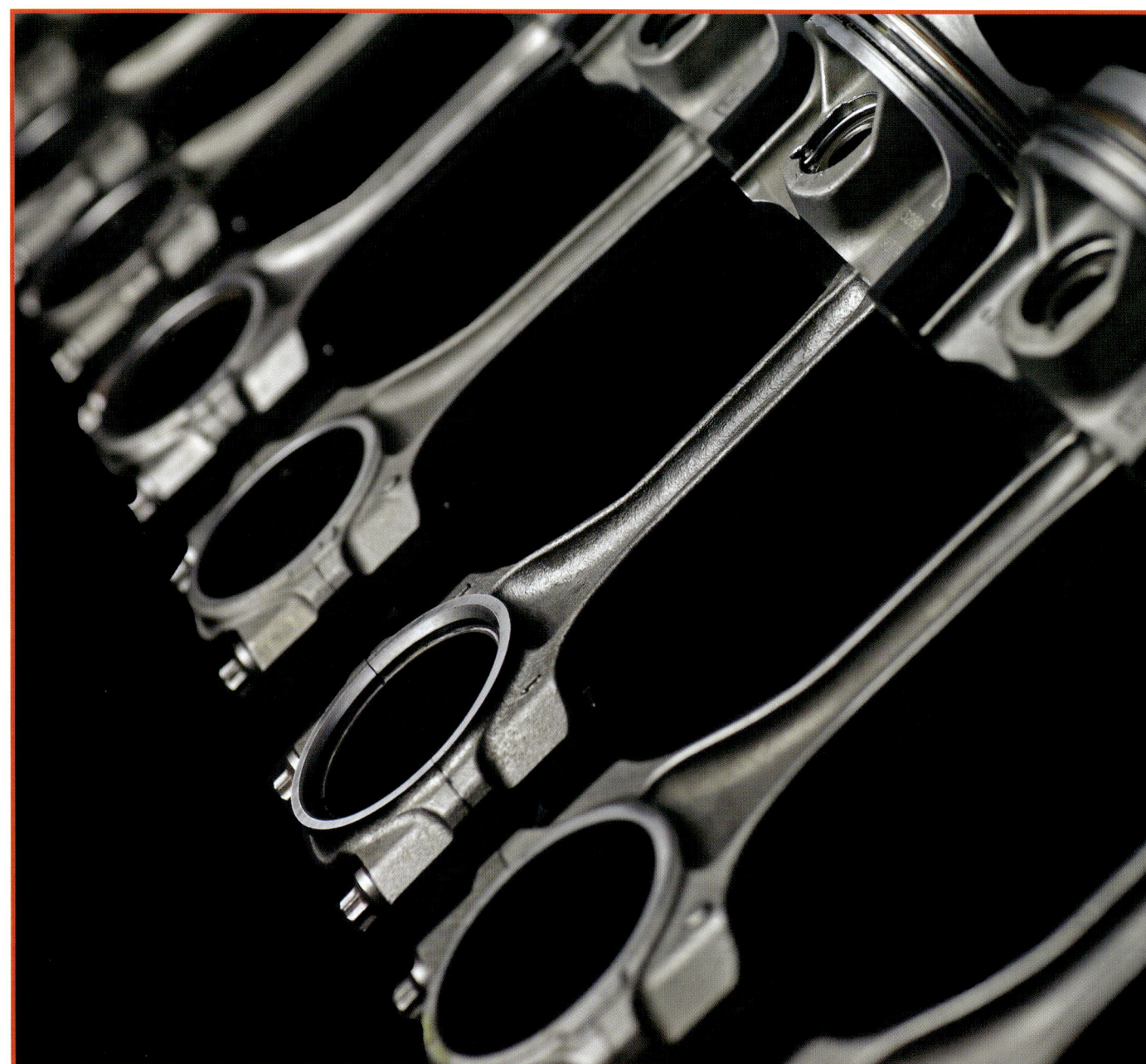

centre of gravity of the new Ferrari four-seater, and to obtain a better front-rear weight distribution (47%–53% for the Scaglietti), the FF engine was located further back with respect to the front axle.

The innovative layout of the four-wheel-drive transmission uses Ferrari's 'E-diff' system at the rear, with no conventional front and centre differentials. Drive to the front wheels is provided by a second gearbox, taking power directly from the engine (via gears from the crankshaft). This gearbox, known as a PTU (Power Transfer Unit) has only two forward gears (second and fourth), plus reverse. The gear ratios for the PTU are 6% higher than the corresponding ratios for the main gearbox (incorporated in the rear transaxle). The drive between the PTU and each front wheel is via independent haldex-type clutches, with no conventional differential. The front clutches continually slip, transmitting a maximum of 20% of the engine torque. The double clutch is integral with the rear transaxle, with one clutch for even-numbered gearshifts and the second for odd-numbered shifts. This system provides a smooth transmission of torque, with an almost seamless gearchange. A seven-speed gearbox is used, operated by paddles on the steering wheel, similar to the system used on the 458 Italia and F12 Berlinetta. Power distribution to the front axle is electronically controlled to optimise traction. The four-wheel-drive system design enabled the main mass of the system to be concentrated at the rear of the car (maintaining a good balance), and also aided weight reduction. The complete system, complete with the PTU and front clutches, weighs only 45kg – approximately 50% less than a conventional system.

The electronically controlled suspension features magnetorheological dampers, which allow the damping characteristics to be controlled by electromagnets, activated by the control system. The braking system features carbon-ceramic discs, derived from those fitted to the 599 GTO.

The powerful F140 EB engine, the first of the 6.3-litre Ferrari family built at the Maranello factory, is manufactured almost entirely from light alloy (pistons, block, heads, timing covers, sump, etc), with Nikasil-treated cylinder liners (94mm bore and 75.2mm stroke). The pistons have extremely shallow skirts to reduce weight, while the crankshaft, connecting rods, camshafts and valves are steel. Camshaft drive is via triple chains. The manifolds from each bank are interconnected, which aids exhaust-pulse tuning to improve performance.

The engine features a direct-injection system, with the Bosch Motronic engine-management system controlling the firing of the injectors, which spray fuel directly into the combustion chambers. Twin ignition coils feed the single spark plug per cylinder.

Despite the weight of the FF (1,880kg), the 6.3-litre engine pushes this four-seater 'battle cruiser' to the astonishing speed of 208mph (335kmh), with acceleration from 0–62mph (0–100kmh) of only 3.7sec. This is aided by the huge torque of 683Nm (504lb ft) at 6,000rpm and power of 660bhp (492kW). The compression ratio is an unusually high 12.5:1.

The first Ferrari engine to feature the 65° vee angle of the FF's V12 appeared in 1992 with the engine type F116 B, fitted to the 456 GT 2+2. In the nineties, Ferrari engineers decided to leave behind the 60° configuration

← **An abstract view of the lightweight piston/connecting rod assemblies. Note the extremely shallow piston skirts.**

of all the previous 'Colombo' V12 engines, to adopt a new vee angle for V12 road cars, derived from F1 experience. Indeed, due to new FIA regulations, 1989 brought the return of V12 naturally aspirated engines into Formula One. The perfect mechanical balance for a V12 revving with minimum vibration is 60°, but with advanced ignition timing control, a 65° V12 was the optimum choice for a brand-new engine project, offering a lower centre of gravity for the engine as an advantage. For all Ferrari V12 engines from the 456 GT to the present, the 65° vee angle has become standard.

The story of Maranello four-seaters begins more than 50 years ago. Indeed, it was 1960 when the first 'proper'

↑ One of the cast-alloy cylinder heads, viewed inverted, with the exhaust ports visible facing the camera.

→ The forged-steel crankshaft, with seven main bearing journals and shared big-end journals.

↓ A view inside one of the cylinder heads, with the valves (four valves per cylinder) fitted, but the camshafts removed. The tops of the valve stems and the valve-spring caps are visible.

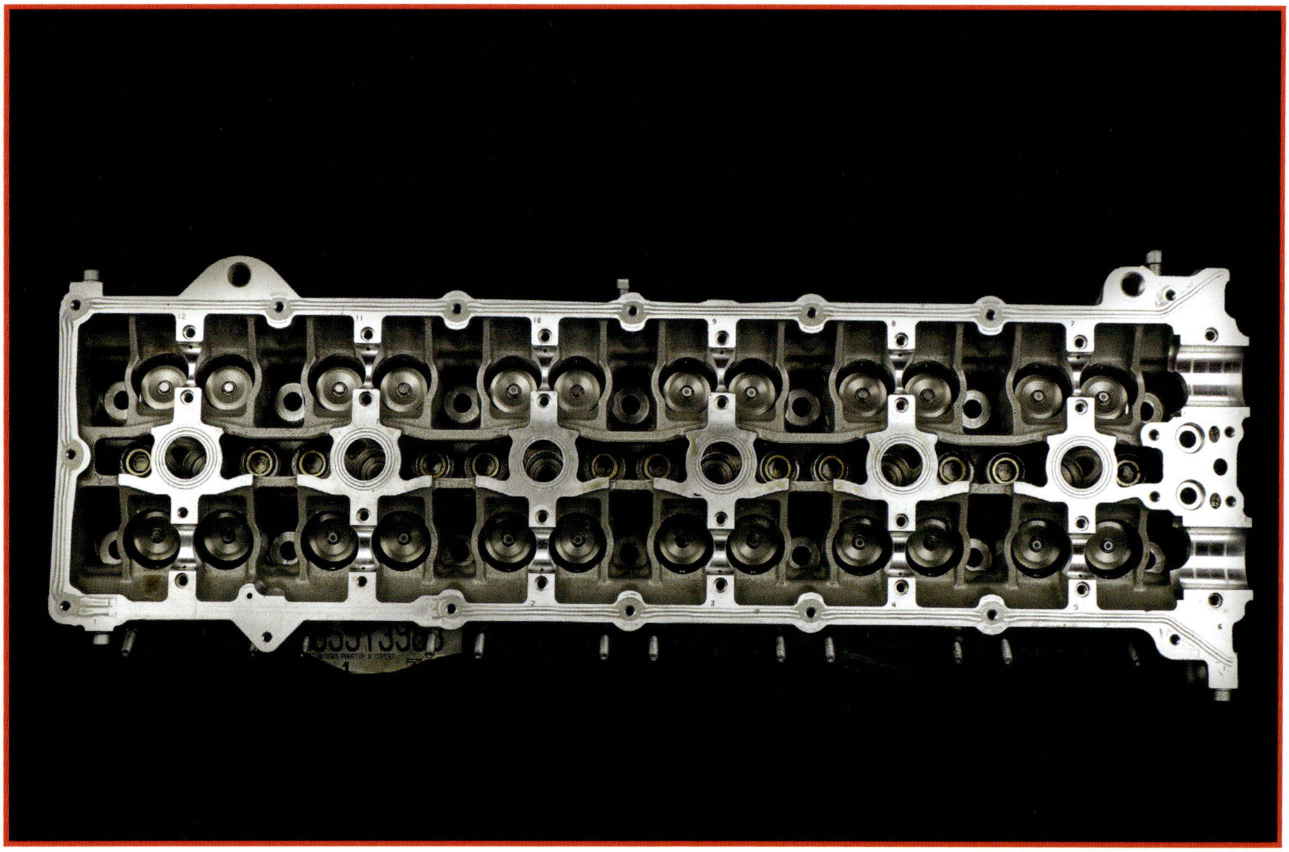

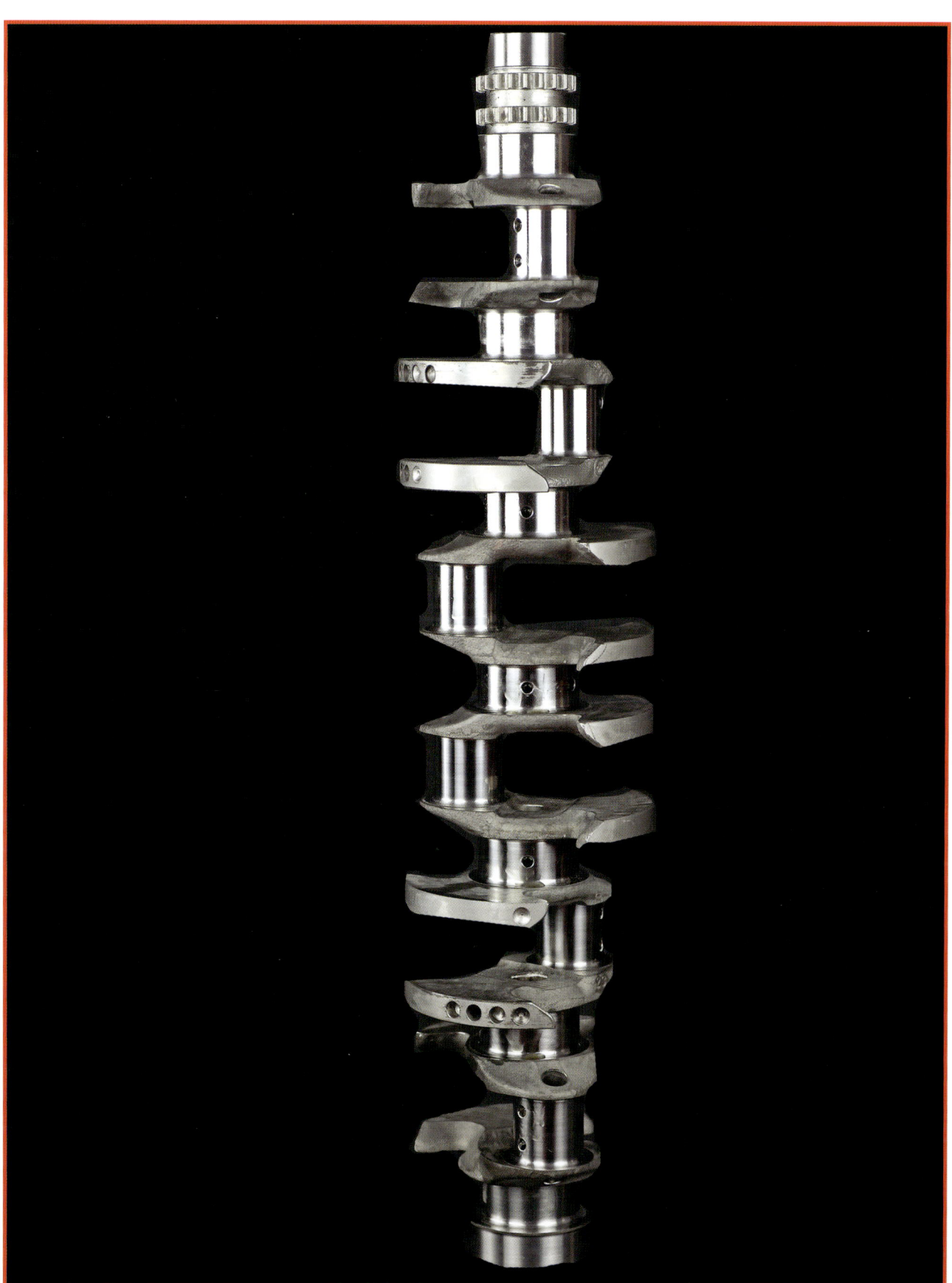

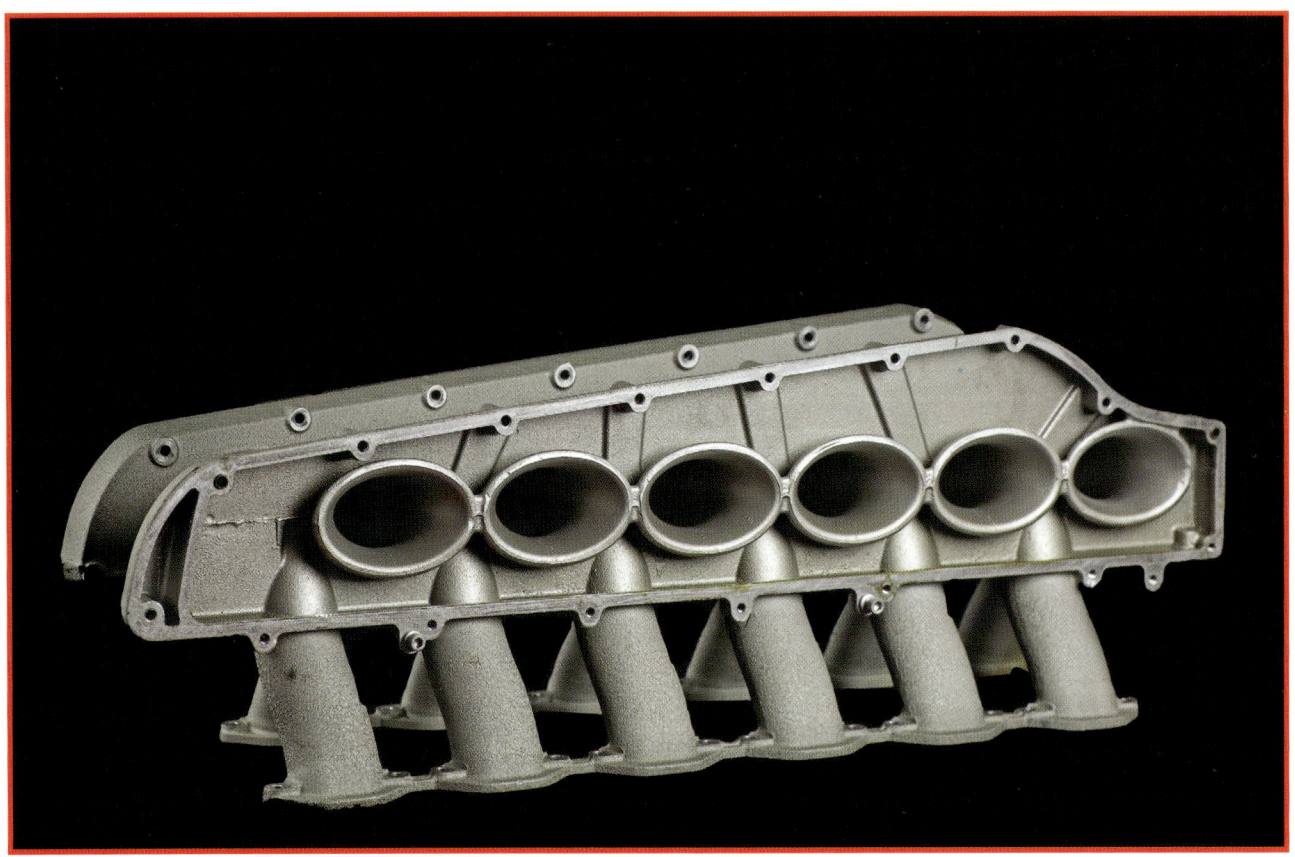

↑ The cast-alloy inlet manifolds, which fit between the cylinder heads and the plenum chambers.

FERRARI FF – TECHNICAL DATA

Engine code	F140 EB
Engine type	Front, longitudinal, V12, 65°
Bore and stroke	94 x 75.2mm (3.70 x 2.96in)
Total capacity	6,262cc (382.13cu in)
Unitary capacity	521.83cc (31.84cu in)
Compression ratio	12.3:1
Maximum power	651bhp (486kW) at 8,000rpm
Power per litre	104bhp/litre (77kW/litre)
Valve operation	Double overhead camshafts per bank, four valves per cylinder
Fuel feed	Direct-injection Bosch Motronic
Ignition	Single spark plug per cylinder, twin coils with ignition management provided by Bosch Motronic system
Lubrication	Dry sump
Clutch	Double-clutch electronic system
Maximum torque	683Nm (503.7lb ft) at 6,000rpm
Firing order	1–7–5–11–3–9–6–12–2–8–4–10

2+2-seater Ferrari made its debut, in the form of the 250 GT/E, which was the first in a long series of comfortable sports cars. There had been Ferraris with four seats produced during the fifties, but these were minimalist in dimensions, only really suitable for children. Even if the four-seaters never received the same love as their two-seater counterparts, Ferrari has still produced a long line of desirable 2+2 cars. As mentioned previously, the first was the 250 GT/E, followed in 1964 with the 330 GT 2+2; 1967 365 GT 2+2; 1971 365 GTC/4; 1972 365 GT4 2+2; 1973 308 GT4; 1976 400 series; 1980 Mondial series; 1985 412; 1992 456 GT; 2004 612 Scaglietti; 2008 California series; 2011 FF and right up to the time of writing with the 2016 GTC4 Lusso and 2017 Portofino.

The most extreme evolution of the 140 engine family to date is the 2017 F140 GA, with the largest displacement ever for a Ferrari engine, of 6,496cc. This naturally aspirated engine is fitted to the 812 Superfast. In 15 years, since 2002, when the first F140 B engine was fitted to the 'instantly collectible' Ferrari Enzo, 400 of which were produced, the development of V12 65° engines by Ferrari has featured continuous technological innovation together with continuous power increases. Indeed, the 812 punches out an incredible 800bhp (597kW), and for the first time in Ferrari history, it has a model designation that refers to its power: 812 – 800bhp

↑ A set of valves, double valve springs (one inside the other) and spring caps for one cylinder.

→ A close-up view of one of the cylinder banks showing one of the cylinder liners in place, with sealing ring at the top.

↘ An inverted view of the end of one of the cylinder-head castings, with the camshaft locations at the bottom of the photograph.

↓ The red-painted plenum chambers have the Ferrari script cast in to the upper face.

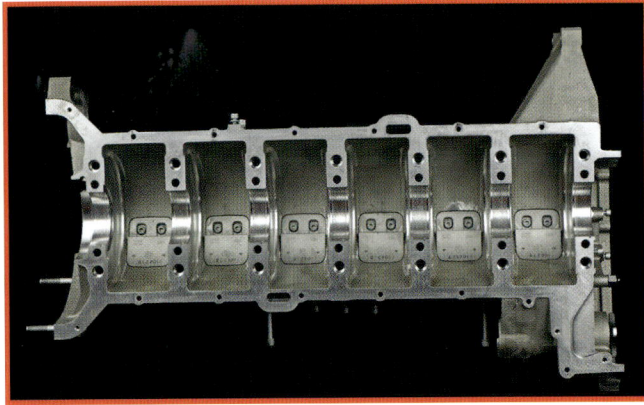
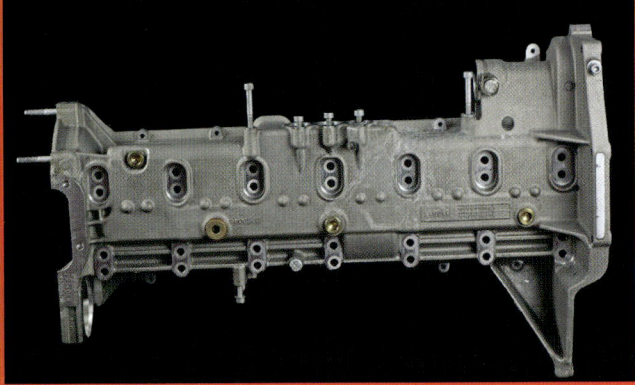

and 12 cylinders. If that is not enough, the F140 engine family also contains the most powerful unit ever produced by Ferrari in the form of the 'Hy-KERS'-supplemented power unit used in the LaFerrari, producing 963bhp (718kW). It seems that the V12 configuration is guaranteed to make a great noise in the future and, together with technology which is constantly evolving, will still produce a great sound comparable to a symphony orchestra. Looking forward though, to the progress of electrical power units and related technology, will the future of the V12 Ferrari symphony remain an astonishing exhaust roar or will we adapt to artificial sounds produced by computers?

↖ A view inside the dry-sump pan casting, which incorporates the lower crankshaft main bearing locations.

↑ The underside of the dry-sump pan casting.

→ The cast-alloy clutch bellhousing, which fits on the rear of the engine and takes drive to the rear transaxle via a propeller shaft.

↓ The complex alloy front timing cover casting clearly shows the 65° vee angle.

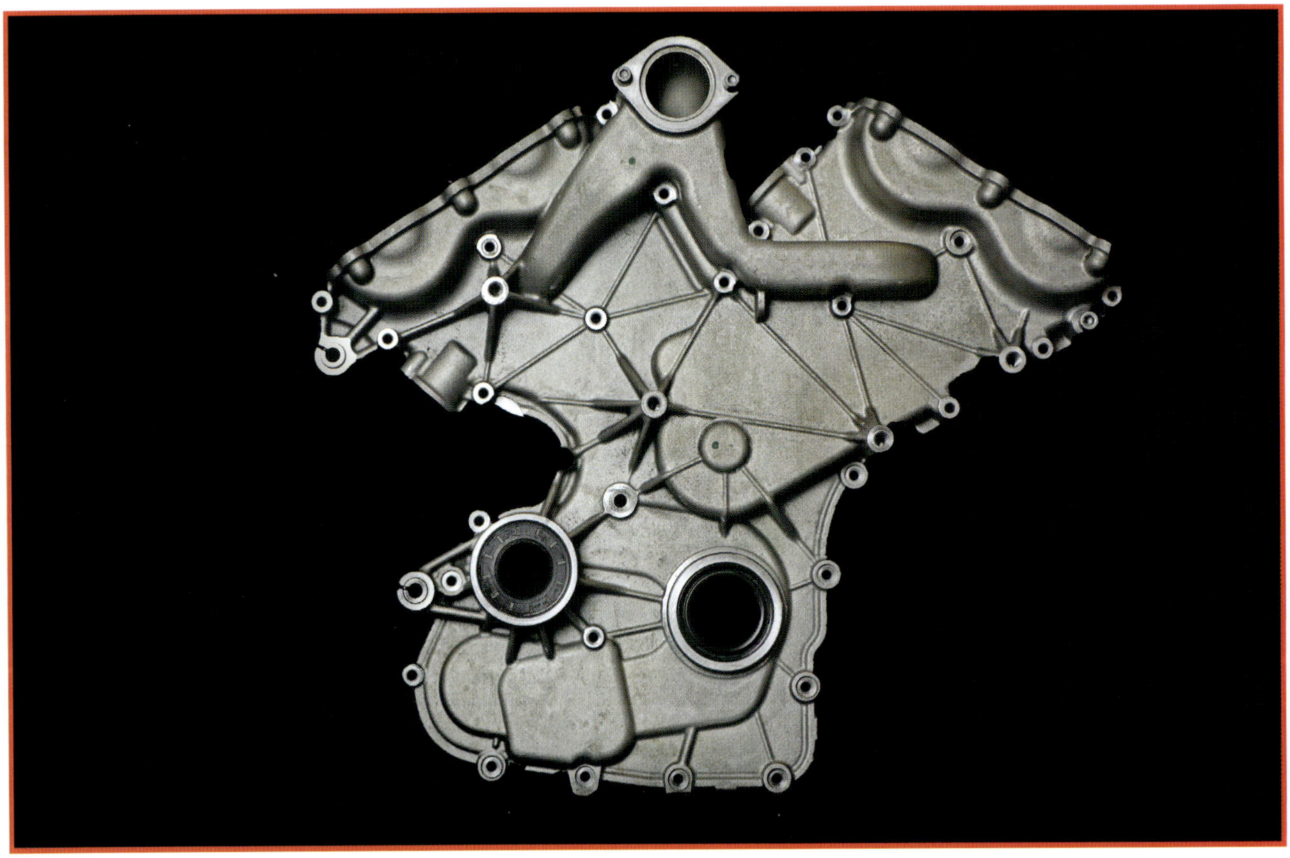

FF: The first Ferrari engine in a 4WD car (2011)

245

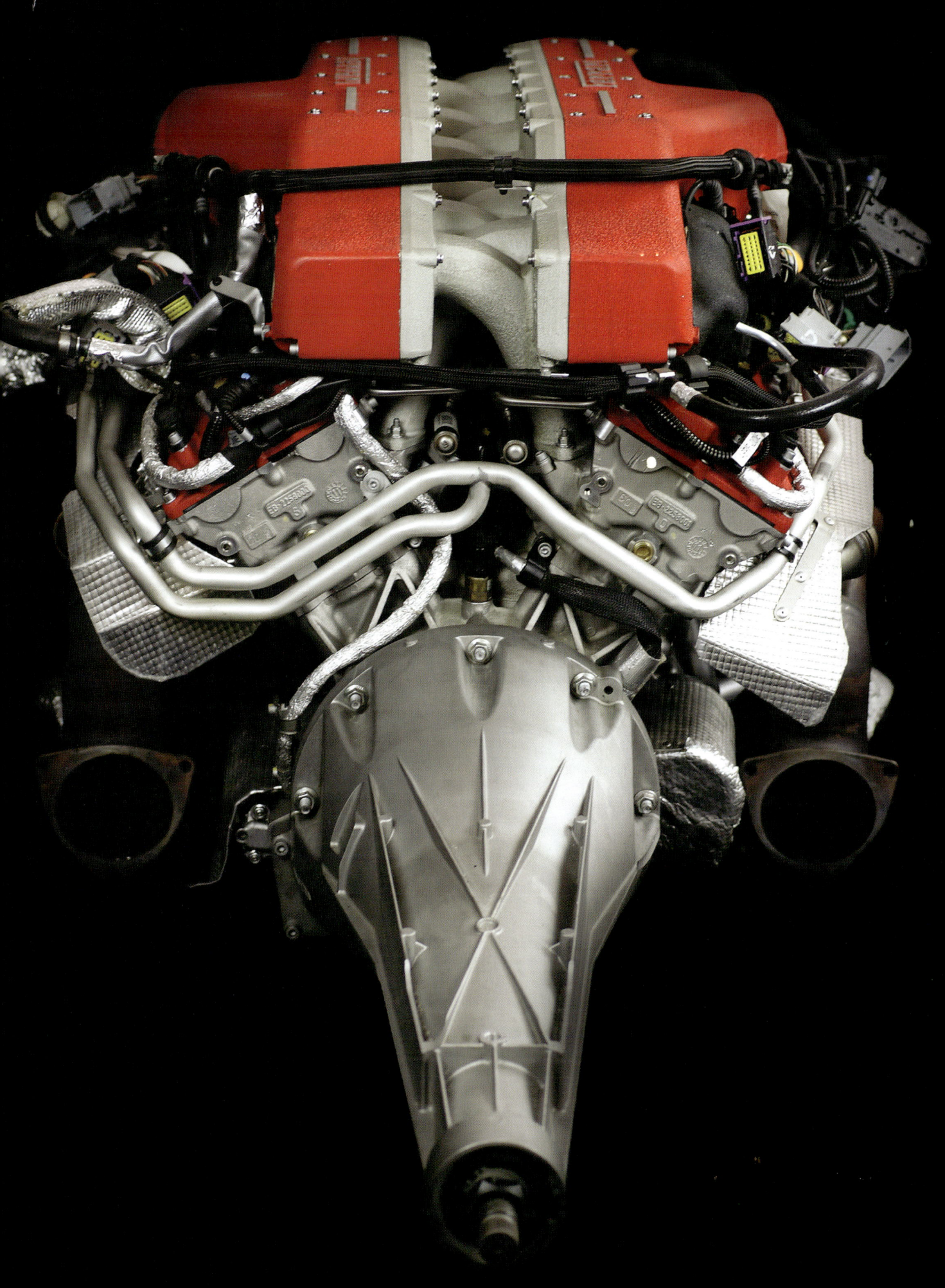

↑ Taking cues from the 275 GTB 'long nose', the front end of the FF displays a curved grille panel routing air to the front engine.

↑ The first production four-wheel-drive Ferrari is characterised by a 'shooting-brake'-style tail treatment.

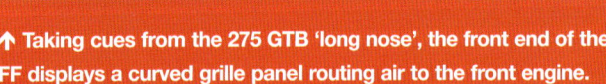

→ The front wings carry the Prancing Horse emblem just behind the air vents, paying homage to Ferrari's racing heritage.

↘ The single, round tail-light clusters sit in sculpted recesses in the tail, either side of the tailgate.

↘↘ The tapered front-light styling is inspired by the aggressive design of the 458 Italia nose.

↘↘↘ In spite of the 235/35 R 20 (front) and 285/35 R 20 (rear) tyres, the four-wheel-drive transmission allows the FF to tackle arduous road conditions with aplomb.

↓ The FF is a full four-seater, but the flowing lines of the car are slender and aerodynamic.

249

FF: The first Ferrari engine in a 4WD car (2011)

250
Ferrari Engines

More road engines

To finish the road-car section of this book we take a look at two engines related to those covered in the preceeding pages. These two engines have powered two of the most iconic Ferraris ever built – the 365 GTB4 'Daytona', which first appeared in 1968, and the F40, built to celebrate the 40th anniversary of Ferrari in 1987.

← The 4.4-litre double-overhead-camshaft V12 that powered the Ferrari 365 GTB4 'Daytona' was derived from the engine used in the 275 GTB4, itself related to the 330 GTS engine appearing on pages 90–105.

↓ The 471bhp (351kW) 2.9-litre twin-turbo V8 powering the Ferrari F40 – shown here with its longitudinal gearbox, which was mounted at the back of the car, behind the differential – was derived from the unit fitted to the 1984 GTO (288).

Competition engines

As mentioned previously Ferrari's philosophy has always been that racing improves the breed, and much of the technology featured on Ferrari road-car engines has filtered down from the Scuderia Ferrari competition cars. What better way to finish this book than to look at a few of Ferrari's beautifully engineered racing engines...

⬇ The Aurelio Lampredi-designed four-cylinder, double-overhead-camshaft 2.5-litre engine, used in the 1955 Ferrari Super Squalo grand prix car. This engine produced 270bhp (201kW) at 7,500rpm.

→ A competition version of the V12, single-overhead-camshaft-per-bank 3.3-litre engine used in the 1965 Ferrari 275 GTB/C, and featured in road-car form on pages 74 to 89.

↓ The V12 double-overhead-camshafts per bank 5.0-litre engine from the 1970 Ferrari 512S sports-racing car. Power was around 540bhp (400kW).

↓ A competition version of the V8 double-overhead-camshafts per bank 3.0-litre engine used in the 308 GTB, and featured in road-car form on pages 138 to 153.